Shape of Community

Realization of Human Potential

Serge Chermayeff
Alexander Tzonis

Penguin Books

Penguin Books Ltd, Harmondsworth,
Middlesex, England
Penguin Books Inc., 7110 Ambassador Road,
Baltimore, Maryland 21207, U.S.A.
Penguin Books Australia Ltd, Ringwood,
Victoria, Australia

First published 1971
Copyright © Serge Chermayeff, 1971

Library of Congress Catalog Card Number: 79–120554

Book designed by Chermayeff & Geismar Associates
Cartoons drawn by Ivan Chermayeff
Manufactured in the United States of America
Set in Lumitype Times

Pelican Books

Shape of Community

Serge Chermayeff is an architect and planning consultant. He was born in Russia and educated in England, where he practised and became a British subject. He went to the United States in 1940 and became an American citizen in 1946. He has been essayist, lecturer and critic, and has worked in the field of education. He was President of the Institute of Design in Chicago, and Professor at the Graduate School of Design at Harvard; he is now Professor Emeritus at Yale. He is a Fellow of the Royal Institute of British Architects and of the Royal Society of Arts. Together with Christopher Alexander he wrote *Community and Privacy*, which was first published in the U.S.A. by Doubleday Anchor in 1963.

Alexander Tzonis was born and educated in Greece and received the diploma in architectural engineering from the Athens Polytechnic Institute. In 1961 he went to Yale as Ford Fellow and he received the degree of Master in Architecture. He returned to Yale as a research fellow in 1965 and worked with Chermayeff on a Twentieth Century Fund project. He has been an Assistant Professor at Harvard since 1968. Alexander Tzonis is an advisory editor to a series of Pelican original books on environmental problems. He is currently writing two books, on *The Non-Oppressive Environment* and, in collaboration with Professor O. Salama, *Programmatic Analysis in Architecture*.

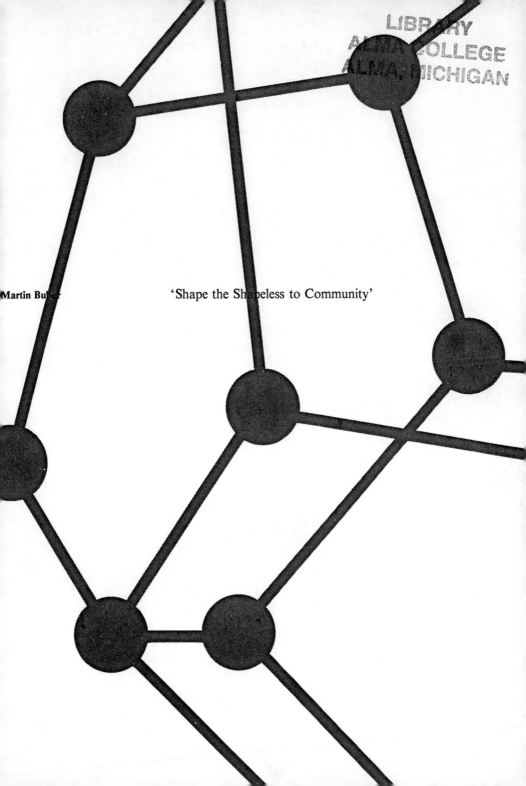

Martin Buber   'Shape the Shapeless to Community'

For Family and Fellow Students

Contents

Human evolution has different tempos. The 'third
ecology' of the man-made environment. The collective
process and institutional lag. Growing interdependence:
mobility and communications.

(a) Growth in quantities, change in quality. Complexity
and simplicity. Man's technological extension and
evolution of his humaneness.

(b) Continuous process or completed form. New
components of dynamic order. An urban theory for a
physical model. A short synoptic view of search for
models.

Chapter 7

Toward a Model　　　　　　　　　　　　　　　115

Commitment into model. Flows, containers, exchanges;
hierarchies of social and technical components in their
natural place. Programming social goals, principles
of organization, operational means in an open system.
Description of some tentative models.

Chapter 8

Theory and Practice　　　　　　　　　　　　133

Who lives where, why and how they move toward
what. Systematic segregation or natural mix. A
description of typical urban failures and of some
excellent exceptions.

Chapter 9

Hierarchy of Community　　　　　　　　　　151

Territories and fields. Containers for concourse,
community, democracy and learning. Pedestrians,

x

passengers and places. A description of some civil places old and new, and some faces of community.

Chapter 10

Building Bridges

The ecology of the intellectual environment. Intelligence, intuition and urban culture. A description of some professional dilemmas and failures. Some suggestions for the education of environmentalists and urban designers.

Epilogue

The Structure of Priorities

A summary and description of some guaranteed norms for all in an urban environment. Urbanism as evolution toward community.

Community in Concourse 192
Guaranteed Urban Norms 192
Urban Warp and Woof 194
Socio-Ends – Techno-Means 195
Contradiction into Complementarity 195
Stepping Stones 196
Which Johnny Does What? 196
Shape of Excellence 196
Pressures and Priorities 197

Grid as Tool for Criticism 217
Critique:
   Reston 218
   Hook 221
   Cumbernauld 223
   Milton Keynes 226
   Dublin University 229
   Berlin Free University 233
   Tokyo: Metropolitan Bridge Extension 235
Postscript 239

List of Text Figures

xiii

Acknowledgements

Some concepts and specific issues described in this book will prove familiar to many readers. Many have been derived from the work of friends and colleagues over the years. The restructuring of these many pieces in a personal way may give the study a measure of innovation. In the last few years universities, if not always in an appropriate manner or with happy results, have been progressively more engaged with technology, which has itself become progressively a more important component of culture. During this period it has been my privilege to work with many colleagues from other disciplines. All were more than generous and kind to a designer who characteristically had no training in either intellectual discipline or scientific method. Their tolerance overcame this handicap to the extent that a modest experiment in interdisciplinary studies of urban environments resulted in some measure of 'bridge-building' which will be discussed later.

It would be impossible to name here all the colleagues and students to whom I am indebted, but some specific acknowledgements must be made. Professors Heinz von Foerster, Karl Deutsch, Edward Deevey, Richard Weinerman, Paul Weiss, and Dr A. E. Parr have been generous not only with their wisdom and time but also with encouragement. Their advice has been both inspiring and crystal clear. I hope they will overlook any errors in interpretation.

A long-standing debt to a friend and colleague in my own field, Professor Charles Abrams, can never be repaid. He has both directly and indirectly helped to extend my design spectrum. John Eberhard, past director of the Institute for Applied Technology in the U.S. Bureau of Standards, was instrumental in obtaining a grant for an earlier Yale study which enabled the authors to formulate the lattice-grid in the autumn of 1967 together with students of the Master Class in Architecture. Professor Jacqueline Tyrwhitt's and Mr John McHale's subsequent incisive commentary on this helped much to bring it to the stage of development presented in this study.

My co-author, Alexander Tzonis, has contributed lucid and systematic argument throughout our collaboration, which started in 1962. His patience and hard work have been remarkable and cannot be adequately acknowledged here. I owe a great debt to many graduate students who helped me over the years to develop the ideas and strengthen the commitment described in this book.

The tedious task of transcribing miles of recording tape, and typing and retyping endless pages of seminars and draft manuscript, was performed with unequaled efficiency and dispatch by Aline Menefee who eliminated much pain from the production process. David Handlin, like a good craftsman-editor, has pointed and polished the prose mosaic.

Finally, without the encouragement of August Heckscher and the generous grant made by the Twentieth Century Fund while under his direction, the study would not have been completed. Thanks are due to the Fund's staff, to Yale University for its assistance and to Jonathan Edwards College for its hospitality throughout the period of the project.

Serge Chermayeff, Cape Cod, July 1968

Preface

by Heinz Von Foerster
(Professor of Biophysics and
of Electrical Engineering,
University of Illinois,
Urbana, Illinois)

Man's biology and culture are closely interrelated. Culture, as a manifestation of man's effective and symbolic behavior, is at the same time cause and effect of man's genetic constitution. As cause, it determines the mechanisms of natural selection in his self-made ecology; as effect it is determined by the cognitive processes that can be mastered by his biological constitution. This interplay between man's genetic potential and his cultural ecology gives rise to an evolutionary process that is distinct in a crucial sense from selecting mechanisms which operate on all other living organisms. While they ultimately compete with each other for limited resources in their finite ecological niche where only the 'fittest' survive, man cooperatively creates his physical and cultural environment within which he sets the rules for degree and kind of competitive behavior, and with these determines *who* is to survive.

This principle of evolution by choice, rather than by chance, has to be recognized if one wishes to assess degrees of stability in man's biology and culture in order either to describe his past or to discuss his future.

Fossil records, studies in primate behavior and the anthropology of stone-age cultures still surviving in isolated pockets today, make it abundantly clear that over a period of more than one million years of evolution, from his ancestral man-apes to his present version, man and his precursors have adopted a way of life which, by comparison with other mammals, is unique in its thorough organization of a social unit, the 'group'. A group may include from fifty to not more than a few hundred members, and it is the organization of all its members – young, old, male, female, strong, weak, and of various personalities – into a functioning social system that is in striking contrast to all other gregarious mammals.

Diet determines the range over which such groups travel. Partly vegetarian, partly predacious, a medium-sized group in savanna country could sustain itself, perhaps, on a few hundred, but easily on one thousand square miles.

Measured by today's standards, this appears to be altogether an unrealizable condition. Half a million years ago, however, the extraordinary rarity of man made space a very easily available commodity. At that time the whole globe was at the disposal of not more than one million creatures, who tended fires, chose materials for tools, produced symmetrical artefacts and used natural shelters. Even if they had been confined to the African continent, the few thousand groups would have had little chance to meet each other: inter-group competition must have been a luxury rather than the rule.

One has to visualize man's biological evolution against this background of contrast between vast empty spaces of freely accessible land and a highly organized group life to which one can relate and which, therefore, makes self-identification possible. In time, the structure of mutual relations between members of the group, and the structure of relations between the group as a social unit and the rest of the world, became stabilized to an astounding degree. These relational structures, which were manifest first in apparently successful patterns of behavior, became later ritualized and achieved ultimately symbolic representation. Until as recently as ten thousand years ago, hunting and gathering had been the way of life over a period of at least five hundred thousand years, during which time the human population had grown from one million to not much more than ten million souls.

While rituals, symbols and, of course, tools are stabilizing factors in external behavior, they are innovators for internal neural activity. Since rituals, symbols and tools have purposes other than themselves, a symbolizing brain knows the world twice: once as the totality of the perceived objects and facts; and second as the totality of the *descriptions* of the objects and facts. Moreover, since a description is itself a fact, a symbolizing brain can make descriptions of descriptions, and so on. The superior survival value of brains exchanging experience and thought through symbolic discourse will favor the evolution of this organ.

Indeed, the differences between the basic constituents of man's motor system and that of his primate ancestors are minute in comparison with the evolutionary changes in the functional and structural organization of the brain that differentiates man from his ancestors and his contemporary simian cousins, the big apes. The evolving new neural organization required more elements and more space, twice its original size. However, the size of a brain is only a secondary indication of its organizational richness, of the individual's cognitive potential. Whether or not this potential is realized to its fullest extent is indeed only a question of chance circumstances in the socio-cultural ecology during an individual's formative and early adult years.

Not more than five hundred generations ago man began to realize his cognitive potential by slightly changing some of his transmitted patterns of behavior. With the disappearance of a smaller brain's biological constraints which would have forced this system back into its stable pattern, new structures of relations began their evolution.

The processes of change that were thus initiated are even in retrospect difficult to comprehend. History – as it was and is now written – is merely descriptive, and even at that highly defective because of the arbitrary selection of descriptors in absence of guiding concepts of communication and control. These conceptual difficulties, of course, arise because man's genetic pool is exposed no longer to a more or less stable cultural ecological system, a constant 'milieu extérieur artificielle', but to an environment which itself evolves as a consequence of his ability to project and to objectivate thoughts and descriptions. It is not merely change one has to contemplate, it is the change of change that complicates the issue of a development devoid of almost all continuities, resembling a cascade of discontinuities, of 'quantum jumps' in kind.

If it took our ancestors half a million years to add ten million souls to reach the stone-age population, contemporary man accomplishes this feat in just two months. In fact, the entire human pyramid that has accumulated since the dawn of man one million years ago amounts to eighty billion people, five per cent of whom are living now. This means that one out of twenty men that ever lived are now alive, and in just three decades from now, in 2000 A.D., the ratio will be one out of ten.

If these dynamic processes, with their intricate ramifications and varied consequences, are not easy to comprehend in retrospect, how can their destiny be seen in prospect? In the face of socio-cultural eruptions, what does planning mean? How does it help? What can still be designed that is not obsolete by the time it is produced? How can one foresee a future?

Change on the bio-socio-cultural level is incomprehensible when seen through the narrow aperture of a mental framework that attempts to describe the world in 'scenarios'. In a completely stationary world, in a museum's world of waxworks, a scenario might be justified: nothing changes, and the time of contemplation is no factor. In a dynamic system, however, 'scenarios of the future' are meaningless, for they are envisioned as being the same as today's, with only quantitative variations of otherwise unaltered qualities: *faster* cars, *wider* highways, *more* people, *bigger* bombs. Nevertheless, 'future scenarios' have become a lucrative pastime for entrepreneurs, who sell them to corporations who profit from designing for obsolescence.

The work by Chermayeff and Tzonis is, to my knowledge, the first attempt to approach on a global level the problem of the shape of community. 'Global' here is meant not merely geographically, but essentially methodologically. As someone who is professionally acquainted with the unpenetrable intricacies of complex, strongly interacting systems, I found it a delight to follow the two authors separating with skill sixty crucial issues from a tangle of controversies and misconceptions, and still keeping the relations between these issues alive.

Merely to present these issues is a major féat, for where is one to begin, where to end in the description of a system whose parts are structurally and functionally interrelated; where B is understood when A is grasped, but A, in turn, is only clear in terms of B?

The authors succeeded in presenting the complex relations of issues by developing an appropriate anatomy of commitments which are located in the same way as atoms at the lattice points in a complex crystal. Their vision of this structure is so consistent that they can keep the reader constantly informed about certain features which may move out of sight here, but reappear there. The relation of issues in the structure of commitments determines the functional part of the author's vision, a set of crucial actions. These three, *issues, commitments* and *actions,* are complementary, generating a concept of community with the necessary and sufficient richness to permit the realization of human potential in times to come.

Prologue   The structure of the book. The analogy of a crystal. How the reader can move back and forth in the book, between bundles of issues.

The cumulative drift toward organization in every aspect of modern life is not due to some conscious desire to convert the complexity of society into the likeness of a smooth-functioning machine; it follows, on the contrary, from an inherent necessity, a principle of organization itself, which demands, imperatively and implicitly, an ever increasing extension of organization in the name of its higher functioning and perfected development. For the principle of organization, as we have seen, carries with it a kind of extroverted necessity to expand: organization breeds organization as a crystal breeds crystals . . .

. . . Hence we may provisionally equate, for purposes of our analogy, the individual with the random molecule; the machine with the crystal; society as an organized entity with a physico-chemical system having a crystal structure; and, finally, a basic change of historic direction with a thermodynamic change of phase.

Roderick Seidenberg, *Post-Historic Man*, Boston, 1957

Man must learn to simplify, but not to the point of falsification. He must learn to concentrate upon the essentials of a situation, but without ignoring too many of reality's qualifying side-issues. In this way, he may be able to tell, not indeed the whole truth (for the whole truth about almost any important subject is incompatible with brevity), but considerably more than the dangerous quarter-truths which have always been the current coin of thought.

Aldous Huxley, *Brave New World Revisited*, New York, 1958, London, 1959

A modern branch of mathematics having achieved the art of dealing with the infinitely small can now yield solutions in other more complex problems of motion which used to appear insoluble . . . and so conforms to the chief condition of motion (absolute continuity) and thereby corrects the inevitable error which the human mind cannot avoid when it deals with separate elements of motion instead of examining continuous motion. . . . The first method of history is to take an arbitrarily selected series of continuous events and examine it apart from others, for there is and can be no *beginning* to any event, for one event always flows uninterruptedly from another.

Leo Tolstoy, *War and Peace*, 1869

For whatever profession, your inner devotion to the tasks you have set yourself must be so deep that you can never be deflected from your aim. However often the thread may be torn out of your hands, you must develop enough patience to wind it up again and again. Act as if you were going to live forever and cast your plans way ahead. By this I mean that you must feel responsible without time limitations, and the consideration whether you may or may not be around to see the results should never enter your thoughts. If your contribution has been vital, there will always be somebody to pick up where you left off, and that will be your claim to immortality.

Walter Gropius, letter to a group of students, 14 January 1964

An analogy between the structure of this book and the structure of a crystal may perhaps help the reader to understand the arguments and act as a deterrent to a simplistic approach to the contents of a book that attempts to describe a difficult process of transformation. Professor Heinz von Foerster·recognized in the authors' argument and in their listing of the components into three categories, structure of commitment, structure of issues and structure of action (priorities), an affinity to the geometry of a regular solid which may grow or repeat itself in any direction, that is, a crystalline structure analogous to the urban structure envisaged in this book. 'Crystalline Structure of Contents' in the appendix describes the components and the structure of the geometry underlying them.

Commitment and Priorities

Exploration of any kind by man is guided by human commitment to human ends of one kind or another, thanks to a mutation of the human brain in the evolutionary process remote in time which has enabled man since then to invent appropriate technologies to meet new contingencies as they arise. Man thus became the first animal to participate directly and purposefully in the evolutionary process, but the products of this activity have had mixed results.

Given the state of affairs of today's urban environment, a reassessment of priorities seems in order before specific proposals can be instituted. Consequently the authors' commitment will be discussed as a foundation for action in the book which follows. Here, in the prologue, the commitment, the issues and priorities, are presented briefly in a random assemblage form. At first glance, the 'random' assemblage or mosaic gives the illusion of three-dimensionality and motion. A second look may reveal a pattern of related 'bundles of issues', then something like a map or geography of our concern and finally the structuring method and shape of our proposals.

The urban crisis which so concerns everyone today is a first priority in our mind. It is potentially more catastrophic than war, and may be described in medical language as 'anamnesis' and 'syndrome', the evolution and concurrence of symptoms of a disease and that which pertains to it. It is susceptible to 'diagnosis', the systematic analysis of the characteristics of the symptoms, and may therefore be expected to suggest 'therapy', an appropriate treatment. We are not, however, concerned with urban pathology and its cures, but, on the contrary, with the prevention of illness, with the understanding of the nature of the man-made environment, with 'prophylaxis'.

Urban Ecology

Urbanization appears to be a significant step in the evolution of Homo sapiens, the social animal. This process in its nature is not dissimilar to the evolution of the universe and other forms of life in it as we know them. On a general level the human community in man-made environments seems to follow some of the laws of natural evolution and mutation – interdependence, conflicts and adjustment – an interaction without end between living things and their environments. Man has simply added another dimension to ecology.

Structure into Narrative

The various components of the urban environment, man's habitat made by man, are pieces in an immense complexity of interaction and relationship, and even the few we have selected for discussion, dictated by our commitment, form a pattern of complex interdependence, which cannot easily be related 'by eye' to one another, and have no correspondence to any sequence which the narrative or graphics may suggest. This is brought to the reader's immediate attention to emphasize the issues, arguments and components of the problem, before and above textual, narrative sequences or conventions of chapter heads and sub-heads.

To emphasize this quality we have placed quotations at the side of the page as supporting evidence in the form of facts, figures and fears, a sort of obbligato to the main theme. In addition, the marginal titles suggest cross-references between any one issue discussed and the same issue in another context elsewhere. These enable the reader to move more freely back and forth in the narrative in pursuit of a special interest or involvement: he is invited to become, as it were, a functionary to help structure the complex urban order with us and in so doing help overcome the restrictions of a linear narrative system.

In searching for the redefinition of the designer's task, we do not want to replace the vague old jargon

with new jargon of the currently fashionable technological vocabulary (hardware, software, systems-
analysis, model-programming, etc.), but to attack the old
and the obsolete on the basis of their faulty logic. This
may still lead to additional confusion at first, because we
are forced at this time to give familiar words a new
meaning. Readers may be reassured, however, by a
glance at the glossary at the end of the book. The term
'urban "system"', for example, is necessary in order to
define a special characteristic of urban environment. No
matter how we choose to break down such an environment for analysis, the pieces derived in the process
cannot continue to exist outside of an organic whole
which is the larger environment or 'system'. In the same
manner the changing of even a single piece may change
all the other pieces. Similarly the term 'environment'
will inevitably become more and more comprehensive.
Our readers must bear with us until the ambiguities and
misleading interpretations, which we believe now exist,
of such words as city, urban, suburban, etc., have been
clarified and perhaps given a new and more accurate
meaning.

This prologue is thus intended to help overcome
the difficulties of one-dimensional representation of a
multi-dimensional order of great complexity. The
unorthodox structuring of the book is perhaps also an
apologia for the inadequacies of the present study. It
is an invitation for others to explore new audio-visual
media, such as film, probably better suited to reveal
this and similar dynamic structures. Man needs to invent
new tools for tackling complexity head on, while
searching for new human purpose.

In the United States the migration of rural folk
into cities is proceeding at the rate of a million people
every year. The great majority of civilized humanity is
apparently moving into urban environments, in the
historic sense of the word 'urban'. But in the study
which follows, this process of 'urbanization' is conceived as creating conditions quite different from those
that characterized historic cities. This state of affairs is
now shared by all forms of human settlements which
depend on contemporary 'technology' for their existence.
This new technology has become so pervasive that it
now plays the role of a cultural catalyst in every urban
environment in the old and the new sense alike. It forces

an ever greater interaction between all settlements and increases their interdependence. Industrialized (developed) societies have already become components in a global 'urban' system; others are following at different speeds.

This universal interdependence appears to operate in much the same way irrespective of the spatial, cultural or other dimensions of settlements: the traffic and communications of national and state capitals operate in a similar way to that of metropolitan centers and their various extensions. Together they constitute a global hierarchy of settlements in constant interaction linked by movement and information sub-systems, which are the two most conspicuous components of a technological super-system now emerging.

In spite of this technological reality, a new condition in the evolution of man and his habitat, most societies continue to be directed by institutions rooted in simpler, self-sustaining economies of an agrarian era, or in ideologies of the early industrial period. Both devices were manageable and satisfactory in various degrees. In the past the effects of the products of the land or of factories were comprehensible to all concerned. Most of the time reality coincided with the illusion of a stable society and economic success. If something went wrong, it could usually be corrected by appeasing the gods or their delegates on earth, by throwing them out, by annexing neighboring resources or by migrating to greener pastures.

These relatively simple remedial steps have become ineffective rather suddenly. In the foreseeable future neither intervention, whether divine or military, nor increased production alone holds much promise. Migration also will probably be limited to search for employment. (Thereafter, in a more distant and equitable future of genuine universal abundance, movement on earth may be limited for the majority of men to the search for rewarding leisure.) An educated, informed humanity in the process of redefining its sophisticated social needs and its control of technical means can no longer remain uniquely pragmatic, curative, palliative or opportunistic in action.

Transition periods have always been critical for the societies involved. The magnitude of crisis in our time is proportional to the quantitative and qualitative changes involved. The present 'urban revolution' has produced unprecedented crises for urban man because in the highly developed societies of our time most men live in urban environments. Existing, crowded cities are hardest hit, but the effects of change extend everywhere. Social and technical conflicts are only magnified in urban situations. Poverty, injustice, alienation, illness, pollution and congestion are failures which reached the existing cities first, but these and other technological and sociological plagues threaten man's entire habitat.

In the United States, the technologically most highly developed society in the world today, people, in James Reston's words, '. . . now have a more solemn vision of the tremendous scope and complexity of human reconstruction'.[1] The crisis of cities has reached in dimension and agony the scale of a third world war. It is the constant preoccupation of thoughtful men everywhere. The multitude of agonies are discussed daily and are too familiar to be described here. Their magnitude now transcends anything previously experienced. The collective crisis has become ecological in scope and effect and has a direct bearing on the environmental issues with which this study is concerned. The city dwellers in developed societies have suddenly become reluctant to leave their destinies in the hands of obsolete institutions controlled by invisible experts, or all too visible politicians, who until recently were believed to be the dispensers of technological cornucopia.

The promises of plenty for all mankind remain unfulfilled, because the emergence of new ideas and institutions has lagged pitifully behind the ecological, sociological and technological realities of the new era. The habitat of the most 'affluent societies' where the citizens live, work and should find their pleasure has been deteriorating and becoming obsolescent at a frightening rate. Technology is racing ahead of social need.

New approaches for the design of environments which might help to deal with contemporary crises are few and the means of implementing them difficult to obtain through familiar institutions. At present the essential redefinition of scope, responsibility and knowledge needed by all those who may be directly or indirectly engaged in the design of urban environments, now and in the foreseeable future, follows the general

1. James Reston, quoted in 'The Sense of Crisis', editorial in the *Nation*, 13 November 1967

institutional pattern. The shift from the obsolete continues to be unconscionably slow. Most of the changes in the last half century, somewhat speciously described as the period of 'the modern movement' in applied arts, were in the realm of aesthetic form rather than in the substance of a great transition in human affairs. With very few honorable exceptions most of the protagonists in the movement were ignorant of, or indifferent to, the changes in need and potential that were generated during the same period.

In the last decade the belated recognition of technological and scientific developments has assumed the proportions of panic among applied artists, those who currently are most directly concerned with the shape of environments large or small, simple or complex. They appear to be divided into two readily recognizable camps: giving an expedient allegiance either to the latest technology, irrespective of its appropriateness for the task at hand (technophiles), or to empty formalism rationalized by an obsolescing humanism (technophobes). Environments are still largely conceived either as receptacles for machinery, or as sculpture or scenery.

In the meantime one can only note with some despair that formlessness is the most conspicuous characteristic of urbanization everywhere. Objects, events and vistas are sadly beginning to look like leftovers from a vanishing world rather than convincing, exciting evidence of a new one in the making. Only very recently have there emerged new, viable ideas for planning and design, which actually correspond to new realities. Almost overnight the design spectrum has been extended and the design priorities have shifted. The erstwhile 'architect', 'artist', 'craftsman' or 'cultured gentleman' has suddenly become obsolete and instead new functionaries have been called upon to comprehend environmental cause and effect, master techniques, and make decisions in a world responding to new pressures of 'technology', which Henry R. Lieberman has described as having components of 'management, education, research, production and technical man-power'. In short they are now involved in a diversified activity of enormous complexity, ranging from the redefinition of human goals to the development of new means of implementation.

Along these lines the authors of this study conceive the urban environment to be the product of a dynamic order, in which interaction between events of growth and change represent a continuous process. Transformation and adjustment in technological society is so rapid that past, present and future melt into one, thus giving the systematic prediction of future events equal weight with the interpretation of the past. In this spirit there is a move now toward planning for a future era to prevent crises, while at the same time attending to emergency cures. Planning thus becomes today as essential an ingredient of man's progress as *laissez-faire* was when it triggered the spread of technical innovation and economic growth during the industrial revolution.

Simultaneous with this new need for planning must be the recognition of greater social flexibility to satisfy and accommodate new human aspirations. Consensus, which has served so well in developing democratic institutions and in providing material comfort through mass-production, may today prove to be a dead center of inertia, arresting the proper function of dynamic order while *laissez-faire* may go dangerously beyond what Professor Karl Deutsch terms 'limits of compatibility',[2] between the complementary freedoms of individuals and their collective good.

It appears to us that maximized choice between opposites within such limits applies to the design of environments in equilibrium. Our priorities may be summed up as the provision of urban public places where human experience is at its richest and most rewarding, and where citizens may be most efficiently served by supporting technologies. The authors' commitment to these general goals has placed the emphasis in this study on principles which might govern urban environments and on a method of programming them. In other words, emphasis is placed on investigating the invisible parameters and the structure behind urban form, as dictated by our commitment, and the systematic approach to problems of design. It is hoped that the formulation of governing principles may one day lead to new models of urbanism which will effect the form of the environment.

2. Karl Deutsch, Yale Seminars, 1966. For details, see Serge Chermayeff and Alexander Tzonis, *Yale Seminars on Urban Models*: a study sponsored by the National Bureau of Standards, Washington, D.C., Yale University, 1967

1. Syndrome

A detached look at the natural and the man-made. City crises are symptoms of human growth and change. The man-made environment has reached an ecological scale. A closer look at the illusions of familiar reality and new realities.

... modern man, and especially the modern American, however much 'know-how' he may have, has very little 'know-what'.

Norbert Wiener, *The Human Use of Human Beings*, New York, 1954

The United States is experiencing a crisis which in a sense is far more serious than the one France underwent during the Algerian war. . . . The Americans are not only divided on a fundamental problem as the French were, but they are witnessing the collapse of the structure . . . that holds their society together.

Jean Bloch-Michel, quoted in 'The Sense of Crisis', editorial in the *Nation*, 13 November 1967

The signs of disarray and discontent are not few or quixotic. They strew the American way . . . from ghetto to campus.

Emmet John Hughes, quoted in 'The Sense of Crisis', editorial in the *Nation*, 13 November 1967

The recognition of crisis in cities is of recent origin. Many people being together, originally an advantage full of promise for the future, has suddenly become a threat. Too many people and too much of their paraphernalia, all new, have begun to spill over the territorial and social limits of the old accommodations. In evaluating the resulting critical conditions men have learned rather quickly about the problems of incompatible quantities of uncontrolled growth. But they are still very slow in grasping the concomitant problems of profound qualitative change.

The crisis of cities is a symptom of simultaneous change and growth. Together these two factors have transformed relatively simple problems, which previously could have been locally resolved wherever they occurred, into immense, complex problems with repercussions beyond the territories in which they originated. This escalation has made the city crisis into an ecological crisis — an eco-crisis. In the larger perspective of human evolution, man's present inability to cope with this condition may be considered transitory and merely a passive expression of the infantilism of the species: a consolation unlikely to comfort the living. However, in this book the authors' intention is to bypass such grim conclusions and to show instead that the problems can be tackled in their complexity and totality in a positive way. The title of this book, *Shape of Community*, conveys a double purpose: to identify changing social and environmental goals and to devise new means of giving these form through design. This conception of design is very different from that which in the past went under the name of 'architecture', and was frequently described as a 'Social Art', a commodity for all men wherever it was made. 'Environmental Design', on the contrary, now has become comprehensive and complex and is indeed simultaneously a science and an art.

While the book discusses, of necessity, the general human habitat as a whole, it is more particularly concerned with the shaping of public meeting places, the key components of a successful environment for urbanizing man. 'Where does man become more human?' is a rhetorical question we attempt to answer in the context of growing and changing urban communities. Our immediate concern is the provision of

4 community places, capable of containing new and old

functions as well as facilities and supporting services. Then inevitably we must also deal with the institutions that will implement them and with the education of functionaries required to design them: tasks without precedent.

The concern for viable urban places is particularly important because, paradoxically, in the process of developing technology man has progressively eroded his sense of community, his moral and responsible attitude towards his fellow men. Affluent societies, preoccupied with immediate material gains, appear to be losing sight of long-term, but basic, goals and priorities. Communication media and mechanized mobility may inhibit direct social intercourse. Reliance on vicarious, 'global' experiences taken on the run may lead to neglect of first-hand, leisurely, daily contacts with 'live' people closer to home. So much has suddenly become obsolete technologically, that urbanizing societies lose sociologically excellent practices, neglected if not forgotten or dismissed: a new and frightening version of the baby and the bath-water adage. This study suggests that man has reached a point in evolution which requires the deliberate conservation or restoration of civic mingling places. These may not correspond in form to historic places, but must serve the same essential function: places in which humanity becomes human; where people in their great diversity meet in concourse and reach their highest potential.

The modern city is losing its external and formal structure. Internally it is in a state of decay while the new community represented by the nation everywhere grows at its expense. The age of the city seems to be at an end.

Don Martindale, prefatory remarks to Max Weber, *The City*, trans. and ed. Don Martindale and Gertrud Neuwirth, Glencoe, Illinois, 1958

In 1965, before the war was escalated to its present level, the President's Message on Improving the Nation's Cities declared that projects were to be 'of sufficient magnitude both in physical and social dimensions to bring about a change in the total environment' . . . .

Life for people in the central cities was to be made better through a radical improvement in housing, sanitation, crime prevention, mass transportation, and the upgrading of education, health and welfare services. Yet rather than starting a vigorous program along these lines, the President asked Congress for only $2·3 billion, to be spread over six years, 'to rebuild entire slum neighborhoods'; to plan the rebuilding of the central cities of the entire nation, he asked for 12 million dollars, less than the cost of developing the plans for the Pan Am Building in New York alone . . .

David Danzig and John Field, 'The Betrayal of the American City', *Commentary*, 1968

Concern for our mishandling of technology has of course been growing apace but with little effect. Pollution of land, sea and air, in one form or another, is proclaimed in newspaper headlines and book titles and is discussed on radio and television. The destruction of hundreds of thousands of animals, birds, fish and plants, including destruction of entire species, apparently has not moved the majority of mankind to anything which could be called compassion for the plight of other living things on this planet. There is not even any widespread concern for the survival of man, since the fear of nuclear holocaust has been at least temporarily allayed. Little wars only matter to those who are killed and dispossessed and they command little attention outside the battlefields. Secure in their scientific knowledge and technical capacity, the 'Great Powers' are watching gladiatorial games being carried on with relatively few casualties in the celestial colosseum. Existing or potential disasters, whether minor or major, natural or man-made, have not shaken the prevailing beliefs in *laissez-faire* or nostalgia for the good old days of untrammeled nineteenth-century freedom. The indifference, the use of pious platitudes and the complacent acceptance of the will of God which inevitably accompany these attitudes have not been abandoned. They are merely operating in another guise.

... Based in Brookhaven, L.I., the EDF (Environmental Defense Fund) went far afield to secure the Michigan Court of Appeals this fall to secure an order restraining the state's Department of Agriculture from dumping three tons of DDT on Berrien County. This agricultural overkill was aimed at an 'infestation of Japanese beetles', which later turned out to number somewhere between 300 and 1,000 bugs. Dr Charles F. Wurster of the New York State University at Stony Brook testified for the EDF that, for every beetle affected, from 10 to 80 birds and mammals 'up to the size of cats and even sheep' would be killed. . . . 'There is no circumstance that justifies the use of Dieldrin and DDT in the general environment, now that concentrations of these persistant pesticides have reached the point of degrading ecological systems in diverse parts of the world' (says Dr George M. Woodwell of the ABD's Brookhaven National Laboratory) . . .

Frank Graham Jr, 'Taking Polluters to Court', *New Republic*, 13 January 1968

Only a very few years ago a tiny minority began to look, first quizzically and later with alarm, at symptoms of new plagues which could destroy mankind. This apprehensive minority does not appear to have been effective. There is much evidence to suggest that the increasing appetite of egocentric producers and consumers alike is more dangerous than the bomb. The majority certainly continues to believe in conventional wisdom and its ability to control most unconventional realities in the wake of the technological explosion.

Predictably, whatever small undercurrent there may be of concern is offset by a cult of escapism. The preoccupation with 'beauty' and its modish expression, 'beautification' of all things, has grown. The comforting slogans of yesterday have become profitable services today. Ugly things are being 'made-up' to look, if not pretty, then at least hygienic. The techniques of the embalmer, traditionally employed to disguise the disagreeable aspect of death, are now being applied to the rather ill, the not quite dead and even the merely dissatisfied. The embalmer's and the beautician's roles have become indistinguishable from one another. Production of disguises, from 'sexy' deodorants to 'elevator' shoes, peddling of panaceas, political and psychological, unscrupulous propaganda and advertising have made deception into a way of life. The deliberate creation of short-term myths is a thriving business. The prosecution of the dubious is more profitable and easier than the pursuit of the reasonable or the inspiring. Ethic, in our time, lies outside the acquisitive world of day-to-day existence.

If there are too many cars, we build new highways. If administration is too cumbersome, we build new levels of administration. If there is a nuclear threat, we build anti-missile missiles.

Paul Goodman, quoted in 'The Sense of Crisis', editorial in the *Nation*, 13 November 1967

Ecology and Expertise

Human ecology became a problem when technological society came into existence. For the first time man is in the unique and uneasy position of being largely responsible for his own environment. At the same time he is threatened by the very technological achievements that made this possible. Dreams of endless plenty and comfort, unmatched by any ancient empire, have been disturbed by daily confrontation with the unexpected by-products of scientific and technical developments. Environmental crisis caused by technology is usually identified with the city. It is, however, not a city crisis *per se*, but simply that the city shows to the greatest extent the effects of 'pollution' which in the broadest

A law on geohygiene must be adopted after broad discussion, and ultimately become part of world efforts in this area.

A. Sakharov, *New York Times*, 22 July 1968

... The founding fathers who wrote the Constitution of the United States did so in an agrarian environment in which, as reported in our first census in 1790, 95 per cent of all Americans lived in rural areas – on farms or in places having fewer than 2,500 inhabitants ...

... [The] metropolitan areas ignore not only township and municipal lines, but also county and state lines. In consequence, our metropolitan areas, although constituting single demographic, economic, and ecological units, are politically and governmentally fragmented ..

... It must suffice to say here that the chaos which afflicts our city, our state, our nation, and our world is the product of the transition we are still experiencing from an agrarian, pre-industrial, pre-urban world to 'urbanism as a way of life', to use the felicitous phrase of the late University of Chicago sociologist, Louis Wirth ...

... This nation became an urban nation only as recently as 1920. It was in the 1920 census that for the first time more than half, 51 per cent, of our population lived in urban places. It will not be until our next census is taken in 1970 that the United States will have completed its first half century as an urban nation.

Philip Hauser, 'Mounting Chaos at Home', *Bulletin of the Atomic Scientists*, January 1968

sense are total and ecological. The man-made and the natural are now inseparable.

Given the new context of the environment of crisis, fresh concepts and personnel are needed to cope with its destructive effects. But, instead, new threats are met by old beliefs that the failures of our day may be overcome by archaic means: city-planning, urban renewal, land use, zoning, new towns, freeways, etc. – while nature is to be preserved in national parks. We suffer from the illusion that technical and professional expertise and scientific knowledge are matched by the political and economic capacity to take curative and preventative action. Unfortunately this is not true. Blind faith in expertise is encouraging para-scientists and para-technicians, to paraphrase Dwight McDonald, and together with blind faith in conventional wisdom, delays the actual resolution of the real problems. The designer's position in our culture is a reflection of the general confusion. Now we have para-professors, para-planners and para-designers.

To ask members of the planning profession to resolve problems of complexity, when they have been accustomed to simplistic analysis of gratuitously separated but actually totally interdependent parts, is no more likely to produce comprehensive solutions than if designers as a profession were suddenly asked to apply themselves to analysis as a prelude to design of something unprecedented. Just as planners have only been taught to deal with irrelevant problems, designers can only produce formal variations in stereotypical situations to serve temporary popularity. Together with opportunistic critics they are only motivated by shortsighted criteria, likely to produce 'structural poverty' instead of 'cultural richness' in the future.

It is ironic that ethical and moral insensibility, as well as relatively greater poverty, should coincide with the greatest scientific and technical potential and economic affluence yet known to man. In the United States, where this new affluence has found its highest expression, the paradox is most apparent and suggests that spiritual poverty is the inevitable first by-product of material plenty. Professor Frankel of Columbia University, for instance, points out that affluence does not necessarily bring about positive results for people: 'The resources of conscience and energy which lie ready

Space travel is a triumph of intellect but a tragic failure of reason . . .

Max Born, Evangelical Academy, Kloster Loccum, February 1953

Los Angeles has been accurately called 'a city on wheels'. Its white middle-class citizens consider a car (in some cases, two cars) a necessity; the Negro citizens of Watts consider it a luxury. Furthermore, Watts has what may be the poorest transportation system in the city. While a trip from Watts to downtown L.A. takes less than twenty minutes by car, it takes almost two hours by bus. One may wait half an hour to an hour for that bus, and then transfer three times, using two transportation systems. In Los Angeles not all transfers are free. A single trip for a single job interview could cost $1.50 and consume six hours of travel time. Children have grown up in Watts and have never seen the Pacific Ocean, for it has been literally impossible for them to get there: their parents have had neither the time nor money to take them . . .

Bernard Duke, 'Festival of the Arts in Watts', Arts in Society, Vol. IV, No. 1, 1967

to be tapped, if those who are professionally and politically engaged in advancing the cause of human welfare have the wit and the will to lead the way, are so great that our very success under the past generation may itself be one of the present obstacles in the way of doing the jobs that now need to be done. The pace of events has left us a little breathless and our progress is a little tired. Our riches seem to have stunned us rather than stimulated us.' We do not intend, however, to maintain that economic affluence, technological triumph and social crisis necessarily coincide. On the contrary they have only now appeared as symptoms of particular stages of technological evolution in human history, but they need not occur simultaneously again.

The authors of this study remain incorrigibly optimistic in a broad spectrum of time. We share Professor Frankel's disappointment in the immediate past and the present, and anticipate tremendous struggles in the immediate future. Optimism must remain a substitute for long-term predictions which we have not yet learned to make with any degree of accuracy. In this book we shall not discuss classification of historical documents and statistical data or categorization of regional differences and curiosities, but will attempt to describe the human ecological condition and the problems, common to all humans, which bring them together rather than separate them. Old problems that still exist and are derived from an intricate past will be related to problems already visible in our present complexity and in turn to even greater future complexity. It is this complex new-old future which we want to describe.

To see the image of the physical man-made environment as an entity, to feel its scale and totality, one should perhaps look at it from a high altitude. This viewpoint, which has been dramatically and splendidly revealed and extended through the technology of modern photography, is particularly helpful to our purpose, not only because of what it shows, but also because of what it does not show. Distant views reveal an image of order to the eye of the trained observer. But order or chaos is only vaguely felt as pleasure or comfort, disruption or discomfort, when the untrained observer is part and parcel of the things observed. To look at man's environment from 'outside' is analagous to taking a step toward understanding ecological problems, that is to say, to see them in a larger framework than earthbound experiences offer.

When untrained men look down over great stretches of the earth from a few thousand feet the visible natural order is undefinable. There is so much variety, so much apparent randomness that it is very hard to comprehend the underlying pattern of relationships unless the observer is a trained geographer. Airborne men, like their sea and land bound ancestors, identify a mosaic of images of visible nature to which they have become accustomed: coast lines, river deltas, valleys, the textures of great forests, the contours of hills and mountains, clouds and blue sky.

When a trained geographer flies over an agricultural countryside, this composite land-water-airscape immediately becomes visually more comprehensible in terms of human intervention, no longer random but rather orderly. The pattern of an agrarian civilization is visible: in the plains the great rectilinear geometry of the flat lands – plowed fields, planted crops, the diversity of color and texture of a patchwork quilt with seams of roads. As the flat plains reach the hills, one sees the more dramatic free forms of the folded landscape – weaving roads and contour plowing following the natural patterns of the topography. On approaching some urban areas one can see suburban and industrial growth around the earlier town or village nucleus. At this point the pleasant pattern seems to be dislocated. One sees either the monotony of repetition – approximately similar lots with more or less identical boxes standing in them – or the mosaic of randomness which

10

does not suggest order but rather arbitrariness. The only visible order by day seems to be that of the natural and the agricultural land patterns. The urban areas in comparison appear, if not disorderly, at least incomprehensible. The geometry becomes more evasive as the ubiquitous roads cease to be identified with direction or target.

The overall geometry of the modern sprawling city's grid of streets or the suburban clusters with roads running in all directions does not provide visual evidence of any comprehensive order. Such pattern as may be perceived in some particular component seems unrelated to other different, or similar but separate, components. Each piece seems autonomous and without any larger organizing matrix.

At night the image changes. The strong forms of the countryside vanish in blackness. One can only pick up the main lines of communication and as the country roads approach the urban concentrations they become streets — great strings of luminous beads of different colors which occasionally burst into clusters of illumination as rich as jewelry. Today the railroads — the communication system of an earlier era — although still there, are practically invisible, especially in the United States. Even their great terminals and yards, now engulfed by the post-railway sprawl, seem plunged in darkness in contrast to the pervasive road system. At night the only conspicuous order is made by the paths of our motor traffic and occasional lights which suggest, but do not explain, activity of some other kind. At night the man-made world appears to be inhabited by machines, not by people.

These images tell us in a simple way several things. The natural order is enormously complex and it is very difficult to identify its separate components even as an airborne observer. The innumerable functions are woven into a pattern of such complexity that it may not be easily deciphered. The natural environment becomes more comprehensible when modified by agricultural requirements, so ancient and relatively familiar to all men in most of their aspects, that it appears as an accompanying order of relatively simple functional elements. The typical modern urban environmental mixture of our day is in appearance more chaotic, missing the obvious focal force of dominant elements in

The increasing use of motor vehicles for personal transportation in the U.S. – from 34 million of them in 1946 to 90 million in 1965 – is a fairly accurate measure of the extent to which rail transit has declined over the same period (from 790 million rides in 1946 to 299 million in 1965). Urban mass transit has suffered a similar fate. Between 1950 and 1960 according to the study by Northwestern University, the man-transit industry lost 45 per cent of its customers and suffered a 25 per cent cut in net revenues.

'The Agony of Getting Anywhere', Newsweek, 9 January 1967

11

the agricultural scene which embraced the fortified, compact early towns.

Pattern of Interaction

In the attempt to evoke a sense of the ordering characteristics in the environment (but not its real nature), we find that the flow of traffic seems to be the only ordering component of this otherwise evasive system visible to an innocent eye. Even at relatively close range one cannot see either pedestrian paths or peopled places. Perhaps they have vanished from the habitat of an automanic society. With the exception of the overwhelming highways, clover-leaf intersections and bridges of precise and giant structural geometry, technology seems inconspicuous. Colossal but more or less visibly ordered structures, such as megaliths of highrise building, may sometimes mark in an unclear way points of confluence of much traffic. Skyscraping giants indicate, if not celebrate, metropolitan nodes of high concentration of the affluent people whom we do not see. The lesser crossing points marked by obsolescing small towns look from above somewhat like neglected cairns, scattered heaps of stone which had once marked some now forgotten event in man's affairs. Man-made mountains, 'megastructures' in modern jargon, foothills and valleys can look deceptively like their natural prototypes, more often than not wrapped in cloud or filled with mist. But, whereas in the natural environment these vapours contain only life-sustaining water, in the man-made they currently hold in suspension elements of danger, if not of death. The picturesque and mysterious mist has been transformed into a poisonous, fearful fog.

In the course of a one-hundred-mile journey I was destined to encounter on the open road no single fellow-cyclist, no single pedestrian, no single horse-drawn vehicle. . . . The occupants of the occasional machines that went whirring by . . . obviously had no connexion in the social sense with the highway over which they were driving. . . . They were lost spirits, hovering for brief periods on another plane, where space existed only in time.

George F. Kennan, *Memoirs 1925–1950*, New York, 1966

Temperate Town – Tropical Metropolis

In the city-scape man has been drastically transformed by the rapid expansion of technology. We have not yet learned that not only have cities become bigger, but their very nature has changed. The historic cities which grew slowly and adapted to their natural environment over the centuries did not prepare 'westernizing' industrialized man for the drastic changes and growth of the last few decades. The four seasons were the only events of change with their predictably gentle rhythm. As the temperate towns grew into 'tropical' cities, the environment suddenly became unpredictable and fierce. In man-made habitats of relative simplicity, comparable to gentle temperate woodlands, the interdependence of living things and their environment was to a great extent understood. Now that the urban environment is beginning to approach the rain forest in complexity, the interactions between living organisms and man-made things have become blurred. The upper sun-drenched layers in the rain forest are filled with orchids and gaily colored birds, the middle layers with monkeys and vines, while several layers below, at the gloomy ground level, other clumsier, larger beasts move around with their infinity of parasites. If we depart from this image of tropical complexity and study the ecological reality of the rain forest, we find that living organisms appear able to make an appropriate adaptation in natural environments of the greatest complexity and they seem to be secure for long periods at a time. The patterns of slow evolutionary processes are invisible and incomprehensible to the inhabitants. Only cataclysmic events of rare occurrence seem to upset the ecological equilibrium and evolutionary rhythm.

Although the new realities of interdependence of all things for urbanizing man have become ecological, the man-made has no natural controls like the rain forest to help resolve the new problems. Humanity at this time has to provide such controls, but this is not possible without a comprehension of the human ecological condition. Until this situation is boldly tackled on a comprehensive scale there can be no remedies, and urbanizing technological society will move through various layers of its habitat, thoughtlessly or callously destroying human ecological balance in the process. For, as the man-made approaches the most prolific manifestation of the natural in richness and diversity, it at the same time becomes potentially more precarious.

Orders and Images

Although we may not immediately recognize the underlying order of natural habitats, we can identify with familiar images of natural physical phenomena: hills, rivers, river mouths, valleys, seashores, mountains, sky, clouds. What we cannot perceive through our senses is the great unifying order behind them, for instance, nature's water-making system, providing the life-blood of all living things on earth. By exactly the same token, we do not see that behind the familiar images of the 13 city-scape — streets, avenues, skyscrapers, which we accept as commonplaces, or civic centers, shopping centers, parking lots, which we accept as essential facilities – there is in fact a constantly changing social order, an invisible controlling system of technological organization, which used to change very slowly, but is beginning to change very quickly.

The urban environmental problem may be considered for the purposes of a designer as analogous to the problems faced by a forestry specialist who is trying to understand the whole process of forest growth, decay and renewal, in order to exercise some measure of control over it. To maintain the forest as a habitat for many creatures and to preserve the ecological balance in spite of invasions and assaults, an assisted adjustment to change and growth is necessary. This interest of a forestry specialist seems closer to an urban designer's purpose than the interest of a naturalist prepared to note and codify his observations but who does not intend to take positive action, and instead leaves adjustments of growth and change to the slow rhythms of 'natural' evolution.

New Forestry

The latter-day urbanists, the new breed of foresters, stand in sharp contrast to earlier city-planners, who, like naturalists, were content to look at the city as something to be measured, classified or categorized. The goal was to provide simple statistics and to extrapolate these findings for future plans in hopelessly over-simplified sets of separate components. We shall not attempt in this book to design new urban end-products, for in the final analysis these must be the expression of particular and infinitely variable situations in time and space. Our concern here is the specification of essential characteristics and functions in more universal terms. We will describe urban situations in terms of human purpose, principles of organization and operational components, in other words in terms of the internal structure of the environment and the interaction of its parts rather than its superficial form.

It has been recognized for many years now, even by the most rigid planners, that a 'master plan', like Utopia, an ideal completed form, can no longer serve the purposes of design in which change and growth may be the essential determinants of order. Forms in their great diversity must become apparent and significant;

14

no single 'master form' can do this.

Urban design cannot be form alone. Purposeful social commitment must precede all action in the design process without concern for the techniques or shapes through which the commitment may finally be translated into physical reality. Although our present concern is for the existence in any urban system of places which may generate concourse and intercourse as a structuring device, before we start this analysis we have to clarify our humanistic commitment.

satisfy the ambitions of persons who use the new technology to serve their own narrow ends . . . the time has come for us to stop being wagged by our technological tails. . . . The time has come for us to start looking at the other end of the human animal – the end that contains the minds and the hearts of the people.

Robert Boguslov, 'Technological Change and Urban Culture', *Urban Exploration Proceedings*, Florida, 1965

I understand planning to be a *method for reaching decisions*, not a body of specific substantive goals. Applied within a fairly stable and widely shared general value framework, planning is a rather special way of deciding which specific goals are to be pursued and which specific actions are to be taken. Seen in this way, it is directly antithetical to the more popular view among some practitioners, who are also called planners, in which planning is a social movement aimed at accomplishing certain predetermined specific goals shared by members of the professional group or by other groups.

Having said this, it should also be apparent that the method is largely independent of the phenomena to be planned.

Melvin M. Webber, 'Planning as a Problem-Solving Method', in *The Urban Condition*, ed. Leonard J. Duhl, New York, 1963, ch. 25

We must find ways of determining the requirements of human beings first and then shape technology. Technology must not be permitted to run rampant in accordance with the whims of the well-meaning technocrats or to

15

2. Commitment and Priorities   Adjustment, interaction and their underlying order. Planning as declaration of human needs and priorities. Urbanization as ends and means. Complementarity of social ends and technical means. Meaningful community.

... harmony consists of opposing tension, like that of the bar and lyre ...

Heraclitus, Fragment 51

Theseus conceived a wonderful design and settled all the residents of Attica in one city, thus making one people of one city out of those who up to that time had been scattered about and were not easily called together for the common interest of all. . . . He visited them, then, and tried to win them over to his project township by township and clan by clan.

Plutarch, *The Parallel Lives*, trans. Bernadette Perrin, Cambridge, Mass., 1914, Vol. 1

... the essential individual randomness from which evolutionary selection and adaptation may be made and the collective rules which enable the organism to exploit advantage of number for survival as a group in the ecological battlefield [are] nature's provision of seemingly contradictory mechanisms ...

J. Z. Young, 'Doubt and Certainty in Science', Reith Lectures, BBC, 1950

The all-pervasive ecological crisis has proved the
inadequacy of present institutions, practices and
attitudes. A new commitment is needed to start the
process of readjusting the obsolete parts of our culture.
This interaction involves the painful transformation of
apparently irreconcilable contradictions into new
relationships. The present study, like any other not
susceptible to exact measurement, is a statement of the
writers' commitment. It contains nothing new in any
particular of analysis or synthesis of the already
observed, sensed and comprehended. Instead it tries to
bring previously unrelated facts into interrelationship so
that design may acquire new meaning through a process
which may be systematically analyzed.

We are engaged in continuous debate, in which our
debt to countless others is quite obvious. Ernst Cassirer
in *The Logic of the Humanities* eloquently describes
such a debate: 'Opposition and clash between these two
forces – the one seeking preservation and the other
seeking renewal – is endless. Any equilibrium which, for
a time, may appear to have been attained is never more
than an unstable balance of forces, a balance that can
break out into a new movement at any point. So it is
that, with the growth and development of culture, the
pendulum widens its swing – the amplitude of the swing
itself continues to increase. As a result, the inner
tensions and oppositions also continue to increase in
intensity. Still, at no time does this drama of culture
become a complete tragedy of culture. For just as it
contains an ultimate defeat so it also contains an
ultimate victory. Instead of mutually destroying each
other, these two forces nourish one another. The
creative movement of the spirit appears to nurture its
own antagonist in those very works which the prota-
gonist has brought forth. For everything created must
by its very nature struggle for position against what is
emerging and will emerge. Out of this struggle through
new effort are discovered new and unknown powers.'[3]

Within such a debate, by pursuing our commitment, we
may find that urbanization may assume forms which
living men cannot imagine. It is not certain that the
present trend toward stable density in urban concentrations of great magnitude will continue in the foreseeable
future. Perhaps this century announces the emergence of

3. Ernst Cassirer, *The Logic of the Humanities*, trans.
Clarence S. Hower, Yale, 1961

technological nomads: a new era in human history in which fluid deployment will reverse the trend of millennia. Perhaps, and this appears more likely to us, fluid deployment will complement more compact and stable urban organization, assuming a complementarity of technological growth and sociological change. In any case the importance of urbanization can only be realized when such potentials can be seen as a system of inter-action between man and environments and man and men, and not as separate pieces, processes or dis-connected events. A technology which is global in scale and all-pervasive in character can only be examined in an ecological framework. It cannot be dealt with in a piecemeal way. The most urgent relationship within such a system of interaction is between the current dominant appetite for technology and its predictable, sociological consequences. This new potential was brilliantly summarized by U Thant, the Secretary-General of the United Nations: 'We can decide what resources we want to have, not the other way around.'

From this it follows that the design of man-made environments must utilize new technological and methodological means, which man has for the first time at his disposal, to build a logical bridge to connect the man-made environment with the underlying order which should govern it. At the same time as the laws governing the environmental order become interrelated with planning, new functionaries must be created as the first step in the process of design. This development in turn will emphasize the necessity of establishing new institutions or modifying old ones to admit the new functionaries into the decision-making process.

Perhaps the central myth is the one that adheres to the very notion of 'a nation of cities' – a notion of which conjures up a vision of nearly 200 million Americans living shoulder to shoulder. . . . The foundation of this central myth is the 'fact' that over 70 per cent of all Americans now live in urban places. This 'fact', however, must be considered in the context of the United States Census Bureau's definition of 'urban place': any settlement of 2,500 population or more. Only when cities are thus defined, is the United States a nation of cities. But, of course, a town of 2,500 – or even 25,000 – is not likely to conform to the foregoing vision of cities . . .

The 1960 population distribution by city size reveals that 58·3 per cent of the nation's total population lived in rural areas or in cities of under 50,000 people (which means approximately 15,000 families) – and that only 9·8 per cent lived in cities of over one million population. Of the more than 6,000 legally constituted cities in the nation, only five have a population of over one million, and only 51 have populations of over 250,000.

Furthermore, while the rural population has continued its decline, the percentage of population in urban places of less than 50,000 has actually increased by 50 per cent since 1920. In the same period, the percentage of the national population living in cities of over 500,000 barely increased at all. At least since 1920, the class of cities with the largest single segment of the nation's urban population (and it is also the fastest growing segment) has been that of the 10,000 to 50,000 group. These hardly deserve to be considered cities . . .

Daniel J. Elazar, 'Is America an Urban Nation?', quoted in *Current*, December 1966

Technological Transformations

The most conspicuous result of the latest spurt in technological evolution is a transformation of the whole environment. Human interference with the ecology of all living organisms on earth is proceeding at a speed and on a scale which varies only in proportion to local economic development, and such differences are likely to become progressively reduced in the future. Material abundance and limitless energy can be provided by the technologies of 'breeding reactors' (already in operation) which produce more fuel than can be consumed from limitless resources of rock and sea. 'Perpetual motion', the dream of ages, has suddenly become reality. But this extraordinary bouquet of affluence will perhaps contain an asp. A sudden extension of abundance, now largely localized, does not necessarily improve the human habitat on a global scale.

Ends and Means

Already the goal of material plenty for future populations is clear cut, has priority, and has become technically possible. Provision of basic necessities of water, food, health and shelter are no longer technical problems. Real problems lie elsewhere – in social goals which include the control of unchecked population growth. These must be re-examined in the face of new realities. In the United States, the technologically most advanced country, the absence of such clear-cut goals is dramatically revealed in the pollution of our air, water and land, in city traffic congestion, in mounting numbers of road deaths, in a climbing crime rate and in the fouling by the private sector of public places. The streets and roads of America are becoming trash baskets; they are among the dirtiest in the world. It appears that in a period of technological transition as drastic as the one mankind is undergoing now, decisions about economic and technical matters are made without reference to possible disastrous social consequences. An insatiable appetite for more material things is not matched by aspiration towards better human conditions. In short, America has many conveniences but few comforts.

Technologically sophisticated societies appear to be sociologically similar. The goals which are generally understood and shared are for the most part high and pious abstractions. Consequently, popular judgements of the success or failure of various technological enterprises are usually hazy or contradictory. Reasonable judgements are not possible if human purpose is not clearly stated. Technologically excellent means may be applied to the achievement of contemptible social ends, because an exaggerated preoccupation with means at the expense of ends makes any viable planning impossible. Therefore the first step in any planning process must be the declaration of social purpose followed by a firm commitment; a deliberate choice of priorities.

From this point of view, as Professor Paul Weiss has observed: 'Planning now appears to be a most planless enterprise.'[4] In familiar situations failures in the performance of a design after its execution can be rectified in the future by improving its design. But traditional methods are no longer useful for evaluating success or failure in new situations. This difficulty may be illustrated by some now familiar examples which show that the historical precedent is no longer a yardstick. How can anyone evaluate the success or failure of such new environments as Los Angeles, which is a mixture of prosperity and poverty, the U.S. new town of Reston, which is an upper crust suburb for Washington D.C. in new guise, or the small Scottish new town of Cumbernauld, which pretends to autonomy a few miles away from Glasgow?

4. Paul Weiss, Yale Seminars, 1966

Defense expenditures for military functions, at $76·7-billion, chew up 41 per cent of the budget. Of this, $26·3-billion is attributable to the war in Vietnam, or 14 per cent of the total budget. The rise in defense outlays is $3-billion, of which $1·3-billion is in the Vietnam cost.

The model cities program, which is designed to combine housing and social programs in a coordinated assault on slum conditions. Outlays will rise from $25-million this year to $250-million in fiscal year 1969.

The public housing program, which provides low-cost housing for poor tenants. Outlays will rise from an estimated $297-million this year to $350-million in fiscal 1969.

The urban renewal program, which helps cities pay the cost of clearing slum land. Outlays will rise from $499-million this year to $699-million in fiscal 1969.

According to the budget, expenditures for housing and community development programs are expected to double, rising from $697-million in the present fiscal year to $1·4-billion in the fiscal year 1969.

Robert B. Semple Jr, *New York Times*, 30 January 1968

Authors' note: Budget allocations for urban purposes have since then been proportionately further reduced under the Nixon administration.

...A Flushing physician complains that 'it is sometimes impossible to have a conversation with patients and even less possible to listen to a heart or take the blood pressure of patients...

A Floral Park mother, finding conversation impossible, spends two hours counting 76 planes passing overhead.... A letter signed by Bernard Landers, president of the Woodmere Park Association, and 100 neighbors [says]: 'Right now the noise is so bad in some areas that not only the comfort, but also the health and well-being of families are being affected. Many people cannot sleep later than 5.30 in the morning when a continuous volume of noise begins.'... Neighbors of O'Hare Airport in Chicago — it is the busiest field in the world; a jet lands or takes off on the average of every 40 seconds — must put up with what their Congressman, Roman C. Pucinski, recently described as 'the unrelenting, unremitting, intolerable boom and whine of the tidal waves of sound'...

If the supersonic transport (SST) is permitted to fly overland instead of being restricted to ocean travel — and Major Gen. Jewell C. Maxwell (U.S.A.F.), head of the SST program, says that overland supersonic travel is 'inevitable' — the plane will drag along a 50-mile-wide sonic boom, coast to coast, which could reach the ears of 20 million Americans.... If all goes well prototype engine[s] will be 20 decibels quieter than anything flying today... the best way to suggest what the 20-decibel reduction will mean is to point out that most big jets taking off today are recorded at 120 decibels and up — about the same loudness as a machine gun at close range.... Community complaint, which can be expected to begin at 9 decibels, usually boils over at about 105 decibels.... Gen. William F. McKee, F.A.A. administrator, [says in] a private memor-

andum... that after much soul-searching they had concluded that a six-to-eight decibel drop is all that they can promise; meantime in the nineteen-seventies...

'I think it is fair to say that as one lives with noise one tends to develop a greater tolerance of it,' said Boyd (Department of Transportation Secretary), in a statement that has been repeated, in one form or another, by every important official of the Department of Transportation.

It is, somehow, a myth that has survived scientific studies showing the contrary. Dr Karl B. Dryter of Stanford University... showed that the more exposure to noisy flights a community is subjected to, the feebler its tolerance becomes...

Eddie Rickenbacker told the National Press Club recently that 'the public will just have to get used to aircraft noise'...

Robert Sherrill, 'The Jet Noise', *New York Times Magazine*, 14 January 1968

...At present it is possible to travel on land — especially selected land — at some 400 m.p.h., but whenever one moves into the heart of a big city like London, the maximum speed may be no more than 10 m.p.h. Even in the off-peak hours traffic in the central area of London north of the Thames cannot go as fast as 12 m.p.h., while south of the Thames, where traffic seems to flow a little more easily, it does not manage to reach 15 m.p.h. Taking the whole of Greater London, which covers nearly 1,000 square miles, the average speed on the main roads in the off-peak periods is only 21·5 miles per hour, and this speed is not achieved during the rush hours.

E. C. Claxton, 'The Future of the Bicycle in a Modern Society,' *Journal of the Royal Society of Arts*, January, 1968

Does our society need flights at supersonic speeds which will provide minimal advantage in terms of overall travel time while ground connexions remain as miserable as they now are? Not only does this involve a colossal outlay from the public purse for the advantage of a few companies, but it also entails interference in the lives of innumerable taxpayers through sonic booms. Is a continuous increase in automobile travel, with its problems of costly traffic congestion in cities, really the best way to provide access to more choices for more people?

Decision Process

It appears that at no time in history has there been a clear-cut demarcation between goals and means, but, in relation to the historic process as a whole, there is a continuous flow of interaction between them. The special goals of yesterday become the commonplace means of tomorrow. As former goals obsolesce, means to new goals emerge.

We accept as a primary goal of our time the increase of freedom of choice for the majority of people. But unfortunately Lewis Mumford's picture (*Men and Machines*, soon to be published in the U.S.A.) of the first machine, the organized, collective labor of slaves, has its counterpart today. As the slaves had no illusions about their freedom of action while fulfilling the tasks of production and service, today the organized, collective consumers fulfill the task of accepting almost anything offered, although they remain content with the illusion of freedom of choice. But now that machines can provide calculating operations which are beyond human capacity, perhaps we have reached a turning point in human evolution: when men cease to be automata. Men and machines need no longer be in contradiction but may become complementary in function. The goal of freedom of choice can be achieved, but to accomplish this social end we must find the right methods and technical means equally fast.

Conflict is discord, and the opposite or conflict is harmony; the words reveal the evaluational bias in the language and common experience. Discord may be necessary to make music interesting . . . but its significance lies in the ability of the composer to resolve discord into some meaningful harmony. . . . The essence of the drama of conflict is likewise its resolution.

Kenneth Boulding, *Conflict and Defense*, New York, 1962

25

In the context of a general theory of urbanization, the whole present process must be questioned in the light of these new potentials. Historic cities were easily comprehended as goals in themselves. In the face of modern urban communication technology, however, the persistence of this idea has appeared obsolete to some who see 'community' undergoing a 'complete' metamorphosis, a view which we do not share. We suggest to the contrary, that far from having outlived their usefulness, intensely used urban communities appear to have changed into means which, within the larger framework suggested, can be enabled to serve the old and new goals alike.

The attempt to answer sociological questions by means of highly sophisticated technology and methodology cannot be more than an exercise. Social systems still elude this form of analysis. A dialogue can be started *ad.infinitum* which becomes in Robert Theobald's phrase 'an analytical dead-end'. At the beginning of any search for viable social goals must come a commitment which can be simply stated and easily understood and can then be demonstrated. Without a demonstration there is little to discuss and nothing to analyze. Robert Theobald puts such a dilemma of a technologically oriented society in these words: 'It is the social aspects of "social systems" which should be stressed rather than the *system* aspect which, when based on ever-increasing cybernation, would result in a final perfect expression of machine needs, the *centralized technological dictatorship*.'[5] Our aim is to achieve a necessary degree of organization without being subordinated by it. In terms of our commitment we believe that after an appropriate resistance period today's prevalent technocracy and technological centralization may become a new technology of a different kind complementary to sociological readjustment.

Commitment and the
Urban Spectrum

In a previous book, by Serge Chermayeff and Christopher Alexander, *Community and Privacy*,[6] the commitment to human goals was at one end of the urban spectrum. Privacy – the option of salutary solitude – was postulated as essential to healthy human condition and therefore to be preserved under any circumstances in the human habitat. The idea that this desirable state could only be obtained in areas of low density was

... the experience of this sharing, of making mine the thoughts of others, and of recognizing from their signals that my signals to them have been received. So, whether or no our activities have made any other contribution to mental health, they have certainly contributed to mine.

Geoffrey Vickers, 'Ecology, Planning and the American Dream', in *The Urban Condition*, ed. Leonard J. Duhl, New York, 1963, ch. 29

5. Robert Theobald, *Free Man and Free Markets*, New York, 1963

6. Serge Chermayeff and Christopher Alexander, *Community and Privacy*, New York, 1962, Harmondsworth, Penguin Books, 1966

aemonstrated to be illusory; the book argued that design could produce the desired results anywhere.

The problem of urban dwellings, both in structure and scale, was deliberately related to high density areas that are generally associated with the greatest interference from technology – traffic, noises, pollution, etc. – simply because such areas are receiving an ever-increasing proportion of humanity. We showed that escape from high density could not provide a useful alternative for all men. This situation was susceptible to clear-cut definition of purpose and at the same time a precise description of the functional components involved. This association, in turn, made possible a systematic analysis of their interaction. The goal being simply described as a commitment to individual privacy, individual men became the familiar and acceptable yardstick.

Commitment and Prediction

No commitment, regardless of its familiar simplicity or its challenging complexity, can provide a solution to a problem, any more than it can be considered as a design process leading to a solution. A commitment is quite simply a precondition without which a process cannot operate nor can a solution be obtained. Lack of commitment, on the other hand, quite often makes technological means useless, and the most advanced methods of problem solving irrelevant. Decisions unrelated to human goals produce technological systems without guidance: a fluid economic growth process *ad nauseam*. To paraphrase Ronald Steel, speaking of the bankruptcy of many scientists and intellectuals now engaged in developing theories of strategy: they have made certain kinds of absurd changes in the environment quite thinkable and even possible by prescribing conditions under which controlled disruption of humanity through the design of the man-made environment has also become possible.[7]

Most prosperous consumers in developed (industrial) countries are content to accept the products of technology as these roll off the assembly lines or to watch out for advertised seasonal 'improvement'. The more literate are willing to turn for assurance to 'specialists' who now, of course, include 'system-analysts'. Consumers, except a few sceptics it appears, are content to stop short of satisfactory solutions due to the lack of humane goals as prime components in

7. Ronald Steel, *Pax Americana*, New York, 1967

the scheme of things they accept. Dr A. E. Parr cites the dangers inherent in a self-drive automotive culture which, while giving a great range to holders of driving licenses, leaves children and elders restricted and frustrated. The disrespect for human values is universal to all industrial societies. Ada Louise Huxtable, in her *New York Times* reports on Moscow architecture, leaves no doubt that the drab apartment slabs on the outskirts of that great city are as 'spiritually debilitating' as similar ones in the U.S.A.

Commitment to Community

In *Community and Privacy*, privacy was of necessity recognized as a complementary opposite to community. This study is concerned with the other end: the aspect of community. Simply stated, our commitment is to the provision of places of concourse, where meaningful community intercourse can become complementary to meaningful solitude.

Since *Community and Privacy* was published, the loss of privacy in urban environments has received less publicity than the increase in the physical pollution of all environments. Pollution and poisoning of air and unbearable daily traffic problems have become every city user's concern. But the 'invisible' and 'inaudible' effects of technology: social disruption, neuroses and crime, have remained somehow conveniently separated from the urban problem as a whole, to be cured like measles or chickenpox.

It seems one can now discuss the greater environmental problems with a reasonable hope of comprehending the issues. This involves putting the 'crisis of cities' in its more convincing perspective of social crises. In dealing with the crisis of urbanization, one has to put the problem, not in terms of the economic statistics of physical patterns, but more directly in terms of the pressures of technological facts on societal issues. A technological society, like all others before it, must have a physical habitat capable of containing it without loss of humanity. Passive acceptance of technology will not lead to compensation for earlier miseries, but possibly to bigger and more painful failures. The evils of obsolete cities may be less than the disasters which will follow the liquidation of the spirit of community.

We thus see that the polis exists by nature and that it is prior to the individual. . . . The man who . . . is no part of the polis . . . must therefore be either a beast or a god.

Aristotle, *Politics*, I, ii, 14

Ecological Scale

Urban problems have acquired a new meaning: on the

Where the world gathers the world learns.

Motto of the International Exposition Hemis Fair, 1968,
San Antonio, Texas

An experience shared can often be called to
view at a glance by those who shared it. Yet . . .
the overload grows, especially if we wish to
maintain values that stress individual men not as
small component parts of the social intelligence,
but as individuals.

Martin Shubik, 'Information, Rationality, and Free Choice
in a Future Democratic Society', *Daedalus: Journal of the
American Academy of Arts and Sciences*, Summer, 1967

one hand, design is now acting within a dynamic order
between innumerable sociological and technological ends
and means. The arbitrarily separated static pieces on
which designers previously focused have lost their
meaning and usefulness in the larger social and ecological complexity of which they are subcomponents.
On the other hand, human ecology, to which this book
is committed, requires that a human community is
understood in terms of places of public concourse. In
the context of existing technological society, however,
places of public concourse either do not exist or are
vanishing because they do not command public support.
We submit, however, that such places must be provided
at every scale.

Commitment and Risk

Every commitment entails 'taking a risk' during the
building of a theoretical structure which can serve as
a basis for action, but it is only through such risks that
man can approach a 'human system', instead of
remaining content with the leftovers of technology or
dreaming of escape into Utopia, which is only an
abstraction used as a protest against existing situations.

A more detailed description of our commitment
to certain goals will be followed by a proposal for a
methodology of design that may be applicable to any
other commitment. This is an attempt to integrate
environmental ends and means in a system of complementarity and equilibrium, that is, an environmental
strategy which, together with its tactics, can avoid the
pitfalls of both Utopia and consensus.

. . . Utopias can exist as realities only if they
die shortly after being born, to be reborn with
new shapes. . . . They act as catalysts
converting the crude materials of reality, the
tools and products of experience and of science,
into civilizations which take the shape developed
first as an image in the mind of man.

René Dubos, *Dreams of Reason: Science and Utopias*, New
York, 1965

. . . A state of equilibrium is not a state of
final rest, but consists of a new starting point,
because an equilibrations process can bring
about the formation of new states of
disequilibrium.

J. Piaget, *Études d'Épistémologie Génétique*, Vol. XV, Paris,
1963

The proposed system relates urban goals to means which can then be defined and structured. The end products of progress, technological and sociological alike, will be the result of the labors of men able to synthesize excellent goals and means into significant form in an environmental design.

Design Extended

This extension of design to embrace the larger environment requires an extension of professional competence to include the mastery of new tools. The relatively simple application of computer methods and techniques to planning urban dwellings and dwelling clusters, as illustrated in *Community and Privacy*, may be extended for the purpose of any segment of the vast spectrum of urban design. The tools of cybernation make it possible for planning to tackle simultaneously sociological and technological issues on the same level. Designing also becomes more comprehensive and competent in function. In this framework contradictions between static separate issues become complementary in a larger interacting system. This system of varied disciplines requires for designing not only a comprehensive theory, but also the mobilization of diversified talent for action. In chapter 10 we will discuss the new design potential and suggest a new catalytic role for this in education. The point we wish to stress is that the tools necessary for tackling complexity as a whole exist but so far have been only partially mobilized. Urban planning, for long a baffling necessity, has become a manageable possibility. The primary task appears to be the framing of searching questions and priorities, not the provision of simple answers.

The integration of opposite elements in the urban units should not be conceived as the establishment of static syntheses but as the initiation of meaningful dialogues carried on in the 'language' of environment. Where such opposites are induced to co-exist, the urban 'breath' is set in motion and an urban quality may be achieved.

Arthur Glikson, quoted in *Ekistics*, August 1967

3. Orbits of Time

Human evolution has different tempos. The 'third ecology' of the man-made environment. The collective process and institutional lag. Growing interdependence: mobility and communications.

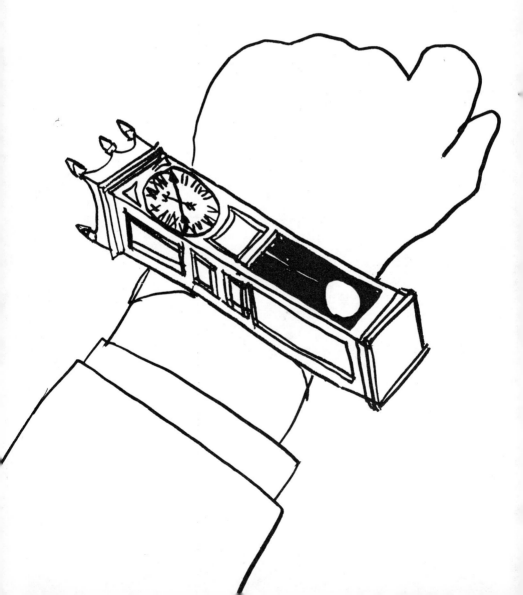

But along with Malthus I had read, and been even more deeply impressed by, Sir Charles Lyell's immortal *Principles of Geology* which had taught me that the inorganic world – the whole surface of the earth, its seas and lands, its mountains and valleys, its rivers and lakes, and every detail of its climatic conditions, were and always had been in a continual state of slow modification. Hence it became obvious that the forms of life must have become continually adjusted to these changed conditions in order to survive.

Alfred Russel Wallace, the Darwin–Wallace Celebration held on 1 July 1908 by the Linnaean Society of London

Where reality does not accord with use, our practice, as frequently noted, is to devise a myth which then serves as a bridge between evidence that cannot be escaped and the belief that is sought.

J. K. Galbraith, *The New Industrial State*, Boston, 1967

The great issues of nuclear strategy, for instance, cannot even be the object of meaningful debate, whether in Congress or among the people at large, because there can be no competent judgement without meaningful knowledge. Thus the great national decisions of life and death are rendered by technological elites, and both the Congress and the people at large retain little more than the illusion of making the decisions which the theory of democracy supposes them to make.

Hans Morgenthau in *New Republic*, 28 October 1967

Innate behavior mechanisms can be thrown completely out of balance by small, apparently insignificant changes of environmental conditions. Inability to adapt quickly to such changes may bring about the destruction of a species and the changes which man has wrought in his environment are by no means insignificant.

Konrad Lorenz, *On Aggression*, New York, 1966

Fig. 1
Evolutionary Clocks
Synchronization Failure

Human evolution occurs in
'four time-orbits'
simultaneously; in the
natural and the man-made
environments. Change and
growth through innovation
and transformation extend
both the habitat and man
himself.
(In this diagram
evolutionary time is on the
horizontal scale and change
and growth are on the
vertical scale.)

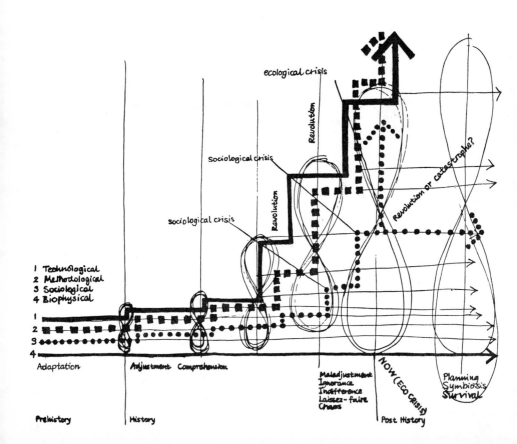

8. Marston Bates, *The Forest and the Sea*, New York, 1960

The ecology of the sea – the 'first ecology' – is a further analogy to the ecology of the tropical rain forest – which is part of the 'second ecology': the land – mentioned earlier. The complexity, intensity and diversity of life in the ocean have barely been explored by man, but biologists have already noted the similarity in the distribution of life and ecological patterns of the forest and the sea. In his book *The Forest and the Sea*[8] Marston Bates describes in fascinating detail his observations of the behavior of land and marine creatures and laments the fragmentation of biological knowledge; a handicap to comprehensive exploration of complexity. Those concerned with the man-made environment, now approaching the tropical forest and the sea in complexity, can join in his lament. If environmental designs are unable to integrate the fragmented knowledge of the human habitat, they cannot develop a theory and a comprehensive method of tackling problems, and no significant advance can result.

The present stage in the development of the human habitat appears to be one of chaos. Humanity is in a state of disequilibrium and its most obvious and dramatic symptoms are to be found in the urban environment. The search for a viable urban theory, undertaken in this study, is the 'third ecology' for urbanizing man.

In order to analyze the dynamics of the development of the 'third ecology' we have adopted a figurative description of the evolutionary processes, 'evolutionary clocks', running at vastly different speeds. These are thought of as homeostatic controls of human behavior operating at different speeds in human evolution, and may prove to be a useful metaphor for understanding the state of disequilibrium in the human habitat.

The 'biological/psychological clock' moves so slowly that time appears at a standstill. Man's biological and psychological needs move in cycles of evolutionary change beyond his control at this time. The 'sociological institutional clock' has been moving at a much faster speed and rate of acceleration. The forms of social organization, the purpose and structure of human groups, change not in a smooth flow and rhythm of progression, but spasmodically in time and jerkily in effect. The various stages in this process may be observed in the evolution of social institutions. These

9. Jacques Ellul, *The Technological Society*, New York, 1964

But the ways of the future are not of one kind. Even if the future society will be completely different from what we know (when perhaps people will not read or write, will not work in offices but will instead communicate through electronic devices) it is possible that the presently known human psycho-physiological behaviour will not change radically. It will only undergo a transformation while keeping largely the same behavioural characteristics.

Dimitris A. Fatouros, 'City: A Macro-Architecture', *Architecture in Greece*, Vol. 1, Athens, 1967

The problem of human adaptation could be presented as a dialectic between permanency and change. . . . Thus persistence of ancient traits does not mean that human history is a mere extension of the past; nor do changes in the ways of life imply a loss of the biological heritage.

René Dubos, *Man Adapting*, New Haven, 1965

operate in a dual manner: as a result of human reaction to environmental pressures and independently in response to new needs generated by the human mind.

The speed of the 'clock of comprehension' – 'methodological clock' – is the product of collective attitudes toward problems and the search for methods of solution: in other words the extent to which theories are able to dominate the basic logic of decision in any period. But while the interactions between sociological and methodological processes are continuous and evident, each inevitably modifying the other, it is even clearer that method is related more directly to the tools which society has at its disposal. Consequently it follows that the 'clock of comprehension' has, up to now at least, approximated the speed of the 'clock of technology', the fourth and fastest clock of all. Technological evolution has been subject to progressively less and less restraint in human affairs. The immediate benefits of science, applied science and technical improvement are clearly visible and hastily accepted. Acceptance and acceleration have become continuous and exponential. Technology has developed its own dynamics: Jacques Ellul has even suggested that it has its own moral imperatives.[9]

It seems that Homo sapiens runs the danger of degenerating into Homo faber by accelerating his technological evolution to speeds which will leave the biological and sociological evolution and the evolution of comprehension further and further behind. That this new discrepancy presents an immediate threat is evident in the proliferation of computer mechanics and the growing acceptance of computerized 'answers' in spite of warnings from scientists. The mind still works quite differently, producing concepts and comprehension by yet unknown processes, while the most sophisticated technology produces nothing more than new means, however superlatively 'useful' these may be at any time.

Man appears to exist in these four 'time orbits' simultaneously. Spread over the face of the earth, exposed to a variety of 'natural' and synthetic events, the human condition has seldom achieved perfect harmony. Occasionally the clock speeds get so far out of kilter that an alarm is sounded. Today, it seems to us, all four alarms are sounding a warning of a vital new transition point in human evolution, requiring drastic revision in methods of thought, in social structure and technological control of the human environment. A diagrammatic statement of this four-part evolutionary process suggests that man has recently moved partially out of the orbit of 'natural evolution' and is operating in a new ecological realm beyond. The unprecedented acceleration of man's extension of his senses and power may be appropriately described as spiraling orbits rather than the motions of regular rotation. The methodological ('clock of comprehension') and technological clocks are producing the most spectacular spirals. One can feel the rate of their acceleration by merely listing some conspicuous discoveries in the history of technology in approximately chronological order: fire, pottery, weaving, the wheel, writing, boats, sailing, timing devices, metallurgy, mathematics, scientific observation, printing, fossil fuel energy, machines, industrialization, locomotion, flying, nuclear energy, electronics, cybernetics. However, sociological/institutional clocks lag far behind even in the technologically most developed countries. The 'established' institutions which are the instruments for decision making do not, or perhaps cannot, respond quickly enough to the newly created realities.

The technological spirals on the other hand can produce only temporary satisfaction, since technology obsolesces as fast as it develops and only the latest technology appears the best. Thus satisfaction declines into indifference, fatigue, nuisance and finally threat, creating a new need and starting a cycle all over again. The improved devices of computer mechanics document evolutionary processes as a watch measures the passing of time. But at this moment the new devices fail to throw any more light than the familiar watch on the process of the aging of the human race. Contemporary man knows the uncontrollable speed of these succeeding cycles all too well but seems helpless – it is hoped only temporarily. The methodological (comprehension) and technological spirals operate in space as well as time, and man's extensions of control over his environment increase the territories of control, extend definition and quantity of needs and create new gargantuan responsibilities and appetites. These continuous extensions require adjustment in the speed of sociological/institutional evolution for ecological balance. If the adjustment is

A 'knowledge explosion' helped by space communications will accelerate the homogenization of society . . . satellites are 'one more example of technology that might be moving too fast for existing social institutions to keep abreast of it'.

Murray L. Schwartz in the *New York Times*, 5 May 1966

not applied, piecemeal material success could finally end in disaster, the destruction of the human ecology from within.

Every living organism exists within certain limits which frame its world. These limits are defined by paths to food, to a mate or to a nest. These form the organism's territory, his ecological container. In the process of evolution living organisms moved out of their habitat in the sea on to the land in search of more favorable conditions. Although their abilities grew and their needs expanded, their behavior was basically controlled by what we call 'instinct'. But a point was reached when this faculty ceased to be the sole governor of behavior. The human species, the thinking animal, either started deliberately to seek more favorable conditions within the accessible environment or to modify the places where they already lived through the use of tools.

Man at some point in the evolutionary process virtually separated himself from all other living things on earth by his ability to modify his environment through the use of tools. The fascinating story of human evolution is, of course, being continuously expanded, documented and described. This compressed, oversimplified statement serves only to remind the reader that there exists a fairly accurate picture of orders of interaction which produced life. The ecology of living things on earth in their natural habitats is now well understood in general, and field studies continue to clarify more and more particulars.

Fig. 2
The Third Ecology
Evolutionary Cycles

The man-made environment, evolved out of previous natural environments, is becoming *total* in scale and unique in complexity. It now requires its own ecology.

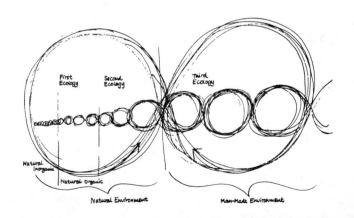

Fig. 3
Ecological and
Territorial Implications

In the course of the
evolutionary process the
man-made environment
changed from being con-
tained and became the
containing one.
Ecological escape for
humanity has become
limited.

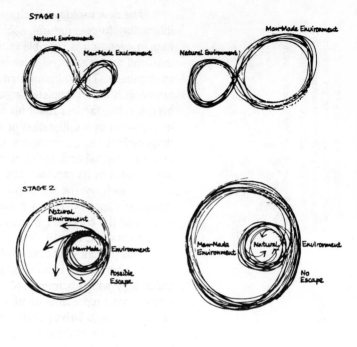

What is not yet clearly demonstrated and understood is that the human species, through its ability to
alter bits and pieces of the laws which govern the
natural environment and its ecology, has in fact created
a completely new environment – a man-made one which
in complexity and scale of containment is comparable to
the natural. This new environment now requires a new
ecology of its own order so that it can be fully comprehended: a third ecology within which, with luck,
humanity may find a new symbiosis with other living
things.

Human Habitats

The human organism grew in ability through interaction
with the natural environment and other humans. The
tools which aided individuals developed into tools which
modified social organization. Collective action in turn
developed the capability of transforming the natural
environment into a man-made one. Thus, the third
ecology environment may be described as technological
in its production and control processes, but at the same
time social in its continuously developing nature. It
cannot therefore be uniquely explained in biological or
39 technological terms.

... Rationality must usually be defined in a social context. . . . Once the limitations are seen, a generalization of the concept suggests itself and a new framework can be constructed.

Anatole Rapoport, 'Escape from Paradox', *Scientific American*, July 1967

The new ecology which we seek is at the center of interacting forces: natural, social and technological. No human evolution is possible outside the social entity of mankind and man's collective interaction with his environment. Thus although an individual may exist temporarily as a complete single organism he may not even survive, far less fulfill his full potential, without involvement in social action at all levels. This requires that the individual participate actively and creatively in the ecological and social process through constant involvement in its modification. Culture and technology are the results of the social process in the evolution of the human species. This is a much more sophisticated version of the collective advantages which evolved earlier among ants and bees.

This human collective evolution has developed to a stage where there is no ideal politic, art, institution or technology which is immutable, universal and everlasting. Each change represents another stage in the evolution of human ecology. Urban environments are the latest products of the evolutionary process and are to date the highest ecological order achieved by any organism. The urban environment which is now operating on a global scale meets not only the material collective needs but in addition provides man with the most effective social extensions: a constantly improving springboard for the next jump in the humane part of the evolutionary process.

We contend that urban facilities which provide opportunities for human, exploratory intercourse create the most favorable environment for the evolution of knowledge and understanding. These human interactions perform a complementary role to technological interactions obtained by other means such as information and communications media. Places where men meet in concourse are not only the physical containers for many men, but may act as crucibles in which humanity is transformed.

The development of the third ecology may reasonably be expected to lead to a theory of urban design. Although the authors are not committed to any particular form which urban containers might take in the future, we do believe that a theory for their design may reasonably lead to new forms of commitment. It is when theory is tested against real situations that purpose must be translated into action. If all concerned with the transformation of the human habitat re-examine their task, they will recognize that they must give form to measurable and predictable events in a world in which existence is synonymous with growth and evolutionary change. This recognition will guide them toward two major groups of components that govern the shape of places: parameters which remain relatively constant, and parameters which are infinitely variable in time, space and culture.

Tools and Obsolescence

Basic tools were originally always directed toward serving simple needs, usually characterized by sameness and repetition. The hunting tools of early man fall into this category. A tool might have become refined but its function remained unchanged. Today the rapidity of change and the impact of succeeding technological events on society are dramatic and disturbing in their indifference to the previously known. Evolution of the human habitat must be seen in its whole complexity as part of the general pattern of evolution of life, while at the same time possessing unique characteristics derived directly from the human component. The redefinition of 'urbanism' enlarges the traditional 'city planning' or 'urban design' approaches by giving it meaning on an ecological scale. It suggests a method of obtaining necessary information for handling the data, and it should facilitate the organization and operation of the design process. Above all, it puts the urban environment, itself a tool, into a new context and provides an alternative to the obsolete method of piecemeal solutions by presenting a means of tackling the problem of urban complexity as a whole. Happily one can assert with safety that methods of tackling complexity have become today simultaneously necessary and operational. Every activity has become affected by this methodological revolution at the same time.

Tools: Quantities – Qualities

When the quantities of tools produced were relatively small, man could stand apart from his products and detach himself from the process, so to speak. Observation and participation looked like two distinct things. Nature, which was the environmental container of man among other living creatures, could always be relied upon to reabsorb the trivial bits of interference of which

41

man was capable. Anything deemed dangerous and unsatisfactory could be abandoned, and man simply moved on to fresh hunting grounds or new pastures. Nature took back its own, and time healed the wounds. In this relatively simple process control of the immediate environment also appeared manageable. Needs were thought of as a collection of independent pieces which nevertheless could be dealt with separately, and this procedure was perhaps a measure of social evolution and stability in early cultures. Later developments permitted conquest of new territories and their occupants; more natural resources and more labor transformed the striving for enough to the quest for more. The trading and industrial production epochs which followed made the appetite for more among men apparently irreversible. More was a good in itself, and any activity which could provide it was expanded.

With the increase of quantities it became clear that previous experiences were no longer adequate and that old ways of thinking were ineffective in dealing with new problems. Increasing stress and strain between man and his habitat became visible and felt. At some point the quantities of elements with which man had to deal became so great that it was impossible to grasp them in the framework of a simple deterministic relationship. The previously obvious contiguity, real and metaphorical, was supplanted by ambiguity.

Nature with us is considered exclusively as decoration. But nature has important functions and they are also society's. That's why when it is misused as useless decoration, it is phony.

Edward Deevey, Yale Seminars, 1966

Runners or cyclists can increase their speed only by a corresponding increase of their exertions; but without any added effort whatever, by merely pressing a slight bit more on the gas pedal, the driver of a car can accelerate his automotive monster, even to the extent where it can take over, and race or rage beyond his control. This easy opportunity for a vast mechanical transmogrifying of our comparatively feeble physical powers can lure us into drastically irresponsible assertiveness.

Everywhere we look, we confront the same fate-ridden disproportion between what I would distinguish as the realms of action and motion. That is: in our nature as persons, we act. Our machines, not being persons, can't act; they can but move or be moved. But their sheer motions vastly magnify our powers of action. And by the same token, they impose upon us correspondingly vast new areas of sufferance.

Kenneth Burke, 'Responsibilities of National Greatness', Nation, 17 July 1967

Chemicals are being used against forested and agricultural lands in Vietnam as part of U.S. military strategy and tactics. This is the first time that chemicals designed to damage or kill plants have been used in war. To damage or kill a plant may appear a small thing in comparison to human slaughter. But when we intervene in the ecology of a region on a massive scale, we may set in motion an irreversible chain of events which could continue to affect both the agriculture and the wildlife of the area — and therefore the people — long after the war is over.

Arthur W. Galston, 'Herbicides in Vietnam', New Republic, 25 November 1967

The theory of planning control rests on the assumption that it can eliminate bad environments and let through good ones. But what is a good environment? ...man's purposes, activities and psychological orientation must be infinitely diverse. . . . Indeed, each man does not so much inhabit a physical environment or habitat, as animals do, as live in a 'world' of his own that may embrace spatially anything that influences him from outer space to Vietnam.

Norris Smith, quoted in *R.I.B.A. Journal*, August 1967

Man lost his sense of antecedents and the measure of permanence on which he had previously relied, and became confused. He had to come to terms with the dynamics of operating forces and to replace apparently accidental connexions with their real, previously invisible, causes. These spiraling changes soon passed the point of being measurable in relation to an immediately visible 'human scale'. Problems became regional in dimension and implication. They have now become ecological. All humanity and the whole earth is involved. The implication of this latest transition point in human evolution is that instead of being a spectator looking at man-made objects in the greater scheme of nature, humanity itself has suddenly become a factor in the evolutionary process. Technology has moved into nature; the man-made environment and the natural environment have become suddenly engaged in a battle which could be fatal to both.

Recent history shows that while man was building his urban habitat and developing new tools, he was also in reality creating a new ecological environment. Perhaps he has already interfered with natural ecology so seriously that he will perish in the not too distant future even without the assistance of the holocaust of nuclear war, because he will have destroyed the very roots of his humanity by making inhuman places in which to dwell.

Change and Comprehension

We can throw our pyramids of scientific achievement into space while our civilization withers from our neglect. Always before one local or regional civilization was succeeded by another. Ours is global and absolute. Mankind has become an entity, interdependent through our common necessities.

Ritchie Calder, 'The Speed of Change', *Bulletin of the Atomic Scientists*, December 1965

It seems evident that trial and error were suited only to the solution of simple problems in small areas. This is not possible any longer. The area of trial has now become the whole world, man's ecological environment. The consequence of error can lead to the destruction of his existence. Man can no longer stand outside his environment.

Change and growth have become so all-pervasive that, lacking underlying order, they can be totally destructive. Moreover, individualized and fragmented specialization, that characterizes change and growth today, has now reached the point that while developed societies are certainly better off technologically, they are often much worse off in respect to the social whole.

The lack of response to realities leads to frustration or irresponsibility; the result is a chaos of conflicting elements. The speed of the increase in quantity is far greater than the speed of adaptation to its pressures. Observation and comprehension are inseparable parts of our mental capacity to operate within a general dynamic order of interactions. With such a methodology of problem solving, man's relation to his environment and his needs is repeatedly redefined and his focus is progressively changed to cope with new problems. It is at points of transition from one cycle to another that the greatest problems arise, crises develop and the failure of tools becomes visible.

Social Structure – Technological Effect

'Urbanization of the world population raises the most serious domestic questions faced by man in the second half of the twentieth century.' In these unequivocal terms the *Scientific American* introduces a book of essays on cities.[10] The great majority of mankind will soon be living in urban environments where men will have to cope successfully with problems of living together. This evidently outweighs all problems of how to live apart, a subject to which man is giving so much more attention today.

The problems of larger numbers of people concentrated in what we may call metro-areas are linked with a concomitant concentration of facilities. 'Massive nuclei' have become essential components of urbanism. Modern technological facilities require progressively larger numbers of users. The visible superstructure of the man-made environment is analogous to an iceberg. What we see above sea or ground level does not reveal the immense invisible supporting technological mass. The greater the quantity, complexity, sophistication and cost of modern technology, the greater must be the intensity, density and frequency of its use, if possible, around the clock. Increase in utilization maximizes effectiveness technologically and sociologically. This is the positive side of large concentrations of people.

In the technologically most advanced, 'spoilt', societies the techno-effects of today remain separated from socio-structures of yesterday. Institutions, government and corporate interests established in agrarian, early industrial, pre-electronic periods linger on in direct contradiction to recent all-embracing scientific techniques and operational extensions of man. The technological revolution continues, while the societies with great social revolutions behind them drag their socio-revolutionary

10. *Cities*, ed. *Scientific American*, New York, 1966

feet. Whether any major physical planning is at all possible in advanced societies in their present state of evolution has come into question.

Territorial Anarchy

The most influential technologies now operating produce interference with historic territories. It is perhaps obvious that most men, even if they do not admit it, recognize that historic territories, which had their particular political and administrative usefulness for processes of decision-making in the past, no longer coincide with the new realities of urbanizing industrial societies. The historic definitions – town, county, state – have become obsolete. It is quite obvious that our technological expansion and extension are involved not only with the surface of the earth itself and its historic clusters of humanity, but also with the biosphere that surrounds the earth. These new systems stretch beyond the rather arbitrary subdivisions of a simpler era, in which places, territories and orbits of interest and involvement could be considered politically, economically, and technically independent.

A great metropolis, being technologically extended beyond its physical boundaries, derives its sustenance, such as its supplies of energy and water, from sources often hundreds of miles away from the political entity. By the same token, its giant metabolic waste spills over areas whose boundaries may not yet be measured. The new territorial and technological realities – metropolitan regions, systems of transportation and the like – have not been institutionally recognized. The Tennessee Valley Authority is an excellent example of the redefinition of a region in the terms of electrical power distribution and irrigation control. The proposal for a north-east corridor transportation system, between Boston and Washington, is a typical technological example. Yet at the time of writing, in spite of the technical excellence of some already designed components, no institutional means to make them immediately effective have been found.

The autonomy of any great metropolis has long since vanished. It began to disintegrate in the railroad age when the relative simplicity of the systems could preserve the illusion of a simple structure. Now the conflict between political structures of the past, and technological realities which are introducing a new stage in human history, is dramatized by the agonies of New

. . . regionalism would provide no real solution, for the definition of a region is not hard and fast, but varies with different functions: a water region, a transport region, an educational region have different 'overlays' on the map . . .

Daniel Bell, 'Toward a Communal Society', *Life*, 1967

45

11. Richard Weinerman, Yale Seminars, 1966

York, the wealthiest metropolis in the world, and is exemplified by the various obstructions placed in the path of the metro-area by the state. There is reluctance, by all concerned, to recognize New York City for what it really is – even if limited to its physical needs – the core of a vast system of interaction, stretching north to the Canadian border and beyond, east to Boston and south to Washington – a vast system, on a regional scale, of supply and waste-disposal and communications. This is becoming a commonplace occurrence all over the world. Even nationalism, patriotism and identity, which now are the essential sociological goals of sovereign countries, are being complemented by a technological, economic matrix of interdependence. Political deployment, it seems, must follow the pattern of physical dispersion, while technological controls, both ecological and economic, must be coordinated.

Urban concentrations require new ways of dealing with public health, education and welfare. What is historically identified as New York City will have to be restructured in terms of its many new and colossal aspects; these may eventually change the political administrative and power structure of the eastern states. Professor Richard Weinerman has indicated such possible future development while referring to health and health services: 'The population has become highly mobile, changing its relationship to fixed points of health service and is now almost 80% urbanized. The nature of health and disease has changed at the same time that the requirements of health service have changed. This change in our population has at one and the same time produced new health problems and new health potential.'[11]

On a smaller but no less significant scale the town meetings of New England had both a practical and a social meaning until recently. With the growth of automobility, and with it inter-town roads and highways connected in a great regional system of transportation, every small town became suddenly a segment of a larger environment, accessible to all kinds of resources and people in unprecedented and unforeseen numbers. The town fathers of the Lower Cape in Cape Cod, who yesterday thought that they were the masters of their own destiny, were suddenly faced with new realities: instead of two million people coming slowly to Cape

Cod every summer, ten million people can now descend there in two hours, twenty million in four hours and fifty million in six hours. In view of the power of attraction of Cape Cod the real problem has become what to do with a seasonal invasion of some twenty million people. The simple problem of making money out of summer tourists has been superseded by the immense problem of the conservation of the Cape's ecology.

Social theory and technological practice thus can drift further apart. Comprehensive, realistic environmental models, however well presented and seductive in appearance, will in all probability long remain on paper and film. Fragments of prototypes may, through exceptional good luck or judgement, emerge whenever they appear harmless to vested interest; or, under even more exceptional circumstances, when they happen to correspond to established economic interests. Probably, as in the immediate past, right things will more often than not be done for the wrong reasons. Even the dilemma of the intellectuals is not dissimilar to the dilemmas of institutions.

Myths and Mayhem

Perhaps the contradiction between technological potential and sociological response in relation to the human habitat is best illustrated by familiar situations about which we can ask reasonable questions in the framework of apparent increasing urbanization. Such questions apply with equal cogency to 'city', 'suburbia', 'exurbia', etc. Modern urban man exists simultaneously in all pieces of the urban environment, whatever their name may be, and employs high (expensive) technology to do so. High technology is a cheaper *per capita* convenience if used in great intensity, density and frequency, but the same technology is more expensive if used in low density.

The continued use of the same transportation techniques for both high and low density situations can now be seen as patent nonsense, a conspicuous symptom of techno-pathology. One contradiction leads to another. Increased mobility in the metro-territory produces increased vehicular pressure on every prime target within the territory, irrespective of the target's location. The pressure of people is an advantage in the sense of concentration of consumers in the same target area, but the pressure of stored vehicles, motionless for long

47 periods, becomes an overwhelming disadvantage. Thus

an inappropriate organizing principle, however sophisticated in its execution as a technological strategy, may cancel out the advantage of other technologies.

Metabolism and Pollution

The physical pollution of environments now being noticed and publicized is a result of the by-products of an abundant technology. Professor William Reifsnyder, speaking of current responses in the free economy of the United States to technological pressures, has summed up the new dilemma rather poignantly by saying that free-enterprise industrialized societies have used their water systems, rivers, the sea and the atmosphere itself, as sewers. The pollution of their environments is now almost total.[12]

Most people have seen the bubbling foam of detergents in country streams and even in larger rivers, coming not only from industry but also from the innumerable residences which in themselves have become sub-factories with their machines and washrooms. The rivers, with this tremendous load of detergents, have begun to look like extensions of a great laundry system. Apparently hygiene cannot be obtained without contradictory filth. Sanitation is still operating on too small a scale. It does not match the scale of the economy. The preoccupation with technological advance, and the corresponding absence as yet of adequate techniques for measuring the sociological effects of this 'progress', conspire together to build a whole new spectrum of ecological pollution. We do not need to dwell here on

It wasn't until the arid 1950s that scientists led by Dr A.-J. Haagen-Smit of the California Institute of Technology discovered that a major source of smog was automobile fumes . . . [that] every car in the nation on an average, emits more than 100 cubic feet of fumes every day. . . . To curb the discharges from its 9 million cars, California set up its Motor Vehicle Pollution Control Board [only] in 1960.

Gladwin Hill, *New York Times*, 28 September 1966

133 millions of tons of aerial garbage is now being dumped into the U.S. atmosphere each year. If it could be placed on a giant scale, it would outweigh the country's annual steel production.

Out of this, 85 million tons are due to transportation media and only 22 million tons to manufacturing.

Edmund Walter Mayer, 'We Can Afford Clean Air', *Fortune*, November 1965

Nuclear generation of electricity on a large scale is finally at hand in the United States, and with it come new and serious problems of environmental contamination. In 1966, almost 40 per cent of the new generating capacity ordered for utilities was nuclear, and it seems that the atom will henceforth provide the main source of low-cost power, even in parts of the country endowed with hydroelectric resources . . . . . . Nuclear generation, it is widely believed, threatens to raise the temperature of our rivers to damaging levels; the most serious drawback to the Portland General Electric's plans is its location on a stretch of one of the richest salmon rivers in the world.

Anthony Netboy: 'Nuclear Power on Salmon Rivers', *Nation*, 9 October 1967

12. William Reifsnyder, Yale Seminars, 1966

the much publicized effects of certain aspects of pollution. We must, however, stress that man-made devices specifically designed for the efficient and ecologically 'safe' disposal of by-products must immediately replace the utilization of nature's flow systems which are no longer able to contain man's vast metabolic wastes.

This pollution can now be joined by other less conspicuous ones. 'Pollution' achieves a deeper and broader meaning if we use a more general term, 'interference'. An environmental-social pollutant also can be auditory. Men suffer collectively from traffic noise, with supersonic flight threatening to raise this to insupportable limits; the individual suffers as a result of the intrusion of communication media into his privacy. We are now told that man can turn a deaf ear to unwanted sounds or ignore unpalatable or fearful events. But there are no controls to protect humanity and there is mounting evidence that such evasions are ineffective in the long run. Outside interference or the individual's own improper responses to environmental realities leave humanity with deep scars, both physiological and psychological, personal and collective.

Urban man is faced with mounting contradictions of extraordinary proportions in his ecological environment. The quantities involved in supply and waste disposal in urban concentrations have reached dimensions never anticipated in history. For many years various aspects of neglect have been brought to our attention without much resultant action. Unless the clocks of our culture are readjusted to the clock of our threatened biological nature, the apparent contradictions of our environment will prove fatal. Pollution in its widest and most far reaching sense is yet another iceberg.

4. Search for a Model

a.

Growth in quantities, change in quality. Complexity and simplicity. Man's technological extension and evolution of his humaneness.

b.

Continuous process or completed form. New components of dynamic order. An urban theory for a physical model. A short synoptic view of search for models.

c.

Search for system. Organizing components for urbanism. Division or cohesion. Stereotypes as technical fallout.

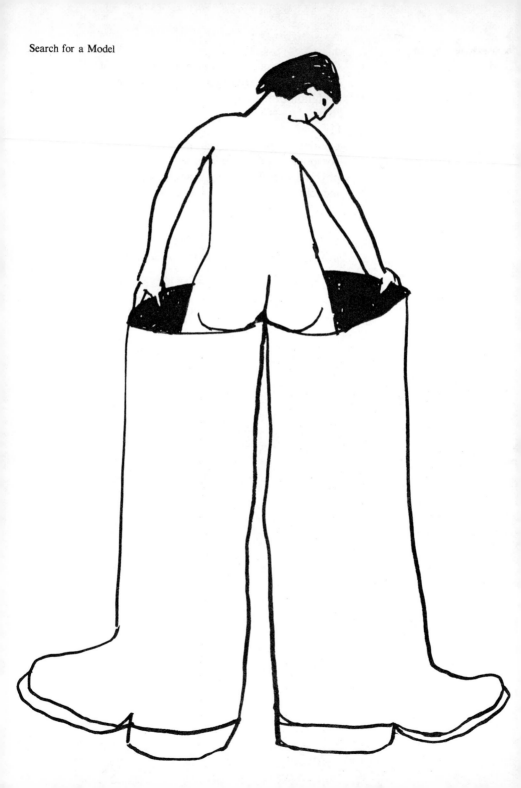

We know more about the planets, such as the moon, than we do about science itself as a social phenomenon.

Maurice Goldsmith, 'The Science of Science', *Journal of the Royal Society*, June 1967

History, like a badly constructed concert hall, has occasional dead spots where the music can't be heard.

Archibald MacLeish, 'The Seat Behind the Pillar', *New York Times*, 21 January 1967

Nairobi, Kenya, 15 December
An inquisitive baboon succeeded in silencing Kenya's politicians for 35 minutes today when it interrupted Nairobi's electricity flow.

New York Times, 16 December 1967

In the long run, whatever proves to be biologically incorrect will never be economically sound.

H. Leibundgut (Switzerland Forestry Congress), quoted by Erhard Rostland, 'Trimming Trees', *Bulletin of the Atomic Scientists*, October 1961

It has become clear that the changes in quantities that technology has created have to coincide with a change in quality of understanding. The agony of disequilibrium is described by Ortega y Gasset: 'Unless we succeed in finding a way to maintain our mastery over luxuriant growth we shall be suffocated by it. The jungle which is life itself lies intergrown with what originally was planted as cultivation in a clearing and has now in its turn become a jungle also.' Evidently it is not only a question of more, it is fundamentally a question of better. The problem lies not in the potentials of production, which probably have no limit, but in the development of a theoretical, systematic approach to all environmental problems facing humanity in a new framework of problem-solving techniques. One of the basic sources of trouble and causes for alarm is the unwillingness, inability or impotence of existing social institutions to adjust to present realities. These conditions currently produce crises, but if they were made comprehensible and translated into correct terms they could instead eventually be manipulated to eliminate those same crises.

Ideology and Responsibility

The gap in synchronization between the clocks of sociological/institutional and technological evolution may be characterized as the incompatibility of quantity and quality. As a result of this lag in the sociological evolutionary clock, there is a reversal in the roles of, on the one hand, ideological order governing a given society and, on the other, individual responsibility for behavior. In the past there was a blind acceptance of the social ideological order which was established by a governing force of religious or temporal supremacy, and this generalized ideological order generated a hierarchy of responsibilities to meet physical needs. But under the pressures of unforeseen forces, old cultures became disorganized. Ideological restrictions became less and

take a stand on such questions as the form, organization and degree of permissible social control ... these issues ... will ... give new urgency to old dilemmas of large versus small scale social organizations, of central versus local government or of a proper balance between social responsibility and individual autonomy ...

Zbigniew Brzezinski, 'Tomorrow's Agenda', *Foreign Affairs*, July 1966

Man's environment and *man himself* will more and more be subject to purposive control and manipulation. The consequence will be a fundamental transformation of our society.... Our institutions are based on the belief that man can and should govern himself. Yet the problems that are likely to dominate our lives in the decades to come may creep upon us without attracting sufficient notice and may not fit into the established modes of our political dialogue.... The concerned citizen will have to

Chaos to Order

less effective and man cultivated the idea of freedom and individual independence. Satisfaction of physical needs gradually came to rely more and more on anonymous mass technology. Humanity grew to accept blindly the physical comforts and conveniences provided by technology while straining at the same time for individual ideological responsibility outside technological control.

There followed the inevitable clash between collective and private interest. Responsibility is the bridge between the two, but once destroyed, conflict is bound to result.

The majority today recognize the obvious limitations of their personal actions but remain largely oblivious to the invisible controls which in reality dominate their lives. They become conscious of their limited freedom only when they are members of the minority of the economically privileged, the technologically engaged or the intellectually sophisticated.

The whole crisis of man's evolutionary state today may be described as a situation of built-in contradictions. Such a circumstance not only suggests that human existence is constantly threatened but also, and more importantly, that at present human consciousness of existence in relation to actuality and new realities is at its nadir. The environmental failures which we now face apply to the urban ecology as forcefully as they apply to the greater ecology of the total environment. In this transition period in human ecology technological society is moving from private to public responsibility in accordance with the emerging need to have massive controls and to take full advantage of community effort. This is happening while at the same time civilized men are trying to retain individual initiative and are indeed attempting to increase it. The public and private responsibilities appear to be in conflict, but actually they are moving toward complementarity.

The crises in human affairs are now global in scale and ecological in character. Man is shaping the environment while at the same time he is reacting to it. It appears that a conflict has arisen because all new goals have to be achieved simultaneously, since traditional relationships have suddenly been upset through the immensity and complexity of the operations involved. Humanity can move from a less ordered to a more ordered society, and in the process individual man can move from a less free to a more free status operating within it. J. Z. Young, a geneticist, suggests that this is part of the natural order of evolution: 'At every stage of the life cycle there are more alternative possible actions available and better methods for selecting the appropriate one. That is, an individual of higher order of organization is equipped with more choices of freedom of wider horizon. Greater complexity of the higher animals enables their life to be carried on under conditions that would have been impossible for their simpler ancestors.'[13]

If we could think of a totally Utopian environment, it could be the product of the synchronization of the clocks described at some point in 'space and time', in Siegfried Giedion's happy phrase. At such a point man could claim to have created a perfect tool. As we are concerned with environment and consider the urban environment itself a tool, an ideal urban environment might appear at first sight as the essence of Utopia: a single pervasive, visible, comprehensible order, an image and symbol of human excellence for all time. Such Utopian organization would in fact not have synchronized the evolutionary clocks, but would merely have stopped them. Environmental design may be considered to be a potential control which operates at some point

Environmental Design

off government, and private, initiative in creating a wide diversity of residential environment offering to all men those vital choices that have too long been denied them.

Edward Mishan, 'The Rights of Man and the Rape of his Environment: a Blueprint for a Peaceful Revolution', Spectator, 14 July 1967

13. J. Z. Young, The Life of the Vertebrates, Oxford, 1950

Machines that are employed to produce services for some simultaneously produce 'disservices' for others ... there are some proponents of laissez-faire who still believe that, given enough time and, presumably, forbearance, it will all sort itself out ... they have failed to observe that as the carpet of 'increased choice' is being unrolled before us by the foot, it is simultaneously being rolled up behind us by the yard.... Legal recognition of amenity rights, on the other hand, would touch

The ancient profession of prophesy has a long and not very honorable history . . . [but its] importance . . . – the moral necessity of anticipation – becomes ever greater as we move increasingly into a world of our own making . . . the very mission of prophesy is changing, from one of almost frivolous whimsy, the role of the gambler's mistress, to one of deep moral responsibility.

Robert Sinsheimer, 'The End of the Beginning', *Bulletin of the Atomic Scientists*, February 1967

Planning is hopeful prediction, based on case studies and norms which can be used as indices to the expected behaviour of a system. The element of hope can be stretched to the point that we wonder, 'Are we planning or praying?'

Eugene Kupper, Yale Seminars, 1966

New Needs – New Tools

of approximate intermittent coincidence between the rhythms of the clocks, where they may interact and complement each other. Environmental design is therefore potentially a catalytic tool. It is generated by the forces of natural evolution and in turn it modifies and changes them. The heart of this colossal interchange is the environment which man hopes one day to be able to control in its totality. Until then men will have to be content to control only segments of the urban environment.

All too frequently it seems that humanity regards the results of its astonishing productivity not as important and influential tools but as toys. They have become very much like Pinocchio. They have an identity of their own, even an image. Such a misunderstanding of the evolutionary process of tool-making, or lack of comprehension of its possible consequences, leads to the violation of the tools themselves. Humanity at the moment seems to be doubly confounded: the new technology in its progress not only violates 'constant' biological and psychological needs, but it also threatens through obsolescence institutions which cannot adapt with an equal rapidity of change. Modern quantities escape the qualitative framework of historical precedent. Previously,

57

men could depend on what they knew as sources of power established by history or experience. Now, historically inherited points of reference have become irrelevant in so many areas that men either have no response to the environment which they themselves are changing or have the wrong response.

Complexity and Simplicity

The tool which humanity seems to need in order to resolve the problems and contradictions which beset the human ecology must, in the first place, appear terribly complex in its structure but may eventually prove to be absolutely simple or simply ordered in its function. Man, one hopes, will one day understand that the ever-present phenomenon of interaction between opposites is essential to the evolutionary process. Once this is understood, the many contradictions will be transformed into complementarities and humanity will accelerate its human evolution.

Technology serves man socially as well as individually. It is, therefore, dependent on a social structure. The institutional framework in turn leads to the structure of comprehension, i.e. the theory of problem solving. The whole of the tool-making process therefore may be in its turn considered and used as a tool in itself; a tool of an extremely high order, an intellectual tool. Professor C. H. Waddington describes in this manner a similar evolutionary process in biology: '. . . as the genetic system is subject to evolution, so in broader terms we may say that the whole evolutionary system, of which the genetic system is only a part, itself must evolve.'[14] Waddington, like Huxley, goes even further to tie the whole biological evolution with the human socio-genetic evolution. 'Conceptual thought and its social transmission were accepted for some time as one of the major defining properties of man, but the view that this process provides a basis for a new evolutionary mechanism is of more recent origin.'[15]

Man's Extensions

The inadequacies of trial and error which lead to contradictions can be first modified and then finally replaced by the complementarity of planning techniques. The multiplicity and complexity of the elements involved in the problem can now be combined in such a way that effects become predictable. Cause and chance can operate simultaneously without contradiction. The

14. C. H. Waddington, *The Ethical Animal*, New York, 1961

15. J. Huxley, 'Cultural Process and Evolution', in *Behaviour and Evolution*, eds. A. E. Roe and G. G. Simpson, New Haven, 1958

decision-making technique can move from the stereotype of an ambiguous authority to a prototype model of rational explanation. Advanced societies already have most of the necessary fragments of the technique but are a little apprehensive in putting these fragments together and forging a comprehensive tool that will help to formulate human decisions. Their newly found freedom appears threatened. We believe that this new technique is not in any way a contradiction of any previous techniques. It is simply a new threshold in the process of resolving problems on a differentiated level of quantity and quality. This technique is appropriate in scale to the human ecological problem.

Humanity can find reassurances in the historic dimension as well as in the evolutionary scale of the future. History reveals that discovery and invention have always appeared as the apparently inevitable response to the pressures of need and in proportion to the maturity of knowledge. Both Leibniz and Newton, for instance, invented the calculus without the knowledge of the other's work and by totally different means, the former through mathematical logic, the latter through empirical measurement. An evolutionary example is provided by the urban environment itself as an extension of man's ability to perform. Scientists tell us that the greatest evolutionary acceleration is in man's most precious equipment: his mind. This is not the product of the evolution of the brain of the individual or of the species alone. It is a mutation in the evolution of interaction between members of the species and the tools that they employ.

High technology, which is the product of the urban community, has in turn become an accelerator in the development of culture. It may prove to be the most important tool developed by mankind and perhaps will produce equally dramatic mutations in the future. During recent years the extension of human intellect has become quite evident. Man is able to cope with increasingly complex problems through the sudden transformation of his thinking tools. He can tackle the physical and technical complexities of the urban environment, the 'third ecology', with confidence. Whether he can learn to attack social complexity with equal confidence remains in question today.

The third ecology is the by-product of tool-making

man, and the urban environment is itself a complex tool. It consists of all the tools in use which were created to control the natural environment. It operates in the final analysis like all tools, changing the environmental forces from man-destructive or man-indifferent into man-supporting.

The development of a general theory of urban organization seems a necessary prelude to the development of methods which could lead to viable programs and measurable solutions. Man's more sophisticated tools, such as cybernetics, provide a methodology to evaluate the complex relationships between the natural, the social, the intellectual and the technological evolutionary processes. The evolutionary factors are so numerous in the total ecological picture that they evade at this moment the exact means of identification. But we are approaching a time when the selection of urban components, typical and prototypical, will be susceptible to analysis and design.

Looking beyond the confused present, man may predict with reasonable hope of success the nature of the next evolutionary cycle and then plan appropriate action: a comprehensible future within a meaningful present. The image of evolutionary clocks out of kilter reveals time lags between various components in human evolution. It is, thus, made possible to assess technological advance in relation to institutional development. The society's comprehension, evaluation and response to new tools can no longer be separated from the tool-making process itself.

Dynamic Order

'Our purpose here is not to define an optimum environment but to design a conceptual approach to its definition.'[16]

'Structural analysis is confronted with a strange paradox . . . the more obvious structural organization is, the more difficult it becomes to reach it because of the inaccurate conscious models lying across the path which leads to it . . .'[17]

'The art of progress is to preserve order amid change and to preserve change amid order.'[18]

We have attempted to sketch the frame for a general

60   theory of design for a dynamic complex order of many

interactions which operate equally in natural and man-made environments, and we have suggested that boundaries between the two no longer exist. We have indicated that, although complex problems until recently evaded all attempts to be resolved, we now have the necessary means which could reasonably relate reformulated human ends in the framework of new environmental realities. We have at the same time stressed that problems within this complex order of biological, sociological and technological components should no longer be separated for purposes of analysis when man has at his disposal a methodology which enables him to tackle them simultaneously. Instead of frames of sub-systems, a comprehensive super-system of interaction which is evolutionary and ecological in scope and scale becomes the real framework.

conceive of world economic problems in terms of the world as one community (a community, admittedly, that has yet to be formally ratified), it will be very difficult, if not impossible, ever to see how the various international components that now exist will have to comport themselves in order to become the macro-economic community of the world.

Harvey Wheeler, 'The World is the Problem', *Nation*, 16 October 1967

At the end, Simon Bolivar said, 'I have plowed the sea.' It was not quite true, but it is the lament of a man who has fought a linear battle instead of an exponential one. The first rule for reformers should be: Fight no linear battles. Find the focus ...

John Platt, *The Step to Man*, New York, 1966

It will be objected to immediately that macro-economics does not exist on the level of the world as a whole. There is no world community.... And if we cannot even

16. C. David Locks, 'Comment on Dubos', in *Environment for Man (The Next Fifty Years)*, ed. William R. Ewald Jr, Indiana, 1967

17. Claude Lévi-Strauss, *Structural Anthropology*, New York, 1963

18. Alfred Whitehead, *Science and the Modern World*, New York, 1966

In looking at human ecological problems in this comprehensive way one can 'see' the separate phenomena in their fullness while at the same time we can 'sense' the pattern of their interaction.

The fallacy of imagining the real world of constant change as separate static phenomena becomes apparent. To freeze this dynamic interaction in some unimaginable universal consensus or in the perfection of a single Utopia is to eliminate life itself. Reality is an ever-changing mixture of maximized experiences of all kinds. It is a process in the course of which any arbitrarily imposed dominance of any single component must inevitably produce reaction.

Human life is thus the outcome of the interplay between three separate classes of determinants . . . : the lasting and universal characteristics of man's nature . . . the ephemeral conditions which man encounters at a given moment; . . . man's ability to choose between alternatives and to decide upon a course of action . . . regardless of the growth of modern science and the speeds of transportation, an evening with a friend, will still call for the transportation factor, will still call for the same amount of time to be expended in the twenty-fifth century as in the nineteenth . . . is personal interaction becoming a luxury that modern man cannot afford, or are there new social forms and institutions that will foster and preserve it?

Martin Shubik, 'Information, Rationality and Free Choice', *Daedalus: Journal of the American Academy of Arts and Sciences*, Summer 1967

Models and Method

The search for models of urban order has of course occurred ever since historic cities and towns began to lose their easily grasped definition and function, and the technological overspill of mechanized communication systems, beginning with the railroads, distorted 'city' boundaries and invaded 'the countryside'. The idea of a search for models can perhaps be clarified by describing a few approaches (probably familiar to most readers) already taken. The brief description of these concepts and their methods does not pretend to give the full historical background or to be complete. They are presented in a roughly chronological order to suggest that the search process is evolutionary in itself and has

followed a development in methodology which is

19. Ebenezer Howard, *Garden Cities of Tomorrow*, 1898 (Cambridge, Mass., 1965)

20. Patrick Geddes, *Cities in Evolution*, 1915 (New York, 1950)

remarkable not only for its increased scope but even more so for its exponential rate of acceleration within the living memory of many men.

In 1898 Sir Ebenezer Howard asked the question: 'The people – where will they go?' and offered a solution of three options: town, town-country and country. His discussion of these alternatives included a thoughtful inventory and balance sheet of their advantages and disadvantages. The three 'magnets', as Howard described them, seemed immutable in their social, economic and technical organization.[19] Patrick Geddes at the turn of the century revised this description of human habitats by redefining social, technological environmental issues as 'folk, work, place'.[20] The abstractions alone advanced the earlier model by removing function from the static context of fixed territories. The most significant contribution of the Geddes model, however, was to put man and his works in direct relationship with nature. But despite this splendid enlargement of the frame of reference, Geddes could not foresee the technological expansion to come and its consequences.

Park Systems – Green Belts

The distribution of urban places of residence or work in natural settings or conversely the scattering of parcels of the natural environment throughout the man-made city implied by the Geddes model had a simple, comprehensible objective: to make nature again accessible for the health and enjoyment of urban dwellers. This end was gradually subverted. Howard's town-country idea grew bigger in scale: the city gardens became parks and the municipal parks were expanded into great national preserves on a regional basis. The green belts of town-country only formed protective outer zones of conservation for beautiful nature around the not so satisfactory man-made towns. Again, the methodology, as a result of over-simplification, led to fallacies. The new stage in technological evolution could not be physically confined and simply defined. It became all-pervasive.

Years of Manifestos

After the First and during the Second World Wars, instead of the pressures of practice, architects underwent periods of enforced inaction which provided a thinking spell, and all over the world they began to construct a

21. Le Corbusier, *Concerning Town Planning*, London, 1947

22. Walter Gropius, *Scope of Total Architecture*, New York, 1955

23. Serge Chermayeff, Institute of Design, Chicago Catalogues, 1946–51

24. R. Buckminster Fuller, *World Design Science Decade 1965–1975*, Carbondale, 1963

25. C. A. Doxiades, *Architecture in Transition*, New York, 1963

The shape that the urban form will take is not 'obviously foreordained'. We are now compelled, as planners, to provide some pretty good management. We are in the position of the framers of the Constitution; we are presented with a unique problem. We must develop a new urban form, using history as a guide in respect to the nature of man, not as a storehouse of previously created forms.

Richard Dodge, Yale Seminars, 1966

theoretical widening of their professional horizon. Manifestos rapidly, and new forms less frequently, followed each other.

A few references to the scope and function of design before the Second World War will suffice to make the evolutionary acceleration of theory visible: Le Corbusier coined the term 'Urbanism',[21] enlarging the architectural spectrum and identifying it with the realities of growing conurbations, and Walter Gropius founded the 'Bauhaus', a system of design education which brought the humanities and technology into partnership and advocated 'teamwork' instead of individual talent as an essential ingredient of the design process in technological society.[22] Architecture was redefined by C.I.A.M. (Congrès International d'Architecture Moderne) as 'a social art' as opposed to the work of an independent, individual artist, and George Howe spoke of 'Master Plans for Master Politicians'.

Serge Chermayeff's 'environmental design' studies after the Second World War attempted to remove the obsolete barriers which separated different groups of designers into fields which no longer bore any resemblance to their professed functions.[23] Architecture, landscape architecture, city planning, industrial design, etc., could no longer hold talent and imagination within these arbitrary boundaries. In the same period R. Buckminster Fuller became the apostle of 'comprehensive design' and emphasized the rational employment of global resources through the greatest technological efficiency,[24] while C. A. Doxiades suggested a scientific framework for environmental design: 'the science of human settlements'.[25]

All these ideas were viable ends in a large measure for designers in a technological society, but all, one way or another, proved individually and collectively too abstract to be translated into action or were oversimplified, and thus produced results quite different from the analyses. The biological, sociological, technological components remained separate and unintegrated. The appropriate methodology for the essential step of relating all 'urban' functions in a single dynamic order of interaction was not there. Ingenious and sometimes remarkable technical inventions were obscured in the proliferating mechanical gadgetry which followed the Wars. But even the best of the technical exponents seemed to lean too heavily on their engineering uniqueness and excellence to make a great impact on society and its institutions, while high-level abstractions, which gave no promise of becoming operational, suffered the same fate for the opposite reason. The two extreme positions for setting out in search of new realities, theory and practice, could not interact and remained disconnected and isolated.

Action – Reaction

The manifestos formulating ends and announcing the methodology of means produced a further retarding process. Sociological and technological clocks got more out of phase after the Second World War: the social deprivations of the war gave way to material expansion which satisfied pent-up public appetites and provided new consumer goods. Impatience with theorists became the mark of opportunism, and anti-intellectualism became overt. Architecture became either commercialized gadgetry complementing other gimmicks then available or became the servant and symbol of the successful and prosperous. The path of comprehensive design, combining inspiration and rationality, remained thorny. The good intentions of planners had to wait. The methodology which they needed would come from the technological expansion in the giant industries then looking for profit primarily from the government through engagement in the cold war. In the words of John K. Galbraith: 'With the cold war, however, the word planning acquired ideological overtones. The Communist countries not only socialized property, which seemed not a strong likelihood in the United States, but they planned, which somehow seemed more of a danger. Since liberty was there circumscribed, it followed that planning was something that the libertarian society should avoid.'[26]

Collaboration in Complexity

Whatever the immediate goals toward which the new means could be turned, one observation became inescapable even to the most reactionary designers: technology had suddenly become so complex and far-reaching that collaborative, inter-speciality action became an undeniable necessity. The romantic, artistic and simplistic notions prevalent in the design professions are now being slowly but firmly eroded by new and harsh realities. The custom tailors, however talented, are

26. J. K. Galbraith, *The New Industrial State*, Boston, 1967

We have not generally grasped the cost and the responsibility of programming before plotting and building. The amount of creative intuition as well as systematic work that goes into it and the effect which this early planning has on the final design solution are only vaguely, if at all, understood in proportion to their true significance.

Richard J. Neutra, 'Programming: A Creative Act', in Building for Modern Man, Princeton, 1949

27. J. K. Galbraith, The New Industrial State, Boston. 1967

28. John Simons, Yale Seminars, 1966

no longer very useful for the vast task of clothing naked millions. New protagonists emerged to deal with the new scale of complexity. To quote Galbraith again: 'Until the end of World War II, or shortly thereafter, planning was a moderately evocative word in the United States. It implied a sensible concern for what might happen in the future and a disposition, by forehanded action, to forestall avoidable misfortune. As persons won credit for competent planning of their lives, so communities won credit for effective planning of their environment. It was thought good to live in a well-planned city. The United States government had a National Resources Planning Board. During the war, post-war planning acquired the status of a modest industry in both the United States and United Kingdom; it was felt that it would reassure those who were fighting as to their eventual utility as civilians.'[27]

Constants and Variables

The collaborative process is, in the language of cybernetics, a feed-back system. In this light, the search for a viable theory confined to intellectual exchanges exclusively becomes, as John Simons devastatingly observed, 'a process of swapping insights'.[28] Theory requires the corrective of empirical field work: an interaction between ends and means to hammer out an extended professionalism capable not only of producing badly needed remedial steps to modify existing stereotypes but also of designing vitally necessary prototypes. This process can be described as a search for an urban system and its model; a combination of interrelated principles to guide the designers of environments. These principles are 'constant' parameters concerned with broad human ends in the framework of human ecology, while means, organizational and operational, are variables in time, space and culture.

Search for Equilibrium

'. . . people driving motor cars don't form a society in any sense. They are frustrated from doing so because the main ways in which we form our society by speech and language and social relations with one another . . . are withheld from motorists . . . the pedestrian is . . . part of this system. . . . There is no doubt that driving produces a change of personality . . .'[29]

66

'Within the discipline of a continuous system we

may achieve a certain liberty in the articulation of function . . . if there is no system, or order, there can be no identity but only chaos of disparate entities engaged in pointless competition . . .'[30]

'At one time everybody who lived in a city was an urbanite and everybody who lived on the farms or outside the cities was a ruralite. We're now reversing this. The people who are the most advanced, most highly skilled, most developed are likely to be living in exurbia and cities are becoming the concentrated pockets of rural folks. We've talked about cities or urbanization as territorial or localization or density phenomena in one instance and about cultural developments on the other hand. They were spatially synonymous at one stage in history. They are no longer spatially synonymous.'[31]

Perhaps the most significant changes and consequent serious problems of a physical nature in urbanization today are directly connected with the technology of communication and transportation. Professor James Tobin has observed that: 'the marvelous products of modern technology – plumbing, electricity, cars, telephones, TV, plastics – have undoubtedly brightened the lives of almost all Americans, poorer as well as richer. But the society's total commitment to them has made them virtual necessities. . . . Legal and social norms make it quite properly difficult for occupants of urban housing to avoid the costs of modern sanitation, central heating and electricity. In an automobile society public transportation declines in quality, availability and economy. When the whole society is geared to communication by telephone, it is more than inconvenient to be without one.'[32]

Division and Cohesion

While transportation and communications are today perhaps responsible for the greatest disruptions in urbanizing society, they are also the most susceptible to systematic planning and design inasmuch as they are already directly and inescapably a major part, technically and economically, of the society now emerging. This planning is not likely to become a reality, however, without a proper measure of public control of essential communal utilities. At present, for example, roads and

29. Colin Cherry, 'World Communication', *Journal of the Royal Society of Arts*, February 1966

30. Shadrach Woods, *Urban Environment, the Search for System*

31. Melvin Webber, Yale Seminars, 1966

32. James Tobin, 'It Can Be Done', *New Republic*, 3 June 1967

highways are a vast piece of publicly owned real estate, along with public rights-of-way and public air-rights. In the foreseeable future with increasing government subsidies many 'private' rights-of-way, such as railroads, may to all intents and purposes pass into the public realm of control.

It appears that technological society may continue either to increase at a rising tempo its subservience to existing communication technologies, or it can reverse this process and make both communication and transportation systems a point of departure for the development of counterbalancing measures through which the purpose of community and public interest must be first served. Community, in the sense we use it here, contains an always available option to privacy. Both community and privacy are becoming curtailed, yet these were precisely the available complementary conditions under which both the cultural and technological milestones were produced.

In developed countries, present metropolitan areas now provide evidence of two apparently contradictory forces at work. On the one hand, convenient, fast transportation, together with instantaneous communication, creates an illusion of 'belonging' to any settlement. This in turn becomes an instrument of 'divisiveness', scattering settlements and facilities of all kinds almost randomly over increasingly large areas. At the same time, regardless of the excellence or speed of transportation and communication techniques, it increases travel time for urban man for the most important and the most trivial purposes and for short and long distances alike. Los Angeles and Houston are examples 'par excellence' of travel without end. Places where cars must be worn like shoes during working hours.

True Travel-Time

Another aspect of the same contradictions in the application of technology is the staggering difference

between the speeds of machines as advertised and the

speed of travel in reality. The measure of travel time begins with the pedestrian and is the sum of his time during transit as well as that between connexions. This includes activities like walking, waiting, parking and minding portable possessions which are usually left out of the reckoning. These neglected segments of travel are just as much part of its time measure as distance, frequency and the speed of machinery. Seen in this way the 1800 m.p.h. one-hour flight of the proposed SST (Supersonic Transport) jets may require an additional three hours or more at each end, reducing its effective travel speed by a factor of seven when measured in true time–distance to a paltry 300 m.p.h. or less. (The sonic boom and other by-products of this folly of course still remain to be measured as nuisance for people on the ground.) In other words, unless techniques of transfer from one system to another are radically improved, even the most spectacular increases in speeds will not substantially decrease travel time. The illusory advantages, more cars, more planes, more speed, will continue to be offset by increases in congestion, traffic jams, discomfort and danger.

Multi-Polar Pressures

Such problems for travelers, however, are the least serious of those presented by the transportation explosion. Technology can easily provide remedies for these matters without changing the sociological and cultural conditions which directly result from an exaggerated preoccupation with them. But blind faith in mobility in general as an 'open sesame' to individual choice may prove disastrous for the community at large. Whatever advantages exist, at this stage of urbanization, in quasi-rural residences and local shopping centers, etc., in suburbia and exurbia, will be offset in the near future by their many growing disadvantages. At the same time we should not minimize the continually rising pressures on the metropolitan cores, old or new. Conditions like the over-building in central areas and traffic congestion on all highways and transit lines leading to and from the urban cores are reaching intolerable limits. Exaggerated reliance on the urban highway systems' capacities to absorb an infinite number of private vehicles exacerbates traffic problems at both ends of the urban spectrum. The cost of moving, controlling and storing sleeping vehicles in crowded places is soaring daily, and this nuisance will continue even if the present pollution of air by internal combustion engines could be modified or even eliminated. More importantly from the point of view of this study, the technological 'convenience-nuisance' of the car will increase daily anxiety, stress and strain and alienation, and decrease opportunities of meaningful human contact for mankind in community.

New York moves into its own core three and a third million people a day. About 850,000 move between 8 and 9 o'clock. 9 per cent come by car and taxi, 72 per cent by subway, 11 per cent by commuter railroads.

Robert S. Bird, *New York Herald Tribune*, 4 February 1966

Already there is an automobile for every one and a half yards of main road; there are forty-five cars to every mile of road, lane, and byway. By 1975, the year of the end of stage two of the New London Plan, there will, at the present rate, be just eighteen inches of main traffic highway to each car.

Atlantic Monthly, report on London, June 1960

$5 million a mile for the Interstate Highway 87 from Armrock to Katonah (six lane) proposed cost.

$46·8 billion for the Interstate Highway program since World War II.

New York Times, 7 December 1966

A person consumes only about 30 pounds of air a day, whereas the average automobile in the United States consumes about 160 pounds. A person contributes only about five one-thousandths of a pound of carbon monoxide to the air in a day while a car produces five pounds. And an individual's production of carbon dioxide is only about $1\frac{1}{2}$ pounds a day, while a car's is 28·6 pounds.

Yet in Los Angeles, the automotive 'population' has reached a point where there is a car for every two persons.

Dr John R. Goldsmith, annual meeting of the American Meteorological Society, *New York Times*, 31 January 1968

Technological Process –
Social Structure

Transportation and communication media have proved to be divisive in their effect, tending to homogenize and stereotype whole settlements in a manner similar to the earlier pattern of the ghettoes. The difference today is that technological society has happy ghettoes too, whose inhabitants enjoy daily travel-time more than living-time and place ever more reliance on canned information and spectator-type recreation, reducing participation in community action. But any communication or transportation medium could obviously have the opposite effect of producing cohesion and could be organized in a manner which would restore to daily life the essential community ingredients of human intercourse which

70   could in turn increase overall social cohesiveness, instead

The effect of circulation is to carry more of fewer things from each of a smaller number of more favored regions, and to spread them and their final products nearly uniformly everywhere ... everyone smokes the same cigarettes, drinks the same soft drinks, and whistles the same tunes. The consumers are homogenized.

Philip Wagner, *The Human Use of the Earth*, London, 1964

Los Angeles, March 25

(1) *Geography:* California is a large body of automobiles surrounded by road signs. It is bordered on the top by sunshine, in the middle by smog, and on the bottom by little old ladies in tennis shoes. It is famous for sunglasses, Humphrey Bogart, saffron slacks, Chinatown and blondes of odd proportion. Its most famous citizen, a household name in every corner of the earth, was the late Mickey Mouse. ... World's Biggest Drive-In. ...

(4) *Points of Interest:* California is the site of the world's biggest drive-in. It is called Los Angeles. Los Angeles is slightly larger than New Jersey, and offers most of the comforts of modern living within hair-raising reach of a nine-mile drive. North and south of Los Angeles lies more of Los Angeles.

Russell Baker, *New York Times*, 26 March 1968

A pocket guide to the biggest state in the union:

of generating, as they do now, scattering, detachment and passive acceptance of faceless propaganda.

The automobile can play only a minor complementary role in this pattern of cohesion since it operates with utmost advantage only in linking destinations towards which relatively small quantities of traffic are directed – where transit line transportation is in fact uneconomical. But when there are great quantities of people to be moved at regular frequencies, it is quite obvious that transit systems have an overriding advantage in efficiency and cost, both economically and psychologically, over the automobile. In addition, even though automotive systems are most efficient only for territories demanding random movement, the mechanical principles on which they are based, together with the road systems being built for them, may already be obsolete.

Mass transportation can serve a double purpose. Once established, it can accelerate the revitalization of densely used central districts, which were in a state of decay because of private vehicles. It can also increase efficient movement and the possibility of cheap parking facilities for private vehicles in sub-urban and ex-urban situations. These parking facilities could then be provided at every outlying point of transfer in the system, where sleeping vehicles, like dangerous dogs, may be allowed to lie.

What is not as obvious as technical and economic considerations in this automanic period is that transit systems can assume sociological significance. A station on any intensely used transit system is not only a transportation exchange, but it can be a community place able to support a variety of facilities. Passengers may then become relaxed pedestrians and enjoy a variety of contacts as a daily experience once more. They will probably not only be more pleasant people but also more responsive customers. Technical and community advantages of an optimum kind begin to work together and can accomplish more in such a situation than fringe facilities around giant parking lots.

The potentially 'divisive' or 'cohesive' effects of systems of movement and communication are introduced as prime examples of the interdependence of technological systems which must be structured and sociological systems which may be shaped. Within the

71

framework of the authors' concern they suggest the interdependence of programmatic planning-design issues which constitute the commitment described earlier in general terms.

Ends and Means

Thus, as we approach the more precise specification of the urban system for which we are searching, the social ends in our commitment take priority and technical means assume a subservient role. There is a degree of high abstraction about human ends, however, which, though indisputable, is too general in nature to be translated into anything more specific at this time than planning principles. Precise design of environments will have to wait a while. But to the satisfaction of physical needs for clean air and water, food, health and shelter, long understood to be essential for survival, must now be added the equally generalized specifications for necessities of a psychological and social kind within the same environments: a sense of security and identity, opportunities for tranquility, exploration and participation, the feeling of freedom and happiness. All these apply with equal force to any form of human settlements whether these be industrial-urban or agrarian-rural, anywhere, at any time.

All these represent human norms which may be thought of as constants universally valid over long periods, whereas the planning-designing changes are subject to cultural and technical variables in space and time. Urbanizing man seems to be faced with a paradoxical situation: the implementation of basic, constant needs through technology often conflicts with the necessity to preserve the sociological and cultural variants and their interplay. As long as these different basic needs remain as contradictions, the developing countries, in many cases still culturally intact, will finally

... the chief sources of social welfare are not to be found in economic growth *per se*, but in a far more selective form of development which must include a radical reshaping of our physical environment with the needs of pleasant living, and not the needs of traffic or industry, foremost in mind ...

E. J. Mishan, *The Costs of Economic Growth,* London, 1967

72

succumb to the very diseases which they are now fighting and which characterize the countries whose technologies they want to utilize and whose material successes they wish to emulate.

Technological Fallout

Once a certain technological status is established, the form of the urban environment can quickly become stereotyped everywhere. Affluence and technical know how result in similar highways, railways, subways, airports, automobiles, bridges, skyscrapers, stadia and slums everywhere. The problem seems to be to adjust simultaneously to technological advance and sociological transition through measures that range from relative simplicity to extraordinary complexity; a problem clearly of transforming contradictions into complementarities within any urban system.

The social priorities which vary must reflect and control the technological components which appear as constants in their organization and function. Technology

'City Life and City Problems Come in the Antarctic': An unsightly garbage dump covers a once picturesque inlet at the base of McMurdo Station, a sure sign that civilization has arrived on the island.

Headline and caption to photograph in the *New York Times*, 22 December 1967

The White Paper on transport, expected to be out towards the end of June, will, it is thought, contain the point that public services should not be treated as 'economic units' (making profit) 'but as socially essential units' with some measure of community contribution.

Daily Telegraph, 20 April 1966

Design . . . means thoughtful solutions to carefully defined problems, which means that the decisions involved are not arbitrary . . . when costs of a new solution are higher, as they often are despite our best efforts, they can be fully justified, without hesitation, because new criteria, new program needs will be met. New benefits are worth new costs. The new priority given to design will prove its value when the benefits, in human terms, are seen and experienced.

Peter Chermayeff, Department of Housing and Urban Development Conference, 22 May 1967

In an ugly and unhappy world the richest man can purchase nothing but ugliness and unhappiness.

In his efforts to escape from ugliness and unhappiness the rich man intensifies both. Every new yard of West End creates a new acre of East End.

The XIX Century was the Age of Faith in Fine Art. The results are before us.

George Bernard Shaw, *Prefaces*, London, 1934

Planners have a duty to urge a change in priorities when considering public expenditure. I agree with former President Eisenhower and many others that the United States cannot afford to spend billions of dollars in preparing for a flight to the moon when there is so much to improve here on our earth, not least in the United States itself . . .

Gunnar Myrdal, 'Too Late to Learn', *Bulletin of the Atomic Scientists*, January 1968

I draw the further conclusion that . . . the common idea that America is an immensely rich and affluent country is very much an exaggeration. American affluence is heavily mortgaged. America carries a tremendous burden of debt to its poor people. . . . Not paying it implies risk for the social order and for democracy as we have known it . . .

of any promise becomes immediately operational and is transformed quickly into technical systems and sub-systems. It is this accelerating process which creates the illusion of decisiveness and constancy, while any notion of planning-designing and investing in any social system, however basic, remains a matter for debate and variability. This socio-technical contradiction rapidly becomes an economic-political one. Those who can afford to ignore the fact that much temporary technology is in contradiction to basic human needs are the privileged minorities in society engaged in the preservation of their private satisfactions. While repeating democratic clichés, the 'fat-cat' debaters remain content to ignore the cry of havoc from the 'lean-cats'. The current dispute rather than debate (contradiction) between the ends of the 'haves' and the 'have nots' obviously cannot continue. No democratic society can afford it. Any viable urban system of the third ecology which can be translated into a workable model must be capable of serving democratic, public purposes. Within such a model every component, without discrimination, has an equal position of interdependence with every other in the urban system.

Neither the programming spectrum nor the plan-design process can be meaningful in itself without the other. Contradictions, apparently irreconcilable, when put together become revealed as complementary opposites which may be enjoyed as meaningful options to satisfy man's constantly shifting purpose or his unchanging characteristics.

5. Exchange is Meeting

Maximization of choice. Where man and machines meet. Exchanges between transportation systems as places of concourse. Urban weights and measures. A tool for sorting complexity.

It is sometimes assumed that the fullness of ideal city life can be brought within the reach of people not living in cities by modern media of communication and transportation. This error is based on a misunderstanding of the nature of this fullness, on the inability to distinguish between vicarious and genuine experience. The vicarious may be characterized as a tendency to maximal passivity coupled with a minimum of choice, as in watching images on a screen or listening to a program determined elsewhere. The genuine means active participation and a maximum of choice, with all the risks involved.

Physical planners have caused more damage than they have achieved good. They discovered that they are in fact dealing with problems that ought to be addressed by comprehensive planning, however presumptuous that term may seem. In fact this has turned planners, in some cases, away from the role of inventing the future, away from the role of attempting to direct that future, into one accommodating to it by skilful prediction.

John Dyckman, 'Planning in a Context of Change', *Urban Exploration Proceedings*, Florida, 1965

Man's rather small tolerances in physical environments are simple examples of the limits of compatibility between opposites. Tolerable climate is confined to a very narrow spectrum of temperature and humidity. Death waits outside these special environmental conditions. Too not or too cold, too dry or too wet, kills. Even the acoustic climate, which is less harmful in many ways, also has strict limits. We can be killed by sudden sound volume and may be debilitated physically and nervously by continuous exposure to excessive noise or meaningless sound interference. Prolonged absolute silence is equally intolerable. Continuous exposure is psychologically ruinous, as is continuous isolation.

The intolerable limits of either a physiological or psychological kind such as those cited above suggest immediately that similar intolerable limits exist in sociological and technological situations. Therefore the system of the designed environment, which here is assumed to be a sub-system of a larger ecological order, must contain, if it is to be favorable, stimulating contrasts within a tolerable frame.

Within it, options of enriching individual experience can become a planning goal instead of the compromised gray middle of mass-culture consensus; exciting choices somewhere between one's own heaven and someone else's hell can be approached in imagination with the reasonable anticipation of being able to oscillate safely from ecstasy to levels which may be optimistically characterized as social equilibrium with no harm done.

Complementarity and maximization become less abstract and more real when we apply these principles to pairs of environmental options, such as, for instance, community and privacy or mobility and tranquility. All four are recognizable as desirable and should be viable options, at least in theory, to all men. Mobility–tranquility represents, of course, a spectrum of experiences through hierarchies of functional components. Close to the maximized tranquility option may be found those ranges of mobility which include various means of slow motion, which in turn permit leisurely unhampered observation and exploration of the small and intimate. Western man's current intoxication with motion and speed *per se* of course inhibits this; focus is lost and a generalized or superficial view only

Unlike other South-east Asian capitals, which have exchanged Oriental charm for concrete and the automobile, Phnompenh, despite its growth in population from 300,000 to 500,000 in little more than a decade, retains an unhurried, uncluttered manner and appearance. . . . As a result motor traffic is light, and tree-shaded streets are safe for sauntering pedestrians and three-wheeled pedicabs, which proceed at a patrician pace . . . .

. . . In this setting the crowding and speed that afflict other South-east Asian cities have so far passed Phnompenh by . . . Phnompenh [Cambodia], with few cars, goes its leisurely way.

Tillman Durdin, *New York Times*, 2 December 1967

Fig. 4
Urban Parameters
Complementarity and
Maximization

Maximization of
complementary opposites
in a spectrum of compati-
bility creates choices
between abstract maxima
and minima of life-
enriching experience.
Intermediary points
between any pairs of
opposites may be plotted
on a hierarchical curve.
Within the public and
private realms we list some
typical complementary
options:
Communications – Contact
Mobility – Tranquility
Community – Privacy
Controls – Freedom
Continuity – Change
Concourse – Solitude
Exposure – Isolation
Consensus – Choices
Conservation –
    Construction
Stereotyping – Prototyping

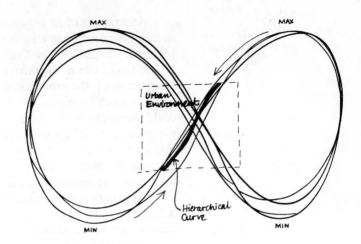

remains. This appetite for motion and speed is being
constantly fed by technological advance, and if it is
not placed in its proper context, appetite can become
addiction.

Under such circumstances, a priority in any urban
system must be the development of environments which
induce slow or non-motion facilities as well as those for
fast travel. The advantage in increased speed tends in
any case to be canceled out by increases in travel time
between destinations which if measured as time/distance/
frequency might well have been planned close together
for excellent reasons in the first place. Our mobility–
tranquility spectrum suggests therefore an entire new
hierarchy of movement which will include the pedestrian
and give him, if not primacy, then at least complementary status with vehicles. It seems that we must
soon establish car-free places and man-full places as
complementary options. Perhaps the parking lot life is
already losing its flavor, and death on highways, which
is no longer a news item but a frightening familiar
experience, has already become as real a horror as
cancer or war.

79

An example of an extended hierarchy of public transit was provided in a most convincing manner in Montreal's Expo '67. The Central Cities 'Metro' subway system linked one of the three islands in the St Lawrence River on which the exhibition was staged with the opposite south bank toward which future Montreal could grow. The three islands were joined in turn by an overhead 'express' system, and, at the same time, the major events on the three islands, in this case exhibition components, were linked by a slower overhead mini-rail with more frequent stops. In addition, moving at close to walking pace were electrically driven, clean, silent 'Charrette' trains, a safe mechanized assistance to the tired, elderly or burdened pedestrians. Similar electrically powered carts for goods and luggage are ubiquitous in warehouses, railway stations, docks and airports everywhere. Their cousins serve as passenger carriers on the broadwalks of Atlantic City and Miami. The latter had not been intensively used until the Montreal Expo. Few paths exist for any such leisurely movement.

This admirable Montreal demonstration of a transportation hierarchy obviously invites extension through many already available technical means and many yet to be invented. Perhaps bicycle paths, safe from motorized vehicles, will eventually spread beyond Central Park in New York and become part and parcel of a new larger network with a strong bias toward walking and slowly moving people all over that city.

Flows and Containers

Mobility–tranquility, given their equal complementary value among our parameters, influence the definition of two major operational components and tools: hierarchies of movement (flows) and of inhabited places (containers). In this manner the hierarchies of places may be thought of as 'targets': terminal destination points and 'exchanges', transfer points between any number of transportation media in which passengers may regain their uninhibited pedestrian state and become complementary independent components.

The old natural flow systems, the waterways of seas and rivers, had their containers and exchanges, the harbors. The caravan routes provided by historic man across whole continents linked market places along valleys and mountain passes. The pattern of markets and routes persists to our day in the man-made and natural habitats alike. Flow systems of technological society have of course added lately the new dimension of air space, but perhaps we can extend the usefulness of nature's flow media today by exploiting again water transport technologies along the world's crowded riversides and seaboards as is most efficiently and attractively done by Istanbul's and Hong Kong's ferries.

The urbanization of man's flow systems has recently undergone a drastic transformation and has become a compound of many sub-systems moving men, goods, fuels, water, energy, waste products, information: life-lines, in fact, without which urban man could not survive. The diversity and quantity of systems of flow in the post-historic, man-made world have magnified the possibilities of unforeseen and dangerous consequences for humanity.

Commitment and Priorities

A multi-dimensional, program-clarifying and process-classifying tool for dealing with problems of this magnitude can also determine priorities by including a commitment. It may join theory, which alone can describe any fact but can explain none, with proposals for implementation in a system which provides for the interaction and interdependence of all components and thus makes abstract theory as effective as technology. The commitment determines the framework, its components and priorities and can never be confused with any other framework, starting with a different commitment, even if this is plotted in terms of identical organizational, operational, functional and technical components.

The heart of our commitment is the maximization of human contact at the human goal level: provision of opportunities for face-to-face leisurely intercourse to complement communication sub-systems of increased and accelerated mobility and instantaneous information. Maximization on the level of community interaction may assist man to become more human *where* and *when* he can do so. Technologically considered, dispersion, scattering and deployment all appear as advantageous to the increase of choice. Sociologically there may well be a flaw in this theory which we will discuss more fully later.

Our search for an urban system and model has

All great civilization has been in a certain measure a Civilization of the Dialogue. The life substance of them all was not, as one customarily thinks, the presence of significant individuals, but the genuine intercourse with one another. The future of man depends upon a rebirth of dialogue . . . and most especially of genuine dialogue between men of different kinds and convictions.

Martin Buber, 'Hope for This Hour', *Pointing the Way*, New York, 1957

therefore been dominated by the idea that territorial identity and community identity is primary, at least until such a time when man's bio-psychological nature is radically and unequivocally changed: probably a somewhat remote reality.

Urban Realms

If our contention is true and flow-container systems are basic to urbanization in any form whatsoever, we can ask a question about priorities. Should not efficient (long-term, cheap) flow systems come first and be thought of as omni-ducts containing all reasonably predictable accommodations for utilities (such as communications and transportation), and the 'plug in' of essential containers, in proper relationships of accessibility and importance one to another, come second? Flow systems such as sewers, pipes, ducts, cables, corridors, malls, passages and alleys will act in the same way and are susceptible to modulation and modification through plan-design. It may change the rhythm and speed of flow, not only of utilities, according to well-known laws, through diverse means, such as widening or constriction, physical slowing or acceleration, but may similarly affect the movement of people through ambiguity or clarity in direction.

The omni-duct service sub-systems suggested here — 'invisible' supporting life-lines which may be designed for great flexibility to receive new technical components — could perhaps replace or supersede the present obsolescent, cumbersome and interfering networks. The priority of public sub-systems seems self-evident. It has been proved for a long time that in dimension, cost and technological complexity this would be beyond the means of private, local and even state capacities. The systematic 'plug in' of private components into public sub-systems could make them both complementary.

It must be noted here that there are in fact only a limited number of sub-systems which can be structured by means of plan-design and this is the reason for the emphasis here on flow and container systems. These are not only major technological operational components, but they are sociologically comprehensible and therefore susceptible to plan-design influence in the immediate future. Public transportation and public functions (flows and containers) invite orderly integra-

82

tion of facilities at many levels and magnitudes in the urban hierarchy.

Public health units, educational facilities, police and fire stations, welfare and social security offices, government local branches, post offices and other agencies which may spring up in the foreseeable future are all potential places of human contact operating before, during and after what we now think of as a working day. They appear to be natural 'pump-primers' for concourse in our imaginary hierarchy of exchanges which will invite private enterprise to follow. The latter may, in the case of a great school or hospital, first play the role of crevice-fillers, that is as servicing rather than prime components.

Concourse exchanges of certain magnitudes will eventually establish their appropriate equilibrium between public and private services and facilities. In any case, what is here suggested is that urban places of high intensity/density/frequency and mix of use could be established in this manner. It is further suggested that utility and communication flow systems, even if privately managed, are so highly coordinated and controlled that, as in the case of mail, they are virtually publicly directed. They are in the community realm and demand responsible protection of the public interest and can be used as instruments for shaping public concourse places.

This suggests the important priority to which planners and designers can apply themselves: they can provide the kinds of concourse places which contain at different scales public services, made accessible for everyone by means of public transportation systems. These may occur as predictable and desirable events along with some elbow room for the unpredictable and perhaps undesirable: a form of safety valve subsystem, probably as essential to community life as are the crevice-filling sub-systems of commerce which cling to all densely used places. The plan-design of containers which are predominantly in the private sector could then perhaps follow the 'public works', thus providing 'planned inevitability', in the phrase of Charles Abrams.[33] That the appetite for such places exists, even among automanic Americans, is borne out by the hordes of tourists who cross the Atlantic to taste the pleasures of leisurely pedestrian concourse in old cities. There

33. Charles Abrams, Yale Seminars, 1966

are no doubt other excellent reasons for travel, but watching people going about their daily lives in their special environment adds to the pleasure of encounter with another land and culture. It is from places of human contact and concourse that both cultural and technical innovations are likely to flow.

When a city becomes too large for walking one may provide technological assistance within the limits of convenience and pleasure for areas that are beyond walking distance, to and from a point of arrival and departure, to and from other destinations. The passenger can be transformed painlessly into a pedestrian and vice versa. Exchanges, at certain magnitudes, become in fact massive nuclei of density/intensity/frequency of use which can then support the most costly, sophisticated and complex technology and structures.

| Targets and Exchanges

What sort of places of community and what sort of concourse are we discussing? What kinds of events, functions and facilities can we imagine within such a hierarchy? Obviously at this stage of our inquiry the answers must remain at a fairly high level of generalization. The urban hierarchy of meeting places does, however, suggest specific situations. Community starts at home where the 'living room', a mini-concourse, can complement individual private retreat. At greater magnitudes a hierarchy of local community meeting places can generate exchanges and perhaps concourse of a progressively increasing public character in proportion to the magnitude or importance of events. At all scales an admixture of housing complements and enriches the other components. Through the device of a declared governing purpose, the commitment, we can go on and describe the qualitative characteristic which we might desire in a given urban organization, either a place or a service or whatever within the system hierarchy.

Our commitment can now be made more specific and closer to physical reality. The 'urban' places, using the term urban to describe a very wide spectrum of the technological environment, will contain a variety of facilities, places of 'mixed use' first and 'continuous use' second. In short, an 'exchange' rather than a single purpose 'target'. The former invites people to gather in a random, leisurely way at all hours; the latter is a

84 short occupancy destination, usually operating during

fixed hours and thus producing peaks of fullness and emptiness. The fullness produces pressures and denies leisure. In the past few years city dwellers have found that the temporary emptiness of certain areas may provoke a wide range of uncontrollable dangers. Clearly this emptying of single function areas can become potentially dangerous in all cases irrespective of the particular character of their function. Such areas do not belong to the system for which we are searching. They are non-urban, 'ecto-urban', they lie outside the framework of community.

Permanence and Change

While planner-designers cannot structure industrial and commercial systems they can learn how these operate. Professor Karl Deutsch has commented on the complementarity of permanence and change, and the resulting dilemma for planners: 'Do we know how much changes how quickly? If you look at half a dozen reasonably new settlements built since 1937 – this is 1967 – what per cent of the major design characteristics have changed by how much in the 30 years that have passed? There may even be records of what they were designed for. The people worked 42 hours in 1937 and they may work 35 hours now. But, if you look at the percentages, it may turn out that even over 30 years the percentage shift in activities per year or per decade, is reasonably moderate – 1% per change per year in almost anything is considered very rapid change in politics.'[34]

Declaration of splendid ends does not therefore inevitably lead to clear-cut, immediately effective means which could implement the former. Many unknown factors concerned with social adjustment to even modest rearrangements in urban structure immediately become apparant. Viable strategies are not necessarily followed by appropriate tactical measures even in most critical matters. Professor Jacqueline Tyrwhitt has observed that in a similar search for urban systems in England, the following occurred:[35] 'The first new towns in Britain were planned according to what people thought everybody wanted. Two great things remained quite naturally out of their consideration: one was the enormous influence of television, the other was the very rapid advent of the second car in almost every middle class family. The first town was planned in ignorance of

34. Karl Deutsch, Yale Seminars, 1966

35. Jacqueline Tyrwhitt, Yale Seminars, 1966

these two phenomena. The result is that the things that were designed to be within walking distance of the residents on their free evenings, are not being used for that purpose at all now. But, as they were not bad things in themselves, they are still presentable and are being used for other different purposes. But, the planned purpose is now requiring a different scale and a different kind of environment. We can still use the measure of validity of both permanence and change, but often change is conditioned by the permanence of the surroundings which can't be changed probably in less than 35 to 40 years.'

Urban Weights and Measures

Within the larger system the 'urban' hierarchy of exchange – concourse places of mixed use and continuous use – may be more precisely specified in terms of meeting, accessibility, frequency of use, intensity of use and 'density' of activity. One can, it follows, include not only a variety of uses, that is of facilities, but also structure the mixture so that facilities of one kind or another are in use around the clock. From this it may be deduced that the mix must include a full spectrum of users in all age groups, from small children to senior citizens. From the sociological point of view this could prove to be a more convincing goal for meeting places: that they become democratic rather than the segregated or homogenous, sparsely populated and separated pieces of accommodation most planners today consider ideal. Throughout this argument it should be noted that in the term 'density' we include not only those living in an area but also those occupying it for any purpose. This then gives a new formula of measurement of density in terms of number, function and characteristics: a hierarchy of containers of intensity/density/frequency of use and choice and variety of mix, in other words, measures of time/space/place.

Once we can systematically examine the operation and organization of flows and containers in this manner, we might see a new set of dynamic measures that could define more precisely the system's structure. Intensity/density/frequency and mix of use describe attributes for containers just as time/distance/frequency, etc., describe the true measure of speed in flows. These attributes can be modulated within the compatibility spectrum, the maximization of opposites.

This study is not concerned with the population distribution as revealed by periodic census-taking of where people *reside*. We are far more interested in where 'urban' people *live*, using the last word in its fullest sense. A new dimension of *life* peculiar to technological, affluent society must be taken into account: the progressively growing travel time. People move about more at all times and for many more purposes. It is evident that the affluent majority today spend an uncomfortably large part of their working lives in cars, nearly as much as their sleeping time in beds. Certainly less time awake is spent in tranquil places than in travel. Enervating and dangerous traffic is already producing traffic jams not only on earth but also in the sky. Death on the roads, however, is democratic. Statistics cover the entire social spectrum and are depressingly higher among the young. Air collisions, of course, involve the more privileged members of society. The separation of commercial planes from private planes in airports will, it seems, guarantee that the elite will eventually die more private deaths. It seems very unlikely, however, that anything as sensible as stricter licensing laws for private vehicles (formidable weapons in their own right) will receive attention. Professional readers will recognize an immediate inequity in such freedom when comparing the overbearing restrictions and the legally established difficulties of obsolescence encountered in architecture, engineering and law. All uncontrolled travel must produce traffic jams, for all means of transportation lead to at least one preferred target at some time. The traffic problem must therefore increase directly in proportion to number and appetite for travel.

The foregoing random examples of measure of interaction, complementarity and maximization of experience can of course be extended in any direction that any commitment or problem dictates. What is emphasized here is that the urban measures must describe the qualitative as well as quantitative attributes of any component. Such a system of measures may be systematically developed both in principle and in particular to fit the context of sociological and technological desiderata alike.

New measures may be now seen as orientation

devices to cover all contingencies in which the plan-design process may be involved. This amounts to a planning-designing tool which can explain urban realities, as suggested above, or expose unusable socio-political and romantic abstractions which grow out of either the false separation of related components or specious analogies derived from obsolete thinking. In sum, it is a double-edged tool of constructive and critical function that cuts through complexity on the one hand and myth on the other. This heuristic device might help resolve, at the most comprehensive scale of ecological control, the complex interplay between constant and variable parameters of humanity.

Commitment and Tool

Our 'commitment' is to a theoretical and social purpose and not to a physical plan; on the other hand, it proposes a principle of urban organization. The idea of dynamic order, a theme central to our proposal, necessarily implies change and growth. Our commitment is not to a Utopian or ideological closed system which, to our mind, would be inapplicable to urban models.

A commitment, however, inevitably suggests a basis for action in the form of organizational and operational principles. It is only such principles that may direct physical form toward desired ends. This is fundamental to our purpose. Appendix 2, 'Sorting Complexity', describes the authors' device for arranging components of our proposed planning method. However, no one model of a physical urban system may ever be derived directly from it. It is, in short, a yardstick and not a design machine.

Design can only emerge from a gestalt-seeing and form-making mind. Man has not as yet invented a machine capable of this function. Consequently our best machines today still await the mind's instruction. We must again stress the limitations of all tools. A sorting, structuring device can tell a designer, once a commitment has been made, *what* to do; it cannot and is not intended to tell him *how* to do it. It can describe a program in considerable detail and can suggest steps in the design process in the order of their importance and indicate the nature and character of the components to be included in the model. Designers can give form; physical tools can only theoretically formulate.

We are witnessing today the fashionable and, one hopes, therefore, short-lived 'planning' activity which rationalizes by means of sophisticated technology most unreasonable social ends. Some of these exercises are ready-made scenarios for films simultaneously hilarious and sinister: troglodyte subterranean communities; a continuous motor-maze condemning suburban drivers to life in a dreadful labyrinth from which there is no escape except into stale arrivals and departures. No goose shall ever wander. Just straight ahead and round the ramp. Thus are physical 'molehills' made out of mathematical 'mountains', a significant reversal of an ancient adage.

6. Social Purpose — Physical Components

Variety and mix. City-scape, water and landscape. Public concourse as urban catalyst. New components and old rearranged. Public mobility in a multi-polar system. Zoning for mix.

I think that one is called upon to have a rather subtle and difficult attitude which combines an unqualified patriotism and loyalty and love of those things in which one is really engaged, those communities of which one is a member, those parts of life which are one's own . . .

J. Robert Oppenheimer, *Arts and Architecture*, Vol. 77, No. 6, May 1960

. . . informal learning plays a part in . . . skills of abstraction and inference. . . . . The toys children manipulate, the conversations they listen to all contribute to the attitude and skills they develop . . .

Francis E. Dart and Pamia Lal Pradhan, *Science*, 10 February 1967

... the evil is in Greenwich and Great Neck, not Greenwich Village. ... The new generation is rebelling against the nothingness breeding in the suburbs ...

Benjamin B. Molman, *New York Times*, October 1967

In the ... 1950–1959 period during which central cities gained 1·5 per cent in population, the suburbs spurted ahead by 44 per cent ... [consuming] ... more land per capita than city growth.

Edward Higbee, 'Strangulation of the Suburbs', *Current*, December 1960

The lamentable consequences of the fragmentation of the man-made environment – lack of focus, specificity and identity – are increasing. Industrial man is seemingly committed to extending the chaos of the environment. The private motor vehicle serves private business and makes for the provision of consumer facilities at random because it has uninterrupted access everywhere. Location priority, then, becomes based on the automobile, and generates a spatial organization that enables private money to be profitably invested rather than public purposes to be usefully served. This condition is rooted in the past knowledge and confidence that the public purse will rush to the rescue and create viable means of access to yet another 'private' place. This haphazard movement caused by the random distribution of facilities privately served by the automobile tends to deploy humanity in an ever more chaotic mosaic. The result is that stereotypical facilities which can be made available everywhere are proliferating; the man-made environment does not invite concourse but simply increases travel. By the same token it may be said that there are no new prototypes, but very few unexpected places, that may be pleasantly surprising. The car is an implement of homogenization because any desired stereotype, the known and expected, can always just as well be somewhere else for the car owner.

The staples of mass-culture and mass-production in stereotyped arrangements and physical containers are the inevitable components in suburban, low-density population areas simply because there are not enough users to sustain anything else. Chain stores and service stations are standardized branches of various corporate interests concerned uniquely in mass distribution. Specialities are sought in places where great numbers over many hours daily provide continuous consumer demands of great variety; that is, in intensely/densely/frequently used places in urban cores.

The endless diffusion of the same kind of people, purposes and facilities contradicts the human need for variety which occurs when great numbers of very different people come together in concourse for common purposes. Facilities randomly dispersed cannot generate this variety and instead become stereotyped as dictated by a market mechanism. A serious question now arises. Can we continue to increase travel in private vehicles if

Monotony is objectionable **not** only because it is boring but even more because it can become an ethnological agent for various types of mental disorders . . . the complete absence of challenge can thus be as deleterious as excessive intensity of environmental stimuli . . .

René Dubos, *Man Adapting*, New Haven, 1965

36. Robert Theobald, *Free Man and Free Markets*, New York, 1963

Scenario for Urbanism

we become conscious that it tends to scatter urban components? Everything which has made man human will suffer in the process of transforming the human environment into the no-place reality of man-empty road networks, parking lots and stereotypes without end.

The genuine increase in choice that modern society supposedly offers does not exist. An illusory pattern of choice, more places providing more of the same, has replaced it. The urban culture dissolves in global provincialism. Pre-digested information and familiar standardized conveniences have gradually displaced intercourse and exploration which accelerated cultural evolution in the past.

As this tendency increases, substitutions by 'marketives', to use Robert Theobald's word,[36] the providers of saleable, prepared experiences, will be the rule for the masses, the exceptions being limited to closed circuits of professional, intellectual and maverick interests of all sorts. Only the privileged and the mad will be able to reach beyond stereotypes. The poor will have to continue to rely on their limited pleasures or their limitless discontent, to eke out whatever tiny piece of collective advantage they can in their given locality. The domination of randomly running vehicles which has already become a direct nuisance in high-density urban areas may indirectly increase the blunting of perception and the danger to social health everywhere.

The pedestrian's view of modern cities is limited and monotonous. With few exceptions, streets, wide and narrow, designed for or turned over to car and truck traffic become as stereotyped as the vehicles themselves. Sidewalk and roadway are indistinguishable from each other. But the areas needed for the smooth operation of rubber-wheeled vehicles demand durable materials of even texture which are irrelevant to many pedestrian purposes. Mixing the two means of locomotion sharply curtails the spectrum of choice in man's condition. With few exceptions architecture now stops abruptly at ground level. Modern city-scapes seem all façade without a floor. Perhaps if we again cultivate strolling and sitting in public places we shall at the same time restore the art of paving, and rich color, texture and pattern will once more delight the leisurely eye.

95

The city-scape seen from highway approaches, the

most common view, is equally dull in its essential sameness in spite of all 'beautification'. But even worse, the pedestrian realm appears to be landlocked or at least irretrievably cut off from adjacent land- and waterscapes. Highways and railroads, surrounding islands of suburbia, or obsolescing storage facilities and industries now occupy erstwhile lovely valleys and riversides. Waterfronts, old and new, which once were the most lively sectors of harbor cities, and sometimes the most precious pieces of cultural heritage, as in Amsterdam and Venice, are lost to the pedestrian. Failure of this kind is exemplified at different scales in New York by a barrier of warehousing and high-speed throughways, or in New Haven by oil tanks and turnpike.

An alternative approach – accepting the pedestrian world as a priority – suggests that cities could with advantage grow back toward their waterfronts wherever feasible as in New York, Boston, London, Istanbul and Hong Kong, to recapture the special flavor of the mixture of work, residence, recreation and transportation. The modern technology of 'hydrofoil' and 'air cushion', which requires virtually no depth of water, may in the foreseeable future bring new craft close to urban concentrations. In some instances water transport could become an integral part of exchange in urban communities. Waterfront activity generates concourse in a setting which joins the natural and the man-made, work and recreation, in a delightful manner.

The pedestrian world, recaptured and consistently maintained, offers an unrivaled richness of experience. The small child looking up at the 'mobile' above its crib or crawling inside and around the dwelling is exploring and learning. He does not have a 'worm's eye view' of his environment. The panorama seen from a skyscraper or an airplane is not a 'bird's eye view'. The groundscape, room-scape, garden-scape, land- and city-scapes, sea- and sky-scapes are a spectrum of environmental experience producing sensual, emotional and mental responses open to man alone. He can move in a space-speed spectrum closed to other species. At the small-slow end man may learn to focus on detail and exploration; at the large-fast end he may learn to perceive the great sweep of landscape. The technological extensions of man are amplifying and enriching his natural

96 perceptions.

At all scales there is a relationship between the essential components of our present urban environments (inhabited places) – the flows (transportation) and containers. The settlements of urban man, 'container' sub-systems, depend upon all sorts of life-lines, 'flow' sub-systems, some of which we have already described. This will probably continue to be true in the foreseeable future; any substantial autonomy appears far-fetched at this moment. Technical services in general, and communication and flow sub-systems in particular, are becoming a large part of the public economic overhead and must be equated with the number of people able to use them. The measure, previously mentioned, of intensity and frequency of use and density and variety of facilities, becomes part of the equation that assesses an urban system's efficiency. The best technology is only useful for extending human efficiency. Urban man is inevitably committed to subsidizing technological advance while keeping an eye on the sociological effects of its misuse. High costs of sophisticated technology can only be fairly distributed and its conveniences widely enjoyed if cost and convenience are placed at the disposal of the many. Technology, on the whole, is the 'invisible' part of the urban iceberg, the vast systems of movement of supplies, energy, waste-disposal and utilities of all kinds which sustain life. Perhaps, economically considered, the visible superstructure is least in importance, although the cost of 'human' containers for urban man is also rising steadily.

It seems that, apart from questions already raised, density, variety and frequency of use combined can lower the overhead cost of all flow systems and permit the shift of investment to many currently neglected but highly sophisticated supporting urban sub-systems. Automobility's overhead is severely time-consuming and unfair in the way its cost is distributed to the poor. The poor, in any case, can ill afford this form of transportation. The purchase price of the machine may be relatively low, but costs of insurance and maintenance are actually proportionately more expensive for the worn second-hand vehicles that the poor usually acquire. However great the cost of public transportation and other services may be, it can still be absorbed and equitably distributed in intense/frequent use situations. Public transit and private car parking at sub-urban

Each driver who travels between Connecticut and New York City is subsidized between $4 and $5 a day.

Robert S. Bird, *New York Herald Tribune*, 4 February 1966

Transportation is the nation's biggest industry, involving one of every five dollars in the economy.

President Lyndon Johnson, *New York Times*, 15 October 1966

Fig. 5
Urban Measures
Flow Systems

Hierarchies of movement
systems are comple-
mentary to hierarchies of
places for people. The
measures of time-
distance, frequency of use
and cost of technical
support are related to the
organizing principle of
public and private
components in comple-
mentarity. This applies
to all systems:
transportation, services and
utilities are all part of
structuring systems of
channels, territories and
orbits of movements
including walking, which
meet at exchanges, points
of transfer between
different sub-systems.

Public Realm

Access to Choices
Continuous Utilization
High Cost Technology
Public Transit
Public Vehicles
Semi-public
Mechanical Assist
Semi-private
Mechanical Assist
Semi-private Vehicles

Walking

Semi-private Vehicles
Private Vehicles
Low Cost Technology
Infrequent Utilization
Limited Choice
High Space Availability

Private Realm

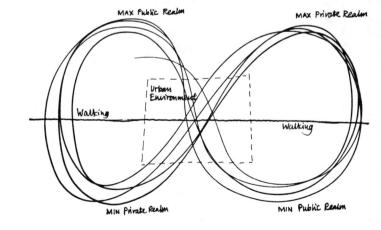

98

Fig. 6
Urban Measures
Container Systems

Places for people may be
organized in hierarchies;
the measures are density,
intensity, frequency and
mix of use. The spectrum
of compatibility lies
typically between opposites
such as
Mobility – Tranquility
Public – Private
Anonymity – Identity
Concourse – Seclusion

Public Realm

Technological Support
Mobility
Accessibility
Exposure
Anonymity
Concourse
Variety

Services

Limited Choice
Seclusion
Identity
Privacy
Space Availability
Tranquility
Technological Support

Private Realm

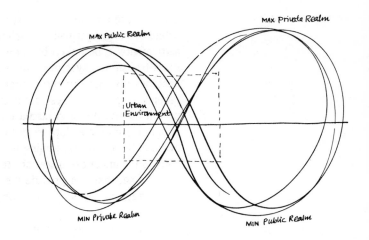

99

... We're making up for 30 years of do-nothingism in mass-transportation. You haven't built any subways. And you haven't done any-thing really significant for commuter railroads since 1913, when Grand Central Terminal was built . . .

Dr William J. Ronan (Chairman of the New York State Metropolitan Transportation Authority), *New York Sunday Times*, 25 August 1968

and ex-urban exchanges might produce a new element of complementarity. Free parking in car silos away from city cores and free transit within them might correct the present high cost *per capita*/journey of commuter car traffic by substituting low cost *per capita* transit.

The sophisticated mass-transportation suggested here is already operating, but too haphazardly to satisfy optimum conditions, technologically or sociologically. Some public transit systems of course exist, but so inefficiently that they currently offer no competition to the pressures of automobile and highway lobbies. So powerful and pervasive is the myth of utmost freedom and option created by private vehicles that technological society has neglected to examine the potential com-munity advantages of cheap and comfortable travel with people living more closely together and has chosen costly spatial scattering instead.

We have already specified the basic ends to which we have been led. What we want to stress is the trans-formation of existing flows through new techniques according to an organizing principle of urban cohesion – that is, accepting a 'topographical' physical fact but changing its organizational principle to serve a definite human goal. In so doing we will try to maintain the same radius of orbit that the automobile provided without the cultural and economic benefits of human cohesion.

Concourse as Catalyst

We propose a change in transportation methods for urban systems that will enable existing and future settlements to be linked by omni-ducts in which a mass-transit sub-system is the major flow. Every station becomes both an organic exchange between transit and other transportation systems that either already exist or will be invented and also a nucleus around which concourse may develop. Places of concourse thus become the catalysts, joining flows and containers in a socio-technical organization. It is this system alone, we suggest, that can provide the basis for the urban revitalization of existing cities or for model cities to be built.

Only this kind of transit can provide the essential cheap transportation required by the urban poor for the long overdue enlargement of their 'orbits'. They need access to a variety of opportunities for employment,

**Fig. 7
Territories, Orbits and
Exchanges**
Complementary
Hierarchies

Social purpose and
necessary technical support
may be organized in
complementary
hierarchies of flow
systems, container systems
and exchanges. Territories
are physically determined
orbits by accessibility of
targets through move-
ment systems. Exchanges
are places where several
movement systems meet.
These components of an
urban structuring system
are nuclei, irrespective of
scale, which can grow into
pedestrian realms and
which may be meeting
places.

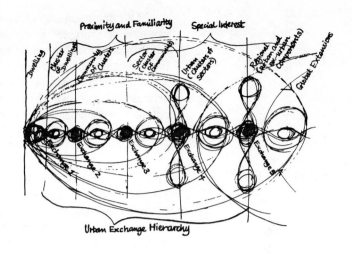

Urban Exchange Hierarchy

education and social services of all kinds to widen their
range of experience beyond the confines of the ghetto.
Cheap and readily available mass-transit may help
dissolve the ghettoes of the poor. Rebuilding slums may
provide pleasanter and healthier environments, but it
solves only one part of the problem of the deprived
urban area.

Urbanizing society need no longer start at the
cheapest end with the purchase of 'unimproved' land,
for example, and proceed to add progressively more
expensive components of 'improvement', such as roads,
utilities, etc. Already land cost for most enterprises is
quickly written off, as are simple technological servicing
sub-systems. The long-term investment process could
now with advantage be reversed and technologically
sophisticated societies could be encouraged to invest
their money in the most costly basic sub-systems first,
with the certainty that these too may be quickly written
off. Examples of such investment are the modern
subway systems, like those in Moscow, Montreal, San
Francisco and the gigantic bridge structure proposed
for Tokyo's extension.

Our commitment, in summary of this argument, can now be expressed in general terms as community advantages through planned cohesion, supplemented by the advantages of great mobility and communications: a techno-social spectrum of viable options ranging between optimum withdrawal and the complementary optimum community. Complementarity becomes the basic organizational principle for making the system a physical reality.

Theory and System

There are many techniques for creating a new system. The selection of a particular technique depends on circumstances and its relation to what is to be organized. The urban problem with which we are faced is immensely complex and constantly changing, but there seem to be two appropriate ways to develop a system for its resolution. One is to introduce new parts; another is to rearrange existing parts in a new way. The priority at this time in urban environments is perhaps not the creation of new parts so much as the rearrangement of existing, already functioning, but conflicting parts. The basic notion of complementarities is just a technique to attack problems and find a way to resolve a conflict: one finds the two poles of a contradiction, and instead of minimizing the opposite forces within the arrangement to keep them at peace, one reorganizes them. Six sets of such maximized opposites, physical urban components, emerged out of our commitment: urban–ex-urban, flows–containers, meeting places–communication systems, exchanges–targets, prime uses–crevice fillers, government components–private enterprise components. They are all operational components in an urban model. They are typical and universal for the reorganization of the urban environment.

Starts and Priorities

One way to reconcile the desirable and the possible is to search for an existing urban component which not only is unequivocally important socially and comprehensible in its operation, but also may be fitted into a new system: a ready-made peg upon which to hang our planning hat. To this expediency, often forced upon the planner, we have been able to add a rationalization quite logically derived from our commitment.

To realize our ends we require in the first place an extended hierarchy of means of transportation; secondly,

102

Fig. 8
**Complementary
Maximized Systems**
Public Transportation and
Private Vehicles

Optimum utilization of
machinery; continuous use
by large number permits
economic use of
sophisticated movement
technology in costly space.
Public transit keeps all
vehicles moving in areas of
high density, where their
storage and control are
uneconomic and socially
debilitating. Optimum
utilization of private
vehicles is in areas of low
density where public transit
is uneconomic

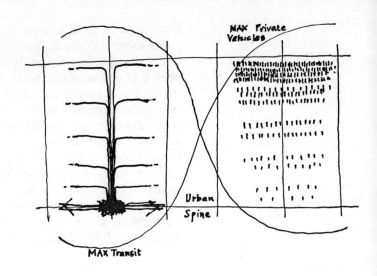

Fig. 9
**Maximized Comple-
mentarity of Choices in
Hierarchies of Places**

Territories and exchanges
which give access to them
can be arranged in
complementary hierarchies
between the areas of
highest density of
occupancy in a
metropolitan spine and
those of lowest density
in peripheral areas. Access
to many movement systems
in any one place can make
this into a pedestrian
realm acting as a bridge;
providing uninterrupted
pedestrian movement and
community focus.

103

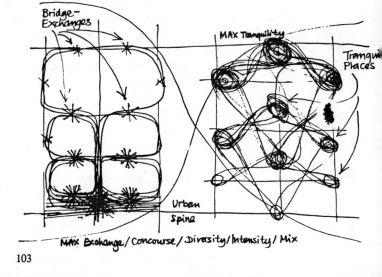

a vast increase in all forms of public transit; and thirdly, public ownership and control of all public rights-of-way which all public service flow systems require. This last point is of course of primary importance; it implies that regular travel, long or short haul, of great frequency will be almost entirely in the public domain and may eventually supersede, through the efficiency and comfort and safety of coordinated mass-transit, much of the travel in separate private 'luxury' vehicles along public rights-of-way. A sensible comprehensive public transit system will substantially reduce at once the pressure on terminal facilities in urban cores and perhaps eliminate them entirely in the future. Designers will then be able to concentrate on containers for life.

Panacea or Solutions

The increase in transit and the reduction of private vehicles in direct proportion to intensity/density/frequency of movement of people and goods outlined here represents a major shift in transportation, irrespective of the technology which may be employed in such reorganization. Urban transportation effectiveness, we suggest, must be measured in terms of the efficiency of the option to be mobile at any moment as well as in terms of the inefficiency of vehicles which remain in the metro-core immobile, at rest, waiting and expensively stored.

But besides this obvious practical disadvantage, we would like to point to a hidden social disadvantage of the utmost importance. Technological solutions which propose to extend indefinitely the 'door to door' conveniences of the private car (and these are many) ignore the many human consequences of such a system and concentrate exclusively on technical and mechanical improvements. An extended hierarchy of passenger movement suggests that the car is not a panacea under all conditions, a single, universal, glorious way of travel, no matter how safe it may become in the future. It suggests on the contrary the extension of modes of travel in accordance with their specific efficiency and comfort under many different circumstances.

The provision of excellent transit for the majority of urbanites does not eliminate auto-advantages under quite different sub-urban and ex-urban circumstances. We suggest that to exploit to the full the advantages of either the private car or public transportation, it will be

A single set of rails – given trains that move fast enough – could carry 50,000 passengers an hour, 20 times as many as a single highway.

Lawrence Galton, 'Commuting at 1,000 m.p.h.', *New York Times Magazine*, 24 October 1965

necessary to curb the activity of the car and improve and extend transit immediately. In any case, proposals based on the blind assumption that cars 'are here to stay' in increasing number, and that they must run faster, more frequently and freely everywhere, means that the stereotypes of today's market will, with the aid of high technology, under the direction of the new breed of young technocrats, launch urbanizing man on another dangerous technomanic period. 'The car will have stayed to dinner' with devastating effect.

It is urgent that urbanizing societies stop thinking of transportation only in terms of problems to be cured. The goal is to provide a system which will eventually prevent the recurrence of conditions requiring cure. But since no operation in the urban environment can exist in a vacuum but must be based on the present conditions, we have to proceed by examining the minimum necessary changes to be applied in the urban environment to achieve our basic organizing principles.

We are suggesting that existing publicly owned rights-of-way, highways and roads be considered as omni-ducts carrying any flow systems whatever – public transit and utilities, private vehicles, etc. – on their proper runs. To this publicly owned ground-level and underground real-estate can be immediately added superstructures utilizing air-rights for the accommodation of public purposes and facilities. The integrity of both public and private domains can thus be organized and maintained. The rights-of-way and air-rights already publicly owned represent an immense reserve of precious, socially useful spaces which must be protected from private exploitation. This public domain can then accommodate the essential new inhabited container components without disturbing already established and functioning components.

Transit and Pedestrian Primacy

Our great national highways and railway lines can very easily accommodate bridging exchanges between mass-transit sub-systems and road sub-systems of all kinds. An extended hierarchy of flows could grow naturally. More importantly, there could develop simultaneously a new hierarchy of special containers which would generate, at every stop on the transit-system, points of exchange. The road-building spree of engineers in affluent societies everywhere has disrupted, in one way or another, well-established communities by cutting through them instead of relating to them. These roads and highways lead away from the community; they contribute nothing within. They cannot be conveniently or safely crossed. As a result the community, large or small, is forced unnecessarily to duplicate many of its facilities and services. It becomes physically divided and this is followed by social disruption.

This contradiction between essential components – flows (transportation) and containers (inhabited places) – is a commonplace at all scales and requires transformation into complementarity in all cases. By bridging the existing transportation channels and making this bridge a transfer point, a station between many movement systems, the bridge can become an 'exchange', serving the needs of adjoining territories, and in the process restoring the social entity of a divided community by providing a new focal point, in which the primacy of the pedestrian within the community may be re-established. (One recalls with pleasure the architecture, now almost vanished, of the pedestrian overpass in railroad stations; why not bigger and better pedestrian bridges to restore community continuity where this has been disrupted by the highway engineers?)

The public ownership of urban air-rights can be modified to any extent in relation to particular situations. But, as a start, it makes it possible to plan catalytic pedestrian places at each bridge/exchange such as public, institutional services and functions of education, health, security and the like. Thus the essential priority given to public facilities may guarantee the support of private enterprise at all scales in and around this pedestrian realm designed for human contact, allowing variety and concourse to develop almost inevitably by providing an ever-present clientele.

Compare the active environment of railway stations in any pre-automobile age city with the obsolescing transit systems (especially in the case of the U.S.) now isolated from the highway flows that were built to supersede them. Here the underprivileged stations look like slaughter houses in which dead cars lie like carcasses by the hundred. The cars have reached the exchange point from some place and occupy the immediate environment of each station so effectively throughout the working day that they preclude the possibility that tnis may ever become a place inhabited by people. It is, in our sense of the word, a non-place, evidence of the decomposition of the urban tissue. Pollution of this kind in its broadest sense, direct technological pollution of environment and indirect sociological pollution, is an unexpected deadly Pinocchio; not a toy but a monster. Charles Abrams in this connexion has asked if '. . . dispersal from the central city isn't itself a sort of a manifestation of an illness'.[37]

Public transit in a metropolitan region – a hierarchy of exchanges linking the focal metro-core with well-established sub- and ex-urban cores in a single transportation system sustained in regular channeled flows – is an effective and economic way of moving large quantities of people or supplies all the time. At each major stop in the public transit system other sub-systems join it, such as buses, taxis, semi-private vehicles for hire, and private cars, which may be temporarily stored in car silos, a more efficient use of precious land than the space-devouring parking lot. Thus all modes of transportation meet to form an exchange. This brings together all sorts of people and provides opportunity for pedestrian movement and creates concourse. The coincidence of the number of different transportation sub-systems will be in inverse ratio in the hierarchy to intensity/density/frequency/mix of use at each exchange: private vehicles requiring prolonged storage become inefficient at the urban-core and become more efficient in ex-urban situations. The transfer from any one sub-system to another, for maximum public advantage, in a comfortable and pleasant manner, may be compensation enough for the 'deprived' motorist.

These points of transfer can be designed as places to correspond to the ages of man: the crawler's, toddler's, walker's and traveller's territories, precincts and orbits. The first stages, on foot, and locomotion without mechanical assistance, establish the first frontiers of individual exploration and learning; these are orbits of movement in familiar territories. They can be gradually extended into orbits determined by interest and involvement which may become global in scale. These should logically reach toward and be identified with the further frontiers open even to children as independent travelers mechanically assisted. Each point of transfer from pedestrian to passenger provides opportunities for design appropriate in scale and character to the hierarchy of exchanges. The physical form of each can celebrate a different condition in the human life.

The commitment to concourse dictates the nature of the model of intra-urban transit we have described, serving and linking places for pedestrian primacy. It also suggests inter-urban long-haul transit between concentrations in a metropolitan system centered upon a historically established core. It may be concluded that most demonstration 'cities' can only be new nuclei of well-established, growing metro-areas, an exchange point in interaction with an established core. One can now begin to see some features of the various components which so far have been deliberately made as general as possible in the context of a theoretical study. These aspects of the urban people-containing sub-system can be plugged into the flowing life-line systems sketched earlier.

All inhabited areas form a hierarchy of meeting places distinguished by differences in occupancy and use, which can be measured in density/intensity/frequency/mix. The basic ingredients of maximum community, mixed use, occupancy around the clock, machine-empty and man-full places, lie at one end of this hierarchy. Our proposal is related to the neglect from which these places have suffered.

As has been suggested earlier, pedestrian concourse may be induced by the judicious mixing of public service components such as education, health and government facilities on the one hand, and private enterprise on the other, together with a mixture of housing for different economic levels both private and public, all in close proximity and sharing equally the benefits of local facilities. Again it must be emphasized that the commitment to restore man-full places is not intended as a panacea. Other environments may provide for other experiences. A wider spectrum of events than the prevailing ubiquitous vehicle-full, man-empty road and parking lot life, does perhaps commend itself to many.

Fast-growing, fully automated processing and manufacturing plants are already reducing even maintenance crews, which is all they need in the way of people, to a negligible minimum. In the immediate future, these may reach a vanishing point as cybernetic techniques perfect self-regulating systems. In the place hierarchy, high technology with its specialized space-demanding production facilities thus stands in opposition to human needs of intercourse, concourse and variety of social opportunities.

The location of manufacturing plants will thus depend on purely technological and economic considerations. If they now happen to be within any metropolitan region this is usually a matter of historic accident or economic or political expediency. Clearly these supra-urban components lie outside the urban fabric. In marked contrast to these machine-full places is the hierarchy of man-full places: the 'intra-urban' community and variety of experience resources. These are at the heart of our commitment and their role is primarily social in function and organization.

Somewhere in between the two extremes of 'ex-urban' and 'inter-urban' function lie many specialized, single-purpose facilities which serve physically identifiable large territories. Obvious examples are recreational areas, such as national parks, great stadia for mass-spectator sports, power plants and wholesale distribution centers of mass-produced consumer goods. The magnitudes required by these cannot be efficiently or conveniently accommodated in the urban core. Their uses and movements fall into periods and rhythms which cannot be easily synchronized with intra-urban organization. The sporadic use of mass recreational facilities tends to build up traffic peaks and valleys which contradict the continuity required for the operation of the intra-urban sub-systems. The dimensions of such continually increasing facilities would make for further disruption of the central urban environment and magnify the already existing problems of single-purpose places in a density/intensity/frequency use matrix. The quantities involved, in any event, make all these centers depend on greater numbers than may be provided by any single urban territory. They belong to neutral ex-urban locations with ample space and optimum access to and from many people and places.

All these various urban and ex-urban components which constitute our theoretical urban system have both technological and sociological ingredients that can act
in complementarity in any pattern of distribution and

at any scale which may satisfy the urban demands. The urban inner components tend toward specialties in mix of great variety and of relatively small quantities, functioning at high density and frequency: the urban outer components tend toward concentrated staples, functioning at great speeds.

Multi-Polar System

This proposed system of organization shifts the historic image of the urban environment as a centrifugal-centripetal system pumping between core and periphery to a new image of an organism which pumps between different kinds of complementary urban choices, a multi-polar system. The former is by implication a concentric system which is either deliberately closed, limited in territory, or which fails when it spills over the limits of efficiency. The latter, on the contrary, is by definition open-ended and based on an ordered organization of mobility. It is capable of accommodating growth and change in both flowing and containing components.

It must be noted here that the operational principles described would apply equally forcefully to any system of urban organization, irrespective of the form. A centrifugal dynamic, expansion of historic cities over greater territories, increases urban areas of occupancy and travel time for the many, as has happened in the United States. A centripetal dynamic, for instance, the immigration of peasants in search of better conditions, increases density of population in urban concentrations, as in many cities in Latin America or Asia, without appreciable increase in the cities' areas. Density of population *per se* is not a measure of urban decline. Appropriate systems of sub-systems, properly designed, could make life very pleasant in densities now considered dehumanizing. The measure of human condition lies closer to qualitative change than to problems of territorial growth.

The authors' commitment suggests that the operational components, urban and ex-urban, exchanges and targets, are logically derived from the organizational principles of complementarity and maximization of choice expressed in opposites; place-proximity or space-availability and exchanges or targets can become an important index of their location.

The proposed system then is a complex of hierarchies of inhabited places in interaction and inter-

110

dependence, which may be physically and socially organized and can include both constant parameters which are independent of the specifics of a location in space and time and the variables reflecting needs of culture, period, climate, geography, resources and technology.

Information and Contact

Communication-information systems require constant utilization by the greatest number to support a very sophisticated and costly technology and they therefore are in the category of global resources or of inter-urban components and operate in fields which are already coming close to being independent of the location of people. Relayed information, irrespective of technologies involved, provides vicarious experience with only occasional glimpses of spatial or territorial identity. However, there are ways of communication that operate through direct physical contact and require participation, confrontation, exploration, in sum, first-hand experiences. It is in the case of such physical realities that the planner-designer is directly concerned, i.e. hierarchies of meeting places and physical environments in identifiable territories that are defined by and dependent on physical access. Information through concourse is the community end of the message sending-receiving spectrum. Technologically transmitted messages provide the illusion of autonomy for those who can afford communication paraphernalia in their private domain. In some developing countries, however, a community owned and operated radio and TV can on the contrary become the nucleus of a meeting place as in remote villages in India.

An urban model begins to emerge from these considerations which is made of physical contact, on the one hand, and a hierarchy of degrees of dependence and autonomy from communications media. Total independence from electronic, instant communication and information systems is impossible. Radio and TV provide indirect, vicarious access to a variety of experiences on a global scale, and in that sense complement the variety of first-hand experience through contact that can be provided on the urban scale.

Specialties and Staples

The principle of complementarity operates at every level in the programming spectrum and within all functional physical, technical components to which planning-designing may be applied. This complementarity can be directly connected with the varieties of choice open to man in technological society at every scale in the hierarchy of information media and place-exchange-bridge, etc. Any set of facilities in any one place in our proposed system will contain in varying degree a mixture of functions: primary and secondary, host and parasite, central components and crevice fillers. Whichever way you may describe these functions they fall into the same classification at the sub-system micro-scale as at the large metropolitan system macro-scale. Either, in any pair above, may be a specialty or a staple. A standard 'chain' movie house showing staple films may be close to the most specialized restaurants and bars. A very special opera house might be surrounded, as in Paris, by very staple cafés. In either case, they represent a nucleus of the variety of concourse which is at the heart of our urban commitment. They are the very opposite of single-purpose places, however staple or special in their function, which vacillate between the extremes of being uncomfortably full or dangerously empty.

Mix in Place

The principle of complementarity then turns out to operate in such a manner as to provide a mixture of experience at all scales in space and time, producing what Jane Jacobs,[38] among others, correctly calls community interest in community events, vigilance and security around the clock. There may be some reasonable doubt that the physical form these desiderata will take will be the narrow city streets which Mrs Jacobs has learnt to love, the mixture of people and vehicles down below and watchful 'mamas' at their windows above. All traffic has turned out to be dangerous and watchful 'mamas' have turned inward toward TV.

Recent highrise buildings in Milan express the old pattern of the neighborhood street of mixed use in a new form: apartments are frequently placed above offices, with community facilities at street level, each building becoming a street put on end so to speak, with concourse on the ground. This represents an example of reorganizing old components in a new meaningful way, or in other words, producing prototype organizations. What is here recommended is that the principle of multi-use should supersede the rule of single use which is now

38. Jane Jacobs, *The Death and Life of Great American Cities*, New York, 1961

predominant — that single buildings, clusters of buildings, neighborhoods and sectors should all be subject to mixed-function zoning and that the obsolete, bureaucratic, anti-social single-purpose zoning stereotypes be replaced as quickly as possible.

7. Toward a Model

Commitment into model. Flows, containers, exchanges; hierarchies of social and technical components in their natural place. Programming social goals, principles of organization, operational means in an open system. Description of some tentative models.

The world is now rapidly entering upon a new era of civic development, one in which 'progress' is no longer described as in mere quantity of wealth and increase of population, but is seen to depend upon the quality of these. The last generation has had to carry out great works of prime necessity, as of water supply, sanitation, and the like; elementary education, too, has been begun; so that to some, even pioneers in their day, our city development may seem well-nigh complete. But a new phase of civic development has become urgent — that of ensuring healthier conditions, of providing happier and nobler ones.

Patrick Geddes, *City Development: a study of parks, gardens, and culture-institutes, a report to the Carnegie Dunfermline Trust*, Birmingham, 1904

To a very considerable extent when we talk about controlling city size and keeping cities independent and so on, we're talking about a bygone non-extant type of city.

Britten Harris, Yale Seminars, 1966

The 'lattice-grid' (described in Appendix 2, 'Sorting Complexity') was devised for the purposes of urban plan-design and remains an open-ended spectrum for all contingencies. It sorts out and interrelates ends, means and functional components as a first step in urban model-building in the plan-design process. It may be described as an urban 'system of notation' that allows several issues to 'participate' simultaneously in the urban system and its model. The manipulation of this 'game-grid' makes the design process more precise and conscious and brings about more accurate predictions in complex urban situations. The readers are invited to 'play' with the grid for their own purposes.

At this stage in our study we can begin to visualize a model which corresponds to our commitment. The plan-design process has taken us from general abstractions which represent constant parameters to certain particular technical or functional means. The model must, however, remain semi-abstract so as to avoid proposing an arbitrary solution. On the other hand, an actual solution can only be provided by feeding into the model the measurable set of variables of a particular situation that is related to geographical, social and technological factors. This is the method of urban problem-solving analysis that we propose.

Model-building can never be quite objective, in a realistic sense, in the urban-design process. The diversity and nature of the urban issues preclude this. It does not, however, necessarily invalidate the method of problem analysis suggested above. Systematic analysis of urban problems would not, we believe, produce contradictory results. It could within a common framework lead to a variety of conclusions, depending on the group of people involved, their cultural background or the discipline to which they belong. It could produce different reactions for different groups of people. A series of such comparative studies could give a picture of entirely new urban requirements which could then be structured into the model with the aid of computers.

Perhaps a closer analysis will suffice to illustrate the method for planning purposes. A hierarchy of urban movement, for example, contains perhaps the most readily grasped functional components of a circulation sub-system. On the other hand, we suggest that each of the many pieces of 'human' and 'technical' circulation components, for example pedestrian and diverse vehicular movements, although less readily 'visible', can still act with equal force on the structure of a comprehensive organizational principle at every level in the multiplicity of urban orders. This is a typical example of components' interaction which must be taken into account in its totality for the purposes of any socio-technical system. For instance, the method relates the interaction pattern which joins mass-transit with all other individual vehicles which are passenger carriers and pedestrians in a single 'flow' sub-system.

This flow system with points of exchange suggests a 'container' sub-system: for instance a hierarchy of public health components, the types which the advocates of preventive medicine believe should form part of a public service cluster and become a nucleus in a community place hierarchy directly attached to an exchange in an urban transportation sub-system. 'Health facilities' constitute a hierarchy of vital importance in any urban system. They depend for their effectiveness on a wide range of accessibility, varying from direct physical access to quick access to information. A large segment of the hierarchy of health components in any case will depend on physical accessibility through various means of transportation and as a result will generate some concourse at the exchanges where they are located. Thus, 'health facilities' and travel systems are indissolubly related. Dr Abram Zeichner, chief of psychological services in the Department of Public Health of Connecticut, suggests that the method described should be able to help determine the desirable general distribution and location of public health facilities in a given territory as part of a concourse hierarchy.[39] Functional urban components such as passenger-carrying and health-facility sub-systems provide easily understood examples of interaction between sociological ends and technical means which can be plotted in the lattice-grid. It is further possible to extrapolate this method of relating functional components to each other and to ones which reflect socio-technical parameters. This, in effect, is a means of ordering which Charles Abrams has described as 'cutting through the jungle of the city'.[40]

39. Dr Abram Zeichner, Yale Seminars, 1966

40. Charles Abrams, Yale Seminars, 1966

Fig. 10
**Typical Urban
Hierarchy**
Components of Private
and Public Health

The health spectrum
includes both prevention
and cure, and stretches
from individual care to a
data bank providing
instantaneous information
to medical personnel
anywhere. The physical
health components can be
made most accessible
through location in
exchanges of movement
systems. At certain
magnitudes health and
other public facilities can
become nuclei of places of
concourse.

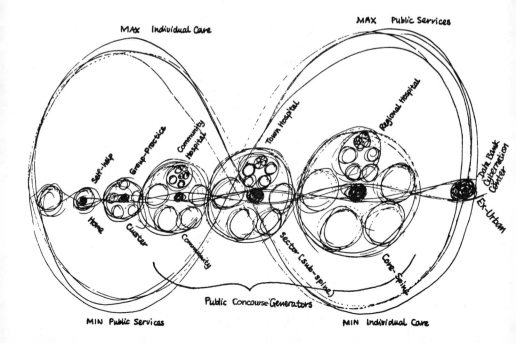

MAX Individual Care

MAX Public Services

Self-Help

Group-Practice

Community Hospital

Town Hospital

Regional Hospital

Data Bank Cybernation Center

Ex-Urban

Core-Spine

Home

Cluster

Community

Sector (sub-spine)

Public Concourse Generators

MIN Public Services

MIN Individual Care

The flow and container hierarchies together suggest a mixed use of public services and urban private enterprises in a hierarchy of meeting places at exchanges of certain magnitudes big enough to generate civic concourse.

Nature of Space

We agree with the ecologist Edward Deevey that: 'It would be a very salutary discipline for designers if the system constructed, first has no physical dimensions, second describes certain urban purposes, and third suggests enjoyment of certain relations between people and function.'[41] He goes on to recommend an assumption of two widely differing availabilities of such factors as space, technologies, etc., in order to see whether two different physical designs with widely different physical characteristics could be produced, which in fact satisfied some of the same performance standards. Deevey points to an analogy between the usefulness of abstraction in the analysis of urban environmental design and its use in his own field: 'It's the abstract language of niche theory in ecology.'[42] The relationship of many different animals and plants with their physical environments and each other – an extremely complex interaction of many dimensions which are infinitely varied in space and time – cannot be easily translated into graphic abstractions. Deevey goes on to say: 'What gets people confused is the dimensionality and the particularity of the way in which you have to draw graphs on paper.'[43] The authors' lattice-grid permits the inclusion of the most generalized parameters as well as the most particular.

A different image was offered by Professor Jerzy Soltan, who saw the grid as the expression of a system, a device to help an urban designer before he became involved in the design process and during the process itself: '. . . a slot machine in which by the method proposed, data will be prepared, put in and processed . . . a method for the good and growth of urban designers . . .'[44]

The grid is precisely as described by Deevey, Soltan, John McHale and others: a 'device' for revealing and organizing dynamic order. McHale contrasts the principle of 'pull' (which, he felt, applied to our model) in opposite directions to the concept of 'fit' in which relationship is relatively passive:

41. Edward Deevey, Yale Seminars, 1966

42. ibid.

43. ibid.

44. Jerzy Soltan, Yale Seminars, 1966

45. John McHale, Yale Seminars, 1966

46. ibid.

. . . a notion tnat something matches and stays tha' way. . . .'[45] To paraphrase McHale: There is no attempt here to produce any kind of ideal urban plan but rather an idealized urban design system at the core of which 'non-ideal structure' there is the principle of maximization of opposites in complementarity. There are certain characteristics of a component, whether it be health, transportation or pedestrian primacy, which the component will demand naturally. All that is done here is to create a system which shows a hierarchy of characteristic kinds of places in which these requirements will seek out their natural place. 'Any space whatever,' in the words of John McHale, 'whether this is a single building or vast territory, is governed and characterized by the flows through it, whether the experience is visual projection, actual walking exploration or acoustic impact.'[46] It is precisely for this reason that the commitment to maximize human concourse repeatedly brings out the importance of certain operational tools which are capable of inducing interaction between hierarchies of maximized opposites in complementarity. All the grid-lattice components in interaction together build up the proposed urban model which is a complex system of unrestricted dimensions, interwoven by overlapping hierarchies of sociotechnical processes in definable specific territories.

A model X was developed by the authors. First it was constructed largely on the basis of experience, intuition, and a commitment. (See Appendix 2.) In the later stages, although the commitment remains partly intuitive, the commitment's priorities were checked through the grid, and plotted in the grid in accordance with the urban measures developed in the interim: density/intensity/frequency of use, community mix, 24 hour occupancy/accessibility, privacy/tranquility/leisure, time/distance/territoriality and so on as discussed earlier. The grid, when employed as a dynamic tool for sorting complexity, continued to 'improve the model' and 'pull out priorities'.

Urban and Ex-Urban

The operational components specified from experience, knowledge and intuition, with the help of the grid, include 'ex-urban' (outer city) and inner city 'urban' components. This pairing, as well as that of flows and containers, is obviously complementary in function.

A curve can be drawn to represent a hierarchy of places between opposite 'urban' characteristics which are in fact complementary. (Described in figures 5 and 6 in chapter 6 above.) One can then plot many intermediate points between these to represent places possessing similar characteristics between the two urban poles. Then each of these hierarchical places can be judged for its appropriateness through the grid in relation to the commitment.

The point of intersection between loops is, of course, an abstraction representing no more than the will of an urban dweller who desires and is able to make choices. The curve can also represent a hierarchy of components which possess physical properties and characteristics; in other words, it consists of many intermediary points varying quantitatively and qualitatively, plotted between maximized opposites. Any one of these points, therefore, may represent a physical urban reality which requires accommodation in space/time. Typical hierarchies of such characteristics are of mobility–tranquility, specialties and staples, public and private realms, community and privacy – properties for use according to declared choice.

Loops of Interaction

Having sketched in our commitment, based on the principles of interaction, complementarity, maximization of choice and urban concourse, we can proceed to the next stage employing the same graphic means to represent the complementarity of physical realities. The same symbol of interaction and complementarity of properties (organizing principles) can be applied to the interaction and complementarity of physical components of infinite variety. Actual places in any physical area of concern – a region, territory, sector, neighborhood, etc. – at any scale may be substituted as components in an urban system, and then the model can become less abstract. Thus a theoretical point of intersection between two places linked by dependence or movements becomes potentially itself a physical reality, an exchange, a place of arrival and departure and thus again potentially a place for other activities: in short, a nucleus of urban growth.

Interaction, being continuous in time, is accurately expressed in a continuous line, which describes loops of two-way motion between existing 'magnets', whatever their nature or purpose in the metro-system. For example, historic cities are established socio-physical magnets. It is not too difficult to project this interaction/growth pattern in any direction and dimension. It becomes a hierarchy of extensions at different scales and media in time-space in an open-ended system.

The time/distance travel measure can be diagrammed in this manner: in loops between points of arrival and departure, the point representing the intersection of movement between two existing points can generate other points, both exchanges and targets, in the urban system. The effectiveness of access to various choices in destination would depend on the relative constancy of time/distance, say a five-minute journey without specifying any particular means of travel. It seems obvious that to obtain parity in time for both inter-urban long-hauls and urban short-hauls different means will have to be used. The former tends to appear in the form of sporadic, infrequent transportation; the latter tends toward more constant (more frequent) movements of people and goods.

Open System

What is sketched verbally here is a composite of overlays of many models which become progressively more complex. These are layers of strategies and principles. The first is theoretical, composed of generalized ends, the second a theoretical programmatic structure, the third a selection of priorities, and so on. Later tactical layers, both organizational and operational, all of which are 'given by the system', are superimposed. Finally layers of functional and technical means take their place. The Model X final version can only be reached if the functional organization insures that continuity and growth, also 'given by the system', is open. In sum this overlay becomes multidimensional, a model of an open-ended system of urban growth capable of infinite extension: a system which can accommodate existing and unimagined contingencies. This is a shift from traditional practice which has accepted the types of closed systems of concentric growth that characterized expanding historic cities. 'Master Plans' which are all too complete, or systems, such as Victor Gruen's in *The Heart of Our Cities*,[47] which are totally closed, leave little room for the insertion of unimagined components. Historic cities

47. Victor Gruen, *The Heart of Our Cities*, New York, 1964

Fig. 11
Urban Growth and Change
A Continuous Process

Movement between existing
places of all magnitudes
can establish a new
exchange and generate new
sub-systems of movement
between new urban and
ex-urban components.

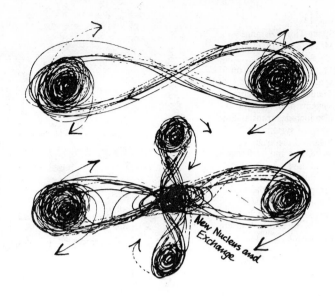

New Nucleus and
Exchange

Fig. 12
**Urban Exchanges in
Movement Systems**

Urban exchanges in move-
ment systems in hierarchies
can be provided with as
many levels as the density,
intensity and frequency
of use dictates. This
optimum utilization of
space can support costly
technology of movement
in three dimensions.

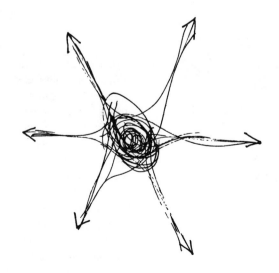

Fig. 13
Space-Time-Distance
Measure of Travel Time

Travel time depends on
space-, time-distance, speed-
frequency of mechanized
systems of movement. It
also includes transfer-time
between systems. A
balanced hierarchy of
movement and exchange
could have a uniform
five-minute time-distance
irrespective of space-
distance and transfer-
time and could include
all waiting and pedestrian
movement.

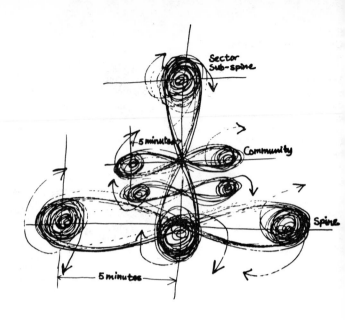

may be conserved, their expansion may be limited or
their breakdown be accepted, but none of these
solutions can work any longer in the majority of urban
situations. Interaction between events has become as
important as any event in itself.

The model's components can be described in
general terms in a dual physical growth pattern: first,
urban supporting and servicing functions which require
space availability and accessibility on few levels and
mobility of a simple flexible kind, and secondly the
urban function creating concourse and providing
'specialties' in goods and activities which need place
proximity, variety, mix and a wide spectrum of mobility
for access. These latter activities are required to
provide community advantage of a social and economic
nature which employs costly technology, such as public
transit and mechanization of travel between many levels
in complex structures. The 'pumping' interaction travel
systems in this model become in the greatest dimensions
intricate omni-ducts on a giant scale through which
urban sectors, zones, nodes and clusters are joined and
126   sustained. The super omni-duct of the urban, metro-

politan inner spine of high intensity/density/frequency of use is complementary to the outer spines of high speed. Residential sectors are advantageously located between the two to create a calibration between a high density of occupancy in the inner spine and relatively low densities toward the outer, with the counterpoint of concentrations based upon points of exchange running throughout the model as various needs arise. The conclusion of this approach is that a complementarity is generated between two incompatible ends which, if physically separated, avoid conflict. But if they are kept in interaction they support each other through the catalytic effect of the residential components which use both sets of facilities.

A thoughtful and comprehensive study reflecting similar considerations was prepared for the Bucks County Commission in Pennsylvania in connexion with a proposed new inter-urban corridor highway, which is to run parallel to the metro-spine that extends from Connecticut to Maryland. In this study particular and conscious emphasis was placed on factors of incompatibility, which hitherto have produced contradictions detrimental to all regional and metropolitan resources and activities. The design decision in this case study was based on '. . . nine design factors: places, roads, urbanization, historic sites, woodlands, stream valleys, soils, physiographic features and slopes', criteria which could be plotted in terms of compatibility. In the words of the report: 'The expressway corridor desire line would be derived from each set of conditions . . . each of the nine sets of conditions was weighed equally. Based on this decision the composite design corridor was formed by simple photographic superimposition of all the nine desire lines.'[48] Contradiction between urban and exurban components was thus resolved.

The measure of incompatibility and complementarity may be applied with equal force and greater complexity on a micro-scale in sectors and sub-sectors of an urban region. The exchanges in our model become at different scales an equivalence of a metro-spine, places of high turnover of intense mobility/activity which find their complement in adjacent places of tranquillity and leisure. Again, these may be described as hierarchies with intermediary characteristics between the two

48. A design decision program for the evaluation of the location of Highway Route 202 in Bucks County, Pennsylvania, 1967. Executive Director: Franklin C. Wood. Assistant Director: James S. Carr. Consultants: Michael Mostoller and Richard Plunz

Models X 1, 2, 3, etc.

extremes, in other words, a variety of places and events which provide a sequence of experiences as one moves through them.

Although all these general specifications were implicit in the search for a system, they were not immediately apparent without the continual, protracted periods of tool sharpening. In the process of this study, several specific urban models developed in broad outline seem to have grown rather like Topsy: each representing a stage in the development of a theory.

In all those attempts spines of high intensity/density/frequency, dependent on mass-transit, were broken down into a hierarchy of exchanges which provided clear-cut sub-systems of flow continuity, such as transit, random vehicles and pedestrians. The exchanges were transformed into bridges each of which not only provided continuity of pedestrian flow but also contained the micro-hierarchies of mobility to tranquility within them: a physical hierarchy of promenade concourse with mix and variety within walking distance of residents in every sector.

The gathering together of lines of flow in our models as they approach the spine demonstrates the 'Venturi principle' of constriction, a law which postulates that this process will act as an accelerator in any flow system. (See chapter 6, figure 8.) We have applied this concept to urban flows in order to increase intensity/density/frequency of use of the facilities at the exchanges close to the metro-spine to augment variety/mix and use in these places. This is a device deliberately aimed at encouraging through plan/design the accretion of facilities and events which naturally try to seek out such a location. In other words, it illustrates that a technological decision may produce the sociological consequences of urban concourse.

Hierarchies and Exchanges

Since the model is conceived as a whole hierarchy of exchanges in an urban system, one can visualize the pattern of interaction, movement and growth at every scale. At the largest macro-scale of a metropolitan super-system, territory or region, the urban component consists of a relatively simple, almost a maplike two-dimensional physical reality. As one gets closer to the macro-scale of physical complexity the levels of occupancy and directions of interaction, movement and growth become a reality which is grasped as being in actuality four-dimensional. The facilities become more numerous, and the technology more complex; the costs become higher, but so do the returns. The resolution of complexity consists of a process of ordering technology and social activity in the same structure.

To summarize this chapter: the search for a system has become the search for a model in which the magnitude, kind, and character of places and circulation are co-ordinated according to a social purpose, an environmental reality and a technological potential. This has been assisted by the lattice-grid described in Appendix 2 which helped a commitment consisting of abstract principles to develop into a physical model. The model discussed here is a product of two complementary processes: an intuitive search, which produced tools and new insights which, in turn, modified the original model while strengthening and clarifying the original commitment.

It must be emphasized that no model is proposed as a 'master-plan' for a new town or model city anywhere. The diagrams include graphically only the parameters which can be expressed in specific principles and organizational and operational criteria. Urban planning and design are part of a continuing process of evolution. All models change and grow. It is evident, however, that some models are less susceptible to this principle – that is, less flexible in their organization – than others.

Ideally the process described in this part of the book, commitment-system-grid to theoretical model, would culminate in comparative tests designed to reveal whatever strength or weakness is present in the tools employed. The theory should be applied to particular, representative problems to see if it works. The model and the measures which make it up have become a yardstick, the value of which must now be put to a test.

There are several approaches for achieving this end through the general method of comparative studies of existing urban phenomena selected from many places in the world. Such studies would fall into four types. The first would concentrate on existing historic urban models if data of change and growth are available. The second would deal with existing urban models, whose data

129

would be produced by field studies, and laboratory simulation techniques, including tools like the lattice-grid. Methods and techniques leading to reasonable forecasts of the consequences of their design could be obtained. The third is a comparative study of existing typical urban components, historic and modern, of sufficient complexity and particularity to demonstrate bio-social and technological forces in interactions of urban scales. This study would focus on, for example, complexes serving government, health, education, transportation, business and so on. The fourth would examine existing special-purpose individual buildings, old and new, in respect to their functional and symbolic purpose.

Any one set of such comparative studies could yield information, which is at present non-existent or uncorrelated, about the nature of each building type or urban complex in relation to its larger urban environment within the third ecology of the man-made. Many examples of critical contemporary issues which should be so studied immediately spring to mind: hidden costs of public health and education in proportion to scattering or clustering; real cost of mass-transit in relation to density, intensity and frequency of use and the numbers needed to support hierarchies of public transportation sub-systems; this could then be compared to the real cost of private automobiles, in public values of all scales, in relation to direct and indirect overheads and hidden effects produced on the total economy and human well-being.

From the point of view directly derived from the authors' commitment, a study to determine minimal numbers needed to sustain public facilities in relation to density, intensity, frequency and mix of use in any place would be invaluable and would supplement the plethora of data already available on numbers of consumers needed by private enterprise. Last but not least, we propose inquiry into the real cost of qualitative environmental standards, social issues of community and individual general well-being which would require new yardsticks. This study would have to be more specific than the usual philosophic and aesthetic generalizations and less biased than speculations about convenience and comfort. In short these studies would

be on aspects of the environmental impact on man,

correlated in an order of their ecological interaction through the methodology of cybernetics. This methodology will be applied to problems of public well-being as a whole, instead of dealing with separate pieces susceptible only to dissection after death by specialist morticians.

Appendix 3, 'Critique Through Commitment', presents some typical urban models from all over the world which were discussed in the Yale Seminars and were criticized in the light of the authors' commitment. 'Critique Through Commitment' is a comparative study which provides addenda to the discussion as a measure of usefulness of a systematic approach to environmental design. We believe that as one approaches the model-building stage in the plan-design process, Model X, irrespective of the authors' particular commitment, would have two complementary advantages over many others. First, that the end product of the model is not limited or static, and second, that systematic analysis as a tool is equally useful for the purposes of both an intuitive and an inventive approach to model building. In the next chapter we will comment critically on the disparity between the theory implicit in our commitment and our proposed model and the present urban practice as exemplified by New York City, 'The World Capital'. Perhaps this is a useful prelude to a model-building process based on a commitment to public meeting places.

8. Theory and Practice

Who lives where, why and how they move toward what. Systematic segregation or natural mix. A description of typical urban failures and of some excellent exceptions.

The future of the city will not be served if the housing projects and the slums become stockades of the kind of narrow separation that permeates the stockades in the minimeadows.

Max Ways, 'Cities to Live In', *Fortune*, January 1968, quoted in *Current*, April 1968

The solution, then, is not to repeal urban renewal, but to transform it from a program of slum clearance and rehabilitation into a program of urban rehousing. . . . This approach is commonplace in many European countries, which have long since realized that private enterprise can no more house the population and eliminate slums than it can run the post office.

H. J. Gans, 'Overview: Success or Failure', *Urban Renewal, People, Politics and Planning*, New York, 1967

. . . we understand our milieu only through the veil of . . . stereotypes. Any political action must therefore be conceived with the distorting glasses always worn by public opinion in mind. One must know a group's stereotypes to know how the group will interpret some action . . .

Jacques Ellul, *The Political Illusion*, New York, 1967

A centipede was happy quite
Until a toad in fun
Asked it which leg came after which?
This wrought it up to such a pitch
It fell exhausted in a ditch
Not knowing how to run.

Taoist verse

Cars passing a single spot in a single lane can carry 1,600 people per hour but a train can carry 40,000 to 60,000 per hour.

Editorial in the *Cambridge Chronicle*

49. Vance Packard, *The Pyramid Climbers*, New York, 1962

London with its vast area of nearly 1,000 square miles has an average daily journey to work by road of under 3 miles, with the maximum average speed falling as low as 10 m.p.h. Contrast this with Stevenage, a new town in Hertfordshire, which has an area of only 10 square miles. There the average journey to work by road is a little over 2 miles and the average speed during the rush hour is over 20 m.p.h.

E. C. Claxton, 'The Future of the Bicycle in a Modern Society', *Journal of the Royal Society of Arts*, January 1968

The mechanisms of mobility are costly, especially those which serve larger territories of urban deployment. The convenience of an automobile operating as a private bus proves illusory in most metropolitan centers and will become more so as the number of urban dwellers increases. The real cost of private advantage includes a gigantic indirect public overhead beyond the direct cost met by the private bus driver carrying no passenger other than himself. In recent years we have developed some direct methods of assessing the economics of this transportation technology. However, the measurement of the indirect social overheads on loss of life, loss of time and loss of peace of mind still wait for an adequate methodology.

In the meantime contradictions between a superficial and costly illusion of choice and a limited reality continue to mount. The median-income middle class can afford to pursue the amorphous advantages of surburbia in their essential cars. But they settle in homogeneous communities with people of similar income, age, and cultural background. Their desires and tastes are assiduously cultivated for them by the hucksters. Vacancies left by the 'pyramid climbers', as Vance Packard dubbed them,[49] are quickly filled by the same kind of people. Private cars, private houses and private clubs are the status symbols at each level, and consequently a suburban subdivision has become an assemblage of private places and comforts. There are few public places in suburbia, if we except the stereotyped school, and in the end these dormitories assume the mediocrity that characterizes shopping centers in all particulars.

The metro-cores are left to three polarized groups. The first and largest are the very poor. They are either born and bred in the metro-core or come there in growing numbers, because they cannot afford to buy the new houses or recent cars essential to suburban life, and perhaps because they cannot afford the commuting time which has to be added to the standard working day. Above all, the poor live in cities because these densely used places hold the greatest promise for economic opportunity in a great variety of service trades. The second group is a small minority of the middle class: the intellectuals, the professionals or officials who either have to be or want to be in the city. Many of these people are cosmopolitans by experience or choice with a taste for variety. Last but not least, in spite of their tiny number, are the really rich, who are, as described by one of them: 'Not people who have a million but who can spend a million.'

The globe trotters, modern cosmopolitans, are exploiting the cities in a very expedient way. They are themselves undergoing a transformation through their very ability to exploit mobility to its fullest by descending on many cities in turn in the proper season. But the majority of consumers cannot afford such mobility and therefore are forced to act as mere bystanders. The new peripatetic cosmopolitans of our time, the jet set, all too often expect in all the metro-cores they visit the stereotyped attributes of luxury facilities; identical comforts, food and drink, climate and companions. Above all, they must avoid direct, to say nothing of deep, involvement in different cultures. The American chain hotels are as homogeneous as the suburbs. They suggest a mad global repertory theater presenting a series of first nights in different theaters with the same actors playing the same parts against different sets to the same audience.

With all these pressures the metro-core becomes subdivided in a contradictory manner to accommodate those who can travel expensively all the time, the tourist who can afford an occasional visit, the commuting suburbanites who must travel daily (thereby producing the greatest pressures) and the resident poor who can only afford the cheapest mass-transit within the metro-core. The intellectuals, the middle-class mavericks and the poor alike occupy housing of varied quality, abandoned in the wake of the suburban exodus.

In truth it is all private consumption: the choice is between a second car and clear air, between a new television set and a park for one's children.

Richard Goodwin, 'The Shape of American Politics', Commentary, June 1967

... more than 800,000 middle class left Manhattan since 1950 ....

New York Herald Tribune, 26 January 1966

The choice between lower taxes and a vast program for the cities is ordinarily posed in terms of the vague and ideologically potent stereotypes of government spending and bureaucracy as against private consumption and initiative. It is natural for citizens, confronted by such choice, to prefer immediate tangible reward to remote and largely abstract benefit.

The National Safety Council provided the following dismal data for the National Center Health Statistics in 1965: Total deaths due to automobile accidents 49,163. The five major national 3 day holidays show a steady increase from Memorial Day 555, 4th of July 740, Labor Day 765, to Christmas 960 dropping off again for the New Year 750. Month by month statistics follow an almost uniform curve from January 3,478 to December 5,022.

Los Angeles is a warning of what happens when the city's obsolescence takes the form not of overloading but of doing away with the centre ... not one of unimpeded movement between a variety of reasonable choices but rather one of immobility for the poor, escape for the rich and a mixture of commuting and marooning for the people in the middle.
Barbara Ward, 'Cities for 3,000 Million People'. The Economist, 8 July 1967

At the moment the New York city's office space is 97·5 per cent occupied, the highest rate in its history. In 1967 an additional 7·5 million square feet of office space will be available. ... During 1966, the city gained 41,500 new white-collar positions. In contrast, it lost 600 blue-collar jobs to the suburbs.
New York Times, 17 February 1967

Segregation as System

The poorer urban dwellers group in communities which are even more homogeneous than the suburban cliques, because their places of residence are longer lasting. Suburbia and expensive highrise apartments in an urban area have a brisk turnover in occupancy, with virtual segregation between the cultural, economic, occupational, ethnic and racial groups, which each occupy their separate residential territories. This practice is likely to continue for a long time. Homogenizing rather than mixing, segregation rather than integration, seem to be the mark of sub-communities within the urban metro-matrix irrespective of income or location. This pattern is the greatest contradiction of them all: while urbanization suggests variety and mix, the reality is actually ghettoization. Perhaps this contradiction, the growing segregation instead of an increase in integration which urbanization implies, can be attributed in large measure to the absence of community places. A new urbanity might be born and flourish in urban places designed for mix with democratic meeting places for concourse: environments in which contact between different kinds or classes of people is invited in an atmosphere of tranquility and mutual confidence.

Democracy and Urbanity

Evidently urbanism of the future will have a multitude of aspects. We may recognize some present types as being likely to linger, others we may predict, but many more we cannot imagine. At the center of our concern is the present lack of public places of concourse where chance encounters of variety, surprises and civic

138

participation in spontaneous activity, antibodies to the prevailing process of ghettoization, are bred. Such exchange events are directly antithetical to special-purpose targets. We cannot tell whether concourse activity will take the form of conversation, dating, debate or discotheque. The design of such places demands a certain relaxed randomness in organization without implying visual chaos (physical contradiction). The character of its architecture must correspond to the character of events which might occur there, a complementary function. Contrived effects, arty garnishing of single-purpose targets, result only in pseudo-places and peak traffic pressure. The concourse here envisaged is the product of natural mix and easy accessibility, the spice of urbanism for men in an unhurried pedestrian state.

Pseudo-Places

The third ecology — urban eco-system, and particularly the problems of its sociological symbiosis — is in a critical condition. On a more specific level the immediately visible components of urbanization, found in places simultaneously occupied by people and traffic in unprecedented quantities, produce 'place-pathology'; pseudo-places have become stock items in democratic America. Symptoms of the same tendency may be observed in most urban situations everywhere. They differ perhaps from country to country in proportion to the degree in which cultural mores may still prevail. But the risk of infection in proportion to technological invasion appears to be the immediately visible human lot. Only uninhabited ruins are real.

In the same measure that places fall victim to the failure of traffic randomness, so apparently people fall victim to the absence of real places for leisurely concourse. The denizens of downtown are always in a hurry. Whether moving in vehicles or on their own feet, they proceed grimly. Distrustful faces distinguish the anxious pedestrian, milling around in a plush world where vehicles and other people alike are enemies. No greetings are exchanged; no quarter given or looked for in the different layers of the urban jungle. Sidewalks are crowded because people have no other public place to go. They have become in downtown New York no more than human traffic arteries which converge together with vehicular streets at the crossroads, a ring in which people and vehicles fight without resolution for supremacy. Occasionally a subway exit (a hole in the ground) contributes its share to the chaos. The non-people have become as antisocial as the non-places which they temporarily fill, as they gravitate with perpetual motion toward private, invisible targets. Because of such circumstances those who live in large towns are alienated from most of the other kinds of people there and are even becoming alienated from their own kind.

In the United States today, and for that matter in many other technologically advanced societies, public places are vanishing, if at different rates. The small open spaces, particularly those now in fashion, are too overtly decorative, too 'stagey' in character or private in location. A growing contempt for public property makes such public places a garbage repository. 'Hygienic' advanced technological societies begin to match their 'dreck',[50] as David Reisman puts it, with the orts and left-overs of 'backward, dirty' savages. The new public places we envisage will be as different from the semi-public emptiness and artificiality of street edges as the latter will be from the semi-private bits and pieces of real activity behind the impersonal façades of commerce.

It has become almost mandatory, it seems, for investors in downtown real estate and their architects to provide scenic effects that masquerade as open civic places. These are shop-window places, uninhabited, unengaged and apparently deliberately so. For no life ever spills into them. They may be superficially pretty sometimes, but they are always dead and unconnected with the activities which go on inside the buildings; life is always somewhere else – wherever some facility or other has been provided either by whimsy or by private purpose. This order of idiosyncrasy, whether through good will or for profit, apparently cannot or will not provide public places for concourse and intercourse – urban foci, images of a life of community. Community cannot be accommodated, either, in the monumental facilities for culture which have today become most uncivic symbols of civic achievement. For the most part they only serve a select minority and are as remote from the poor, who often live just around the corner, as Caribbean beaches.

50. David Reisman, 'The Suburban Dislocation', Annals of the American Academy of Political and Social Science, Vol. 314, November 1957

Different sorts of non-places exist in the metro-core, but they are all artificially created and as empty of concourse as they are empty of function. They have nothing to do with the context of city life and add nothing positive or significant to the pervading formless motion of crowded sidewalks and traffic-jammed streets seemingly stretching out of sight in an endless grid. Being contrived they end up as negative assets. Where in America can people meet in leisurely concourse for eating, drinking, boy and girl watching and all those human activities that Americans travel thousands of miles to enjoy elswhere? Where is it possible to do so in comfort and without haste, dirt or danger?

New York City produces a formidable catalogue of the pseudo, the not so pseudo and some honorable exceptions to the indictment. Rockefeller Center is a giant shop window with symbols on display; super-colossal Christmas trees, gorgeous flowers and pretty, privileged skaters down below, beneath a very golden, very large and very irrelevant sculpture. The whole scene is awe-inspiring and may be enjoyed by hardy visitors who, however, have nowhere to sit and have nothing to do but to take an occasional look at a super-metro phenomenon of affluence. Rockefeller Center is a 'rubber-necking' concourse, where people look on but do not participate themselves. In other words it is an expensive version of the more sordid attractions devised for passers-by on Broadway and Forty-Second Street. In almost all the other places, the moment anyone wants to talk or rest or eat or drink, he must leave the pseudo-place with its aimless milling and vanish into some facility which is, of course, always on private property and has a price tag attached.

Lincoln Center, a later metro-colossus, is inhabited by another breed of sight-seers, who have pretensions to being art-seers, and are here perhaps appropriately introduced to the cultural wonders of New York. The cluster of auditoria for the performing arts, suitably garnished with expensive fine arts, is in itself an over-blown stage set entirely surrounded by outsized back-stage spaces which have to be negotiated by visitors irrespective of their means of arrival – Cadillac, taxi or subway. In the cold light of day, as many excellent photographs testify, this stage is as vast and as empty as any other.

The growing separateness of culture in our cities, with the honorable exception of the Metropolitan, Modern and other museums at weekends, is as debilitating in its context as poverty, poor education and racial segregation are in theirs. An expression of urban mix is almost nowhere visible during the week except in the passage from target to target. In streets and alleys and on escalators all men are strangers.

Vehicles Versus People

We have described the dominant feature of urban organization that we seek as special-purpose pedestrian places linked by transportation systems, places of quick access and short occupancy. Since modern vehicles enjoy priority in streets, there are few public places for leisurely passage or promenade. Pedestrians in today's streets are often fierce and frenetic, hurrying on their way without relaxing even while visiting. Public places are mostly travel places in which people on their feet begin to behave like drivers behind wheels.

As we focus on smaller, more special places, the failure to offer community concourse in a tranquil environment becomes more conspicuous. The formal garden behind the New York Public Library is crowded in fine weather. It is an island of relative tranquility surrounded by a moat of noisy monoxide-spewing traffic. Better than nothing, maybe, but how much better would it be if it were part of the pedestrian realm that offered refreshments more appropriate to concourse than a sandwich and was insulated from vehicular traffic, noise and pollution. Nevertheless, this garden, like a London square, provides an illusion of tranquility which over the years has become a local legend, an image of peace in the middle of chaos and movement. The pleasures such gardens provide, however curtailed, are real. The contact with flowers and shrubs has a seasonal meaning and delight. A similar feeling is provided wherever, as on the lower East Side, one finds segments of carriage avenues left over from an earlier era of slow traffic malls. These areas also give an equally illusory sense of escape in the midst of the different, denser traffic of today. In any case, the benches at least provide rest for the weary.

In this context it is somewhat disturbing to read some suggestions by Jane Jacobs,[51] who has had such excellent insights into the nature of concourse. She

51. Jane Jacobs, *The Death and Life of Great American Cities*, New York, 1961

does not want to separate pedestrians and vehicles. Where would Mrs Jacobs draw the line? The right mix and adequate controls are hard to establish and maintain. It is only in relatively leisurely conditions that man may focus purposefully or respond to various stimuli. Not too many impressions may be absorbed even under the best circumstances; fewer may be taken in on the run. With a somewhat nerve-racking journey just completed and another imminent, the mind remains subconsciously involved with machinery. The mind's eye is continuously half-cocked, so to speak, to deal with the problems of parking, the dangers of crossing traffic, or whatever might occur in arrivals and departures. The pleasurable anticipation and the lingering impact of a great event may only be half felt if the next 'target' to be attacked involves troublesome travel.

What Does Johnny See?

The visual stimuli now being sedulously cultivated through 'beautification' programs, which are not inexpensive, are perfect examples of obsolete thinking about new realities; the separation of theory (social goals), programs (politically controlled means) and end products (physical reality). As a result these stimuli are usually inadequate, redundant, or merely absurd. While admitting that visually agreeable surroundings contribute to the enjoyment of any place, 'beautification' alone cannot generate what we consider a viable public place. The present proportion of the already inadequate governmental effort and spending on slum clearance for such a modish priority as 'beauty', a trivial category, does not bring us closer to resolving the major urban problems. The obfuscated, the trivial and even the dangerous are not necessarily visually disturbing or shocking. Some of the worst objects and environments, in broader terms of human goals, are at first glance deceptively attractive aesthetically.

A few more New York examples will suffice to round out a picture of expensive error. Between Park Avenue and the Avenues of the Americas in mid-town, lesser pseudo-places have been provided in the most affluent area of the most affluent city in the world. Lever House was the first major corporation to allow a skyscraper to include a planned public open space as an extension of Park Avenue, but this has been done so ineptly that the good intention has produced a dead mouse of a place complete with flower wreaths at the foot of a busy mountain. The only signs of life to be seen here are a few hurrying executives cutting the corner. The formal axial arrangement of the Seagram Building on the other side of Park Avenue, with its two pools and fountains, offers a retreat from the traffic in a most perverse way. The only seats provided are the cold granite edging around the pools on which you may squat on a fine day if the wind doesn't give you an unexpected shower from the fountains. These apparently public places were not provided for public purpose. Although they are accessible to the passer-by, they are really only ornamental private spaces through which the tenants pass. In other words these are spaces to look at or to look out from at the panorama of the man-made cliffs, not areas for escape from traffic. It is all too grand to violate with your coffee-break paraphernalia in a brown-paper bag or with a gentle snore.

In recent years there have been few signs that the lesson has been learned. A block away a little canyon, left by the debris of the defunct Stork Club, has been transformed into a decorative public outdoor room for the most privileged denizens of mid-town, through the generosity of W. Paley of CBS, complete with the cliché fountain and some vigilantes to see that nothing untoward occurs. Further west the forbidding elegance of the CBS headquarters towers above another Paley Platz, a narrow, shallow and dry moat seasonally decorated with expensive potted plants.

It appears to the authors that in the context of urbanism, priority must be given to meaningful human purpose in public places of all sorts. Public places, whether they be art or architecture, object or background, must be components of a larger community order and activity. Furthermore, their full impact must be allowed to reveal itself slowly in a climate of leisurely contemplation in a framework of human activity free of interference from traffic, noise and dirt. The latter is a nuisance while the irrelevancies described earlier in no way assist escape from the cacophony which finally hits the urban environment in the form of acoustic pollution. So far the citizens of a technological society have been subtly taught how to ignore and tolerate all

competing detergents made by the same firm, purchase planned obsolescence in automobiles and household appliances, and pay interest rates which are carefully designed for maximum deception. The private sector advertises; the public sector, by and large, does not.

Michael Harrington, *The Accidental Century*, New York, 1965

The public sector of American life, health, governmentally financed housing, education, transportation, and the like, is considered a great burden by most Americans. Yet, this sector contains some of the most important necessities of modern life and is a fundamental constituent of a standard of living. The private sector, on the other hand, is thought of as an area of freedom. Here one may bid for

forms of pollution. But perhaps the time has now come to provide opportunities to comprehend, to criticize and finally to relish the richness of an environment which accommodates leisure, pleasure, human activity or rest in the midst of urban bustle.

Preludes and Epilogues

The suggestions made toward this end in this essay describe the provision (throughout the metro-matrix of a hierarchy) of places of concourse with one essential attribute: a diversity of uses within a pedestrain precinct devoted to places of leisurely movement in which may be accommodated 'crevice-filler' meeting centers – either activities of short duration, or great urban facilities which induce long-term occupancy. These are the kinds of civic places – complementary options to an individual's withdrawal to a private realm – man enjoys everywhere.

Homogenized communities, while perhaps enjoying convenient access for their private transportation to their chosen targets scattered randomly in the metro-area, may soon prove to be something less than socially beneficial unless complemented by a more comfortable, cheaper, more logically organized, democratic order of movement in transit systems linking an extensive hierarchy of places of concourse accessible to the poor and rich alike. Only extensive 'mix' can naturally generate the densities, intensities and frequencies of use in exchanges and create meaningful, controllable compactness.

The suburban scatter may prove, security apart, too uneventful, if not downright monotonous, for the changing appetites of new generations. The symptoms of dislike for stereo-environments among the young may be seen in their drive for independence and adventures with special companions of their own choice. MacDougal Street is more alive, at the time of writing, than Lincoln Center Plaza. The former may well leave a more lasting cultural imprint on urban life in the United States than pretentious stereotypes like the latter.

Complementary Contrasts

The discontent of younger generations echoes the contention of this essay that urbanizing, technological society requires safety valves of various scales for spontaneous mingling for unspecified events, in addition to the nineteenth-century-type 'Central' parks (con-

The reason we didn't move to the suburbs is that I would have become a bitch waiting for Roger to come home every night.

Betty Friedman, 'Beyond the Feminine Mystique', *New York Herald Tribune*, 20 February 1965

ceived as 'cities' lungs', breathing spaces) which have become for most 'city' residents only yet another special target to travel to occasionally.

The compulsive technological tightening and centralization of technical facilities and their control requires the complementary loosening of institutional constraints. This process can lead to new opportunities for maximization of 'real' options instead of the mythical extension of choice, the manufactured mass-produced stereotypes. Every event in such places may be accompanied by a prelude or epilogue event within walking distance without the intervention either of anxiety, generated by problems of arrival and departure when crowded, or of security when empty. How delightful it is to stroll slowly in a leisurely crowd, to sit and drink in an urban vestibule, without interference from the noise and fumes of traffic, but against a backdrop of urban scale and the obbligato hum of human activity. There are many places which leave long, lingering pleasure of this kind: for instance, the small Piazza of Santa Maria di Trastevere in Rome, where the sound of the celebration of the Mass mingles with the laughter of another sort of celebration in the café opposite, or the large Piazza of San Marco in Venice where everything happens. How dismal and dangerous are the deserted monumental single-purpose structures which technological society is building in the wrong places and at the wrong scale in the metro-areas, such as the St Louis stadium and surrounding garages in the precious historic downtown area which all too often goes dead and becomes useless.

Dangerous Diffusion

Diffusion *ad infinitum* achieves the same asocial results through different means in the dormitories of suburbia. Long periods of relative emptiness of endless crooked streets only containing houses provide opportunity for the disturbed, the delinquent and the criminal. This perhaps explains why the well-to-do in their low-density dormitories have a steadily rising crime rate that is now catching up with that of the slums. The separated homogeneous environment anywhere, however spacious and plush, is as destructive as the segregation of the packed slum.

Scattering may bring some benefits, but we believe
146 them to be completely outweighed by the concomitant

Across the continent the sharpest increase in crime in 1965 was in suburban areas where the F.B.I.'s uniform crime reports showed an 8 per cent rise within cities between 10,000 and 50,000, while cities with populations of 1 million and up showed an average jump of only 2 per cent.

New York Herald Tribune, 1 December 1965

serious problems at each end of the technologically controlled urban spectrum, in the metro-core and metro-spaces and periphery alike. In these dispersed environments the tremendous problems of servicing and protecting both men and their machines and other possessions become increasingly difficult. The growing scatter of randomly located and frequently empty places can no longer be dealt with adequately by professional policing. The technologically sophisticated equipment at the disposal of the police can hardly keep up with mobile criminals, equally well provided with the lethal tools of the trade. As a result police energies cannot be concentrated on the most serious duties. In any case the time-energy waste of controlling traffic shuttling between downtown and distant targets of suburbia is as great as that spent pursuing guerrilla tactics in dark jungles or on inaccessible roofs.

The wringing of hands, the voices of doom, the pious abstractions of public officials only produce unfulfilled promises or pseudo-events, such as the contrived farce of 'happenings', in public parks, a frivolous prescription for the relief of grim and tired millions. Even traditional annual parades appear to be losing their significance. It is true that the temporary dislodgement of traffic from its dominance does transform whole avenues into civic places for a fleeting moment. When decorated, as in a New York Fifth Avenue parade for a national hero, by a man-made snowstorm, the rare spontaneous event assumes symbolic stature. For a growing majority, however, it seems that traditional seasonal marches through the streets have less and less significance. Their original purpose and symbolism are becoming too remote, incomprehensible and irrelevant. The pseudo joins the obsolete and the forgotten.

Where Can Johnny Be?

The accidentally arrived-at urban mixtures of public and private enterprise make Coney Island and similar New York public beaches very real during their short season, as urban, democratic places. Like the City's parks, these are a counterpoint in their idle leisurely enjoyment of beach and honky-tonk to the emotionally charged experiences of spectator sports for millions.

A hierarchy of urban places of comparable quality for smaller numbers is perhaps within the means of the most affluent society. The TV camera's viewing advantage is a consumer-citizen's equivalent of the 'Royal Box'. Both are privileged positions, but we also require an extended social urban spectrum to serve the underprivileged. Still missing are opportunites for a maximized variety of less dramatic encounters; these can no longer be left to chance.

Breathing Spaces

There are of course honorable exceptions to the failures which have been described earlier: the public parks and beaches which are within the hierarchy of public places in the metro-areas are not pseudo, but genuine places of public recreation. Bird-watching is still practiced by men of all ages, while a good zoo anywhere invariably provides an agreeable show. Whether breathing spaces of great dimensions alone can be made to serve twentieth-century purposes has become a serious question which remains unanswered for the time being. At present, pollution of one kind or another makes 'breathing' anywhere in or near a great city a matter of hazard rather than of therapy; nature itself becomes most unnatural. As we suggested earlier, the pseudo-natural large-scale parks have now become occasional targets and it requires special effort to reach them. Metro-areas are too large for them to be readily accessible to the majority of urban residents. What is required is the provision of a hierarchy of open spaces, of different scale and character, within easy walking distance for everybody, and fit for all sorts of seasons, weathers and purposes.

Cities, whether metro-cores or sub-cores, have never been either comic or tragic. They have until recently contained opportunities for the spontaneous daily expression of community of a diversified citizenry in a single place. An urban public mixing place is a mirror and magnifying glass for culture, and perhaps can also be its crucible.

9. Hierarchy of Community

Territories and fields. Containers for concourse, community, democracy and learning. Pedestrians, passengers and places. A description of some civil places old and new, and some faces of community.

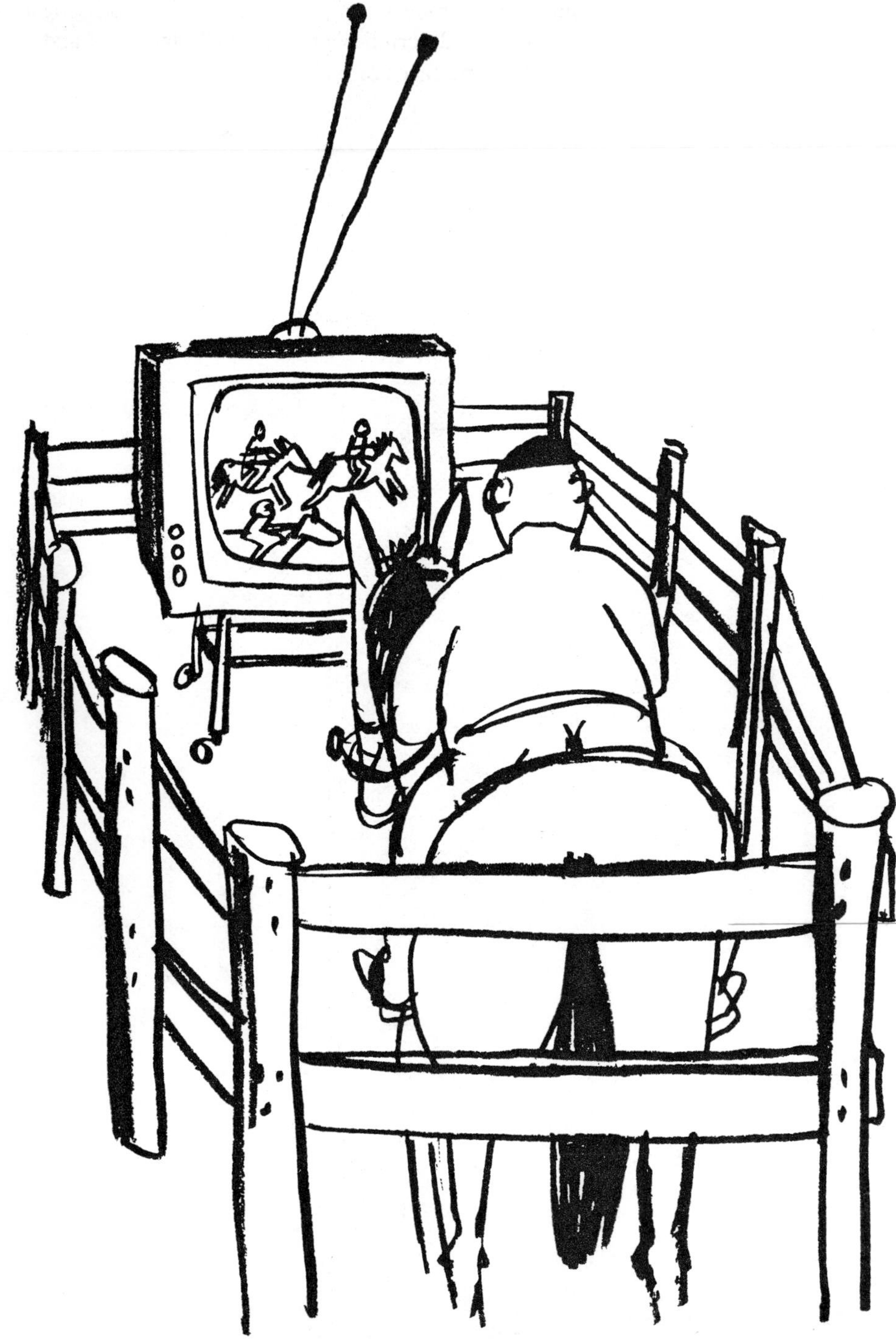

These Cyclopians have no (places) for debates . . . they live on
high mountains in hollow caves; each one lays down the law for
wife and children, and no one cares for his neighbours . . . (they) . .
have no ships . . . and no shipwrights . . . to row in and visit the
cities of the world . . . such craftsmen might have civilized the
island: for it is not a bad island.

Homer, *The Odyssey*, IX, trans. W. H. D. Rouse, New York, 1937

In most animal species . . . each group develops a complex social
organization based on territoriality and on a social hierarchy. . . .
Thus the establishment of an accepted hierarchy in a stable group
of animals almost eliminates the stresses of social tension and results
in a kind of social homeostasis.

René Dubos, *Man Adapting*, New Haven, 1965

. . . Can community and settlement, then, be equivalent? . . .
What is the settlement in sociological terms – an empirical unit
that represents the accumulation of the residues of activities of
people who lived in a culturally meaningful space during a culturally
meaningful time and who left behind a collection of things that
express not necessarily a common culture but one that is exactly
identical with no other in the world, not necessarily a comprehensive
micro-cosmos of the cultural but basically a self-contained system
of complementary parts? . . .

K. C. Chang, *Rethinking Archaeology*, New York, 1967

. . . the possible major change in the future is from the cult of
obsolescence of a scattered field of stereotypes to the 'cultural'
emphasis on caring for things or people.

Karl Deutsch, 'Baselines for the Future', *Daedalus: Journal of the American
Academy of Arts and Sciences*, Summer 1967

In our previous analysis of interaction in the man-made environment, we first discussed the most immediate means of human contact, that which can be achieved through walking. We referred to its spatial limits as territories which can be reached without the employment of any mechanical assistance. We discussed secondly the technological means of transportation which move people, goods and services. The spatial limits of these 'flow systems' we called 'orbits' of interest, involvement and service. A third level of interaction, which is not movement, does not imply direct human contact, and has no spatial configuration, is the communication media. Telephones, radio, television, etc., operate in 'fields' and most of the time have no global limits.

Instantaneous electronic messages have no territorial entity; no matter where they originate, they may now be heard anywhere. Information media have extended intercourse to a global scale, and bouncing messages from satellites have broken the last tie that information technology has with territoriality. Soon direct invoicing for communication services to consumers everywhere may become impractical and both sender and receiver will have to be licensed and taxed. Nevertheless, while messages without limit will be footloose and perhaps free, mobility will continue to involve traffic flow, whether of passengers, goods or utilities. This factor is indissolubly linked with territories or means of access: serving rights of way possessing physical dimensions and directions. Mobility, therefore, despite the extension of communications techniques, still is directly linked to a community structure based on territorial accessibility.

Community as an idea and fact has been extended quite suddenly to an immeasurably greater spectrum of human contacts than ever before in history. Communication systems, global in scale and fast in speed, have provided technological extensions to the traditional entities of family, neighborhood, village, city and country. But the meaning of territory and proximity is as poignant as ever. Because of the many different ways of getting together, the spectrum has acquired overlapping, and apparently contradictory aspects of community. It seems as if the gigantic 'instant togetherness' has produced a reaction of 'separateness' and alienation, to a greater extent than ever before.

Unless people become things, they will always live in the small scale as well as the big scale, and more intensely in the small scale than in the big.

Paul Goodman, 'Two Issues in Planning', *Commentary*, August 1967

The inhabitant of any of the world's large cities – London, Tokyo, Paris, New York – is more likely to find himself 'at home' in any of them, than in any rural parts of his own country; the international cultural milieu which sustains him will be more evident.

John McHale, 'Education for Real', *Ekistics*, Vol. 24, 144, November 1967

The recent acceleration in the growth of urban society has all but destroyed the possibility of man's identification with familiar places. It has also deprived him of encounters with the unfamiliar, which quickens his awareness and can open doors to the excitement of discovery. This has been quickly followed by endemic alienation of large groups from other groups. Everything is simultaneously either quite familiar or quite strange, depending on the observer. The state of equilibrium, the confident and repeated confrontation with the familiar and the strange as complementary opposites, has all but vanished. Man lives in a world in which unpremeditated confrontation is limited to unsophisticated tourists who may be swindled or to innocents abroad in the dark alleys of their own cities who may be robbed or killed.

for functioning in a universe which has temporal, social and spatial dimensions. From this point of view, the loss of an important place represents a change in a potentially significant component of the experience of continuity.

Marc Fried, 'Grieving for a Lost Home', in *The Urban Condition*, ed. Leonard J. Duhl, New York, 1963, ch. 12

Any severe loss may represent a disruption in one's relationship to the past, to the present, and to the future. Losses generally bring about fragmentation of routines, of relationships, and of expectations, and frequently imply an alteration in the world of physically available objects and spatially oriented action. It is a disruption in that sense of continuity which is ordinarily a taken-for-granted framework

Civil Places

The segments of the community spectrum which have been vastly extended by communications media have not been equally stretched to include active confrontations. The indirect communications systems operating in fields have grown in number and have been extended unnecessarily for the majority of individuals, while the orbits of direct access to different territories through transportation techniques have been limited to the well-to-do. Individual consumers can see and hear more through T V and radio, but do so without participation. The listener, spectator or globe trotter in this world, with access to everything, runs the risk of focusing on nothing.

In our imaginary spectrum of community (leisurely, meaningful contact and participation) there is a hier archy of orbits: the privacy of the family, meaningful public concourse in several scales and varieties of mixtures, easy urban circulation of all people and communications systems through many media.

Traditional urban environments are vanishing in technologically advanced societies. Modern urban man needs pedestrian-filled places from which interfering and irrelevant technology is barred and civic and civil intercourse are priorities. These people-places by definition can be fitted into the smallest segment of the community as well as into the greater collective. But whereas in old cities a few special-purpose places of civic mingling were sufficient, our territorially extended community, contrary to current tendencies, requires a great new hierarchy of places which might serve the same social integrating purpose. In other words, we call for a hierarchy of places designed as pedestrian concourses for a greatly expanded variety of purposes and scale, not to replace the existing facilities, but to complement them. Such a hierarchy will depend for its success on an appropriate system of movement, applying the same principles to the problems of both access and distribution. This is an essential complementarity now missing in our society.

It is obvious that whimsical or random distribution of places, however well designed, will prove to be as futile as 'inventing' new meaningless 'events' to fit old places. Environmentalists may only reasonably 'nudge', as Charles Abrams has said, planning toward the provision of places for the conduct of social processes; such a predictable necessity is not unreasonable.

Excellent Prototype

The Greek Agora was a meeting place which to this day remains an excellent prototype of community contact. It was highly accessible and devoted primarily to activity, conversation or listening, or participation in public debate or performance. Trading was the natural accompaniment of 'crevice filling' activities exploiting 'captive audiences'. A hierarchy of new Agoras, or their modern equivalent, may produce a sociological counterbalance to technological power: democratic assemblies in many places to keep decision making in balance and technology under control at all social levels. Jacques Ellul in *The Political Illusion*[52] insists that this need exists in all technological societies including

these determine the success of that communication. For the word 'communication' comes from the Latin *communicatio*, meaning *share*; it does not mean 'I send messages'. It implies involvement.

Colin Cherry, 'World Communication'. *Journal of the Royal Society of Arts*, February 1966

Other people have given different definitions of communication in terms of simple stimulus/response ideas. But here the social aspect is left out altogether. It conjures up the picture of one person making signs at another, who responds; communication has succeeded. But this leaves out the most important factor – who those people are, the momentary situation, and how

52. Jacques Ellul, *The Political Illusion*, New York, 1967

the democracies, and a progressive increase in popular participation in the political process must be provided to offset the technological and administrative centralization demanded by efficient economies.

As physical planners, we believe that suitable concourse places, dedicated to these and similar purposes (that is to say, not dominated by business or its products and therefore designed to attract passive consumers), may be essential 'exchange' environments in any urban system. Modern Agoras need no longer be exclusively outdoor places, only where natural climate permits. Modern men can now make a favorable climate for themselves wherever they are.

Places designed for unspecified events in fact soon develop their own identity and become naturally *special*, thus being quite different as environments from stereotyped, staple places which characterize the single-purpose target areas prescribed by mass-culture. We could even now specify some undesirable and desirable characteristics for the people-containers we have in mind: none should be so monumental or so large as to appear purely ceremonial and by implication occasional and formal. Needless to say none should be awesome, but on the contrary should be capable of absorbing small events. Exclusively dramatic settings demand attention all the time. Doing anything oneself in their shadow is almost impossible. They reduce everyone to the role of spectator or listener; pageantry, message and propaganda get scrambled. On the contrary, the larger segment of our imaginary hierarchy of exchange concourse-places must include containers of variety in which events are seen in detail and the crowd is composed of recognizable persons.

Learning Places

The implication of these specifications can now be extended. Places must invite participation. The confrontation of the individual with the rest of the participants is of the utmost importance both for the individual and the society. It is part of a continuous learning process to exist and behave and think in community: to learn to become human. The entire human habitat, including its urban components, may be thought of as a hierarchy of learning places for that goal. Learning is integral to the process of growing, changing and aging in which observation, information and action

Fig. 14
The Learning Process

Learning is response to all the environments which man can experience: the physical, social and technological, employing his psychological, sensory and mental equipment. Genetic and environmental conditioning can be complementary. First-hand experience provided by the natural and the man-made, operating in equilibrium from the beginning of the individual life, are essential to man's development. Full awareness invites involvement and can become a creative process.

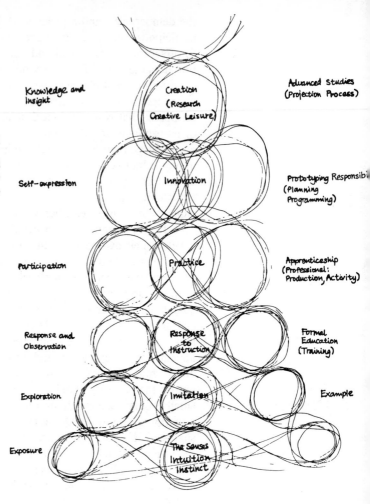

Knowledge and Insight

Creation (Research Creative Leisure)

Advanced Studies (Projection Process)

Self-expression

Innovation

Prototyping Responsib (Planning Programming)

Participation

Practice

Apprenticeship (Professional: Production, Activity)

Response and Observation

Response to Instruction

Formal Education (Training)

Exploration

Imitation

Example

Exposure

The Senses Intuition Instinct

among people, things and events, play an equally important part.

During the critical pre-education years, if we except some nursery schools, the child usually vacillates between over-love or overt interference, over-protection or outright neglect. The provision of places where the learning process for the very young can be productive, preceding formal education, is linked to the problem of simultaneously providing the two complementary means of learning for all children: observation, participation and invention on one's own, while learning from others. Both of these means, once acquired, may be extended into maturity for the enjoyment of self-enriching work, which, as Professor Paul Weiss has suggested,[53] will be the substance of future leisure, the natural extension of learning. Plutarch saw long ago that 'the city is the teacher of man'. It may still perhaps play this role. The passive consumer could be transformed into a creative human being after exposure to the enormous variety inherent in the environment.

Learning combines intuitive exploration, observation, discovery and creative action – environmental conditioning – on the one hand and its complementary opposites on the other: instruction, information, systematic research. Learning in fact contains a feed-back process between intuition and analysis from the womb to the grave.

That part of the growth and change of man which is stimulated by his moving through the designed part of the environment must not be separated from intellectual adventures found in knowledge. It is not a matter of display of objects before 'public view' (a fashionable attitude) but of *access* to places, which must involve the child, the adolescent, the adult and the elderly in regular encounters. However, at present in America, designed environments appear to make few provisions for natural encounters between different age groups. Most children have very restricted orbits which provide only very few opportunities to observe the adult world, outside their own family, which they are supposed to join immediately after graduation, except on rather superficial occasions from the street corner or the back of a station wagon, depending on their status. In our most mobile world children and adolescents are deprived

of independent mobility while waiting for that passport

to maturity and achievement, the driving license. The aged, whose responses no longer measure up to the demands of the auto-age, are equally frustrated by their increased dependence on the over-extended and exhausted adults of the younger generation, who have no time for them.

Where Does Johnny Go?

It seems that wherever there is no public provision for meeting places or social concourse, public purpose of any kind is frustrated. The urban dweller has few public places which he can visit and where he can rest, talk, smell flowers, dance, debate or demonstrate. People, wishing to act in concert, are forced into an uneasy or even inhuman position in public.

The technological society appears to close its doors to democracy. It may invite participation in the decision-making process at many levels, but it fails to provide places where this process of participation may naturally occur. Anger and dissent socially expressed has its physical counterpart. Practically and symbolically the democratic process has no place in our society. It is indicative that currently there are more marches than meetings. Any improvised platform is more than likely to create a nuisance, 'disturb the peace', interfere with traffic or privacy. Forcible occupation becomes a substitute for legitimate use. It may provide temporary consolation in 'sit-ins' and 'work-ins' of others' territories, but even the lawful 'hiring' of a hall for legitimate purposes other than by recognized political parties or for straight entertainment, all too often, under these conditions, gives the false impression of violent protest, instead of the image of peaceful intent.

The church and village halls, not to mention pubs to which all were welcome, seem to be historical precedents of concourse at a certain scale and may perhaps be recreated in function to fill out the modern spectrum of community for which we are searching. In more ways than one, man is environmentally conditioned. The physical conditions of affluent societies provide problems not of a technological nature, which are already soluble, but of a sociological kind for which no solutions are yet in sight. These solutions can grow out of experience only, not out of formal education. We need 'learning places'.

... The continuing tension between representative and participatory forms of democratic government ... . Who is the 'community' that 'nominally' exercises 'control' through the representative process? ... In what sense can the representative system be said to have 'spoken for' this community, during the long years of neglect and decay?

Adam Walinsky, *Sunday New York Times Book Review*, 2 February 1969, on Daniel P. Moynihan's *Maximum Feasible Misunderstanding*

In our society, at least, creating a setting involves one with a variety of existing settings which may have different purposes and traditions but with which one must develop and maintain relationships.

Seymour B. Sarason (Psycho-Educational Clinic, Yale University), 'The Creation of Settings: A Preliminary Statement'

Old conflicts, contradictions and misuses of human potential become paltry when faced with the new promise. Old expediencies, fashionable improvisations, however well intentioned, will not work. It seems that the realization of new human potential does not automatically follow in the wake of the limitless material abundances or the unbounded extension of man's intellectual powers. 'Breeding' nuclear reactors, obtaining their fuel supply from common and plentiful rock, may simply promulgate everywhere technologically based power. 'Cybernetics' and 'automation', the electronic extension of man which may forever release him for debilitating toil and degrading drudgery, may extend passive acceptance of equally debilitating consumerism and leave human need for creative leisure untouched for a dangerously long time ahead. Bigger and better gadgets may make deeper inroads into human ecology and deeper scars in human souls. Man can perhaps shift easily from his preoccupation with survival to universal consideration of convenience. But the shift to different aspirations may yet be too difficult. Maximization of individual and communal advantage as complementary drives may elude man's grasp.

... The importance of accomplishment gives way to values of awareness. The smell of earth, the touch of leaves, sounds of animals calling, myriad qualities interweave to make one not only aware but aware of one's awareness.

Charles A. Lindbergh, 'The Wisdom of Wilderness', *Life Magazine*, 22 December 1967

... Had the choice confronted me, I would not have traded nature's miracles of life for all of science's toys. Was not my earth's surface more important than increasing the speed of transport and visiting the moon and Mars? In wildness I sense the miracle of life, and beside it our scientific accomplishments fade to trivia ...

161

The authors' commitment to equilibrium in human goals, backed by technological and methodological working tools for their implementation, has been described. We can specify general organizational and operational principles and point toward essential functional components. There already exists a large body of agreement on many of these issues among many professions. In other words we have described some general 'constants' in our problem, but have been unable in the context of the study to include all the possible variables. Our commitment does, however, contain a very 'particular constant' not usually encountered in the context of urban design: public meeting places and their supporting mobility systems – a hierarchy of concourse to be devoted to pedestrian, leisurely, public intercourse complemented by a hierarchy of transportation and services accommodated in a general urban system. The questions which had to be answered in our model were: where and why. We want now to make the answer explicit in terms of how the above system of complementarity fits together.

Communications and Contacts

Our argument suggests that public pedestrian places and realms be provided in any urban environment with easy access for the many. This functional hierarchy is therefore related directly to the mode of travel between such places and realms. Whether the concourse lies within walking or transportation time/distance, the general principle does not change. Of course the local requirements will vary in content and scale. The concourse, however, must always be a real area of confluence: an exchange or transfer point between movement systems: in other words, places by definition in which passengers may leave their vehicles and join other tranquil pedestrians for whatever purpose.

In any such place, then, the frequency of use depends on easy access of one kind or another. Pedestrian places therefore represent, within the context of the current pattern of both deployment over an ever greater territory and constantly increasing travel time, a reasonable option. They can be considered, if not an antidote, certainly a complementary opposite to maximum mobility in the form of maximum tranquility, a therapy needed in a restless culture. If such places

Times Square remains a strongly beating urban heart among cool commercial towers, a night and day world of sun and neon against one of New York's few remaining open skies. It has what planners call a sense of place. Even its sordid aspects have failed to dim its vitality as the city's entertainment center or its reputation as a landmark – one of the most familiar in the world.

Ada Louise Huxtable, *New York Times*, 25 March 1968

are located in the metro-area at transit stops, they can logically become transfer points for mass-transit, road vehicles and pedestrians and naturally and properly become mixed-use places, not single-target areas of stereotypes. Twenty-four-hour places are special prototype areas in which many spontaneous activities including leisurely and tranquil ones may occur at any time.

The compactness, previously mentioned, of such places themselves would potentially enrich the larger community because it would produce social cohesiveness, in other words, an antidote to the divisiveness which is apparently the inevitable by-product of perpetual random automobile motion over ever-expanding territories. That this general notion has validity is already in some measure demonstrated by the underground systems of London. The largest part of the central 'tube' system of course has stations serving historically established nuclei. The 'underground' longer-range system has many new stations in the outlying districts that came into being later. In the twenties and thirties these stations, under the direction of Frank Pick, then head of the London Passenger Transport Board, were not only intelligently located but well designed. They became 'exchanges' in our sense, because in character and generosity of design they anticipated urban events in their vicinity and provided room for bus stops and taxicab stands as natural extensions of public transportation sub-systems. To this day they generate modest concourse around them. This type of environmental ordering is by no means beyond the scope of possibility. The various components of the concourse we envisage already exist in separate pieces in many places, but we can imagine a new synthesis to surpass anything now existing, if, as in Montreal, where the public transportation system is already well established, concourse places are next recognized as urban renewal priorities.

The New York subway system is, of course, beneath contempt when measured against New York's extravagances. Every subway stop in the United States for that matter is usually just another hole in the ground inviting an appropriate, quick, ground-hog dive. Grand Central Station, one of the few identifiable New York meeting places, despite being a great space in form, is an uneasy waiting room in function; certainly it is not concourse in our sense. It fails because its facilities are uniquely short-stop conveniences with a thick sprinkling of 'novelty' stores. No one can sit down anywhere. We can imagine, however, a combination at Grand Central scale in a transportation exchange below, say, an equivalent of the Galleria of Milan or the Piazzo San Marco in Venice: a confluence of inter- and intra-urban movements; a civic image of meaning. In a similar manner, if in London the underground stations and their 'crevice fillers' at street level could be combined with London squares with their prohibitive railings removed, together with the ubiquitous parking, the new pedestrian precinct hierarchy could begin to stretch all the way to the great historic public concourse of Trafalgar Square. Perhaps Lord Holford would then finally overcome long-standing obstacles and something comparable to our concourse model would be achieved in Piccadilly Circus.

Community Advantage

Our notion of concourse is a logical extension of mass-transit. Without the former, the social problems of our cities might be hard to solve, for public facilities would continue to have random distribution and random use. Wherever the private automobile dominates transportation, and particularly in the United States, the compelling reasons for extending mass-transit in metro-areas to reduce unbearable traffic congestion may unintentionally coincide with a process for restoring pedestrian concourse to its proper place. Public movement flow systems and public mingling container systems go together in a new metro-system of all-embracing interaction. Open-air and enclosed pedestrian meeting places, as environmental needs dictate, in conjunction with public and private transportation, are as natural to this contemporary urban scene as were their historic equivalents – the village greens, market places, meeting halls, churches and pubs.

Their form and content would, of course, vary from place to place, but the social catalytic function could again become a universal constant. Healthy evolution of modern politics and culture may possibly need the equivalent of the Greek Agora in modern dress.

All great civilizations have been based on loitering. . . . Think of the Greeks, for instance. One of the most interesting adventures in our history. What were the Greeks doing in the Agora? Loitering. Not getting agoraphobia. The result is Plato.

Penelope Gilliatt, 'Le Meneur de Jeu', *New Yorker*, 23 August, 1969, quoting Jean Renoir

164

The industrialist today has to think not
only in terms of labor, but also in terms of
being close to government, banks and the
major skills, the very high skills which you can
draw upon in a very big city, and above all to
rumors.

Charles Abrams, Yale Seminars, 1966

The United States . . . wants to do the thing
it is good at. . . . What the United States does
best . . . [is] performing technological stunts.
Some of these serve humanity, some are pointless and some make the human condition
more difficult than it already is. . . . The supersonic commercial jetliner, or SST . . . is a
gesture of technological indifference to
humanity. No power on earth
can prevent its development . . . building SSTs
is the kind of thing we do best.

Russell Baker, 'Why Hardware Always Wins', *New York
Sunday Times*, 8 October 1967

Pedestrians, Passengers, Places

The advantages of plenty may logically be equated
with the advantages of community which can operate
in complementary ways – first, through supra-territorial
communication systems and secondly, through direct
human contact. This study puts the world transportation
systems at all scales into complementarity with meeting
places at all scales no matter whom they serve. The
traffic exchanges may thus also become human exchanges: places where men become more human. The
time lag between the sociological and technological
evolutionary clocks may be shortened. Technology
properly structured could play an important role in
promoting community advantage.

Designers cannot design an ecological system, but
they can comprehend its workings, influence its direction
and participate in the process of transforming it on
many scales and in many ways. The abstract notion of
concourse can become a reality in a planned system
containing visible, comprehensible, spontaneous events
of unpredictable variety, where people of diverse mien
and purpose participate daily as a matter of course in
community action – to gossip, to learn the news, to
trade and to debate issues in public. Such public meeting
places lie at one end of our urban hierarchy of community. At this end, the scale and intensity, variety
and number of people involved provides opportunity for
anonymous activity. At the other end are to be found
the psychological comforts of individual identity. The
hierarchy of community then may be said to begin at
home in the privacy of the family and stretch out to
meetings everywhere at every scale.

The optimum enjoyment and proper utilization of two
major complementary components, the meeting of men
and machines, can only be obtained if both have their
own integrity. This integrity of both 'containers' and
'flows' does not imply segregation of people from vehicles.
It does, however, suggest reasonable separation within
limits of compatibility, mutual tolerance and mutual
reinforcement. The range of compatibility of movement
systems and man-full places will no doubt be further
stretched by a technology controlled by more humane
considerations than is now our custom. Land, water and
air vehicles will become appropriately dimensioned and

165 powered, clean and quiet in relation to their special tasks.

The gamut of choice between these extremes is curtailed if the city has an inappropriate form. Every lack of differential in its physical pattern means a negation of choice, and thus a negation of true urbanity. An inhuman anonymity then results, that of particles in an amorphous mass, whereas a genuinely urbane anonymity is comparable to the full splendor of the whole without losing any of its own lustre – in fact, the individual *tessera* only asserts its real significance within the total complex.

Edward Sekler, *Daedalus: Journal of the American Academy of Arts and Sciences*, 1960

We will investigate now the kinds of physical paths that are implied by such an organization of flows. In low-density areas road vehicles may well be separated from pedestrians at ground level. New short-haul, frequent-stop, relatively slow mini-trains may be usefully raised to the flowering-tree level, allowing the pedestrians to pass below while remaining within easy reach. The mini-station of land or water transportation belongs within the pedestrian precinct anywhere. Sharing the actual pedestrian paths, there may be motorized 'rickshaws', 'bubbles' and mini-buses, gentle and clean mechanical aids for the elderly, the tired and the laden.

In our imaginary hierarchy of movement, increase in intensity/density/frequency of use of exchanges demands a concomitant increase in levels to provide vertical separation in closer quarters. The needed space would be 'folded', becoming a three-layered 'sandwich' at the sector scale with the pedestrian realm properly in the middle, leaving the lower 'ground' level to road vehicles, public and private, of all kinds. The upper level would accommodate the midi-trains, swifter, longer-haul intra-urban transit, which would here be added to the sector mini-trains. Two-way vertical access would provide quick and convenient transfer between three transportation systems. As one gets further into the busier metro-core or spine exchanges, the simple three-layer sandwich becomes a 'club-sandwich' with as many layers as function demands.

The increasing number of transfers makes mechanized vertical movement here essential and economical. Moving ramps, escalators and public elevators enter the movement hierarchy and generate new levels for pedestrian activity while increasing the efficiency of transfer between many more systems at several levels added above and below. In these central layers the basic sector-sandwich described above can in this new complexity rise and fall with the tide of preference or need – down to swift long-haul maxi-trains and water transportation serving the metro-area and beyond – up to vertical take-off, quiet aircraft serving the region or providing shuttle flights to trans- and inter-continental airports. At each stage in our hierarchy of exchanges, new systems of mass-transportation are added, vehicles which move through but are never stored in the city. This essential continuous movement increases and declines in proportion to the passenger and trip number in each exchange in our transportation hierarchy. At the lower density/intensity exchanges, private vehicles may be conveniently and economically parked; at the higher they may only call.

What Johnny Sees

The many modes and levels of movement modern man may employ to explore his environments, natural or man-made, have much more than functional significance. A very few fortunates may recall their first venture on horseback, when a childhood's landscape was suddenly extended by that lively elevation. Looking over and beyond walls, the widening of horizons is made possible by increments of free movement in the land-scape or city-scape alike in three dimensions.

Faces of Community

The hierarchy of exchanges and movement systems implies simultaneously the hierarchy of community expression, the urban 'windows' displaying the social shape of a small-town neighborhood, sector, and core or spine nucleus in the metropolis. Arrival, departure and utilization of place are the three pillars of concourse at every scale. Exchanges as conceived by us may become modern equivalents of earlier concourse places established during the cultural evolution of man. These may be 'village' or 'town' centers and greens or Agoras as suggested earlier. Our commitment to concourse is rooted in the belief that public places designed for community action are needed as an antidote to scattered innumerable activities now conducted behind closed doors. Community in action must be made overt in all its forms, socially, symbolically and technologically.

Many activities now out of sight in private realms can and should be made visible in the public realm. Others with advantage could spill into it: various men at work, machines at work – printing, relaying messages, cleaning – people of all ages, kinds and colors, going about their daily tasks, people eating and drinking, reading and gossiping, resting and hurrying, having their hair cut and their shoes shined, people making music, singing and dancing, running, walking and strolling in pedestrian precincts designed to accommodate human activity and dialogue at every scale.

Community places sketched in here have the power to revitalize and extend the pageantry of people;

167

different modes of movement linking them may enrich and extend the urban panorama.

... The city spreads out with new buildings. ... Any man here, if he is healthy and not a good-for-nothing, can earn his living with the decorum appropriate to his station. ... On festive days, when one looks at the merry crowds of dignified men, both of the nobility and of the people, also at the bustling throngs of children incessantly scurrying here and there, and at the comely gatherings, the comely groups of ladies and girls walking back and forth or standing on their doorsteps, as dignified as if they were the daughters of kings, who would say that he has ever met such a wonderful show of people on either side of the sea?

Fra Buoncicius della Reva, in 'Eulogy of Milan', quoted in Robert S. Lopez, *The Birth of Europe*, New York, 1967

Extended and Deprived

One must equate the anticipated increase in leisure, as a result of technological and methodological advance, with the increase in material abundance and continuing 'urbanization' in an entirely new sense. Technologically advanced societies have developed new social inhibitions in direct proportion to technical conveniences. Machinery carrying travelers at home or abroad, it appears, always ends up in hostile territory. Even the most devoted globe trotters among tourists often take a jaundiced view of strangeness. Foreign lands are usually visited very much like zoos in which exotic creatures are safely behind bars. At home curiosity about the familiar environment often reaches the vanishing point. Only the exceptional have any interest in living things in their own backyard

... We may be caught in the irony that at the very moment when by our wit we have developed the means to give us considerable control over our resistant natural environment we find we have produced in the means themselves an artificial environment of such complication that we cannot control it.

Elting F. Morison, *Man, Machines, and Modern Times,* Cambridge, 1966

Until the end of World War II, or shortly thereafter, planning was a moderately evocative word in the United States. It implied a sensible concern for what might happen in the future and a disposition, by beforehanded action, to forestall avoidable misfortune. As persons won credit for competent planning of their lives, so communities won credit for effective planning of their environment. It was thought good to live in a well planned city. The United States Government had a National Resources Planning Board.

J. K. Galbraith, *The New Industrial State,* Boston, 1967

unless they have put them there themselves. Familiarity does indeed breed contempt. The mechanized traveler even at home leaves everything unexplored except stereotyped targets.

The urban environment, if man can only learn to shape it properly, is not only becoming an essential component of the total environment, but has great promise as a springboard for rediscovery of the wonders of life everywhere, and simultaneously of man's own humanness. But time is running out and mankind may be running the risk of losing its humanity before it reaches its highest potential. From this point of view it seems reasonable to tackle the problem of readjustment at both ends — not only the conservation of the natural, but also the restructuring of our collective selves, thereby satisfying simultaneously an ecological adjustment and a sociological evolution.

10. Building Bridges

The ecology of the intellectual environment. Intelligence, intuition and urban culture. A description of some professional dilemmas and failures. Some suggestions for the education of environmentalists and urban designers.

My present interest is that of identifying urban systems in terms of what they are capable of containing that is useful and meaningful for the human beings which inhabit them. I am taken aback when I hear someone who is very willing to accept the decisions of the market as the governing organism of city life.

Eugene Kupper, Yale Seminars, 1966

Neither unstructured chaos nor unstructured ennui has room for the exercise of free will and option which we claim to require for a democratic way of life.

Richard L. Dodge and Frank Eugene Kupper, Graduate Architectural Design Thesis, Yale University, 1967

This book has argued that in the framework of the third ecology the evolution of man depends on his responses to the man-made environment, which is actually two complementary environments: the physical and social. In an advanced technological society which uses sophisticated methodology to arrive at complex social ends and employs technically complex means there is, so to speak, a fourth ecology within the third. This operates within the framework of the evolving human mind: the intellectual environment. Its mechanisms can perhaps be explained according to the same principles discussed in the book. The systems of interaction, complementarity and maximization of choices, upon which our commitment was based for the purposes of a physical urban environment, can be usefully applied in the analogous context of the intellectual environment, in which man must also develop new responses to new realities. A new bridge-building is necessary; this amounts to intellectual exchanges between sociology, methodology and technology, the goals and means. The intellectual environment can no longer be left to chance any more than the physical habitat; it must be systematically structured to respond to new discoveries through the learning process.

There is an extraordinary technological gap in our society . . . the difference between traditional productive technique and social technique. Our social technique here is, in a number of specific areas involved in city and regional planning, so primitive as to account for some . . . pessimistic overtones.

John W. Dyckman, 'Concluding Remarks', *Urban Exploration Proceedings*, Florida, 1965

Professional Obsolescence

The concerns of the intellectual and the physical environments come together in considering the question of educational means toward the ends we have sketched. The design profession has the ability to contribute to the resolution of critical problems and give visible and comprehensible order to the new complexity, but it is handicapped. Architects and planners are by tradition and training collectively uninterested in research and unsuited to the new task. At this moment they appear to be less able than other professionals, educated in fields intellectually more disciplined and perhaps methodologically more efficient, to make a meaningful contribution to interdisciplinary studies and research.

174 The current fashionable, simplistic insertion of courses

in computer technology in professional design-school curricula, without adequate preparation at the college level for the student, is only matched in futility by the practice in real situations of throwing self-appointed heroes without reasonable notice, innocents in fact (non-swimmers), into complex urban problems (deep water), forcing them to escape into purposeless form making. Lack of skill is not compensated for by sensibility; skill and sensibility of course play different parts, but both are quite able to ignore any sort of theoretical base for action.

If the professional schools for designers are on the whole inadequate, the traditional design professions appear to be completely obsolete, and since the schools prepare the students for the profession, there is evidence that this form of education will also become obsolete. Professionals in the field currently require continuity in attitude, in interest, in skills and in the practice of expediency. The result is that they are conservative by nature. Yet these are the people who are asked to inspect and to accredit the schools of architecture from which they draw their assistants and, more often than not, their 'inspiration'. But schools should be by definition scholarly, exploratory, adventurous and philosophically concerned with the broad scope of questions. At present their interest is exactly the opposite. It often is not to deepen and widen the field or to investigate, to understand and to predict as a whole without being tied to the temporary demands of the market. In a school devoted to architecture and planning (environmental design), and more particularly in a university, this search for the widening and deepening is both a moral and an intellectual obligation. But students and teachers alike, no matter how well intentioned, have in spite of themselves become opponents of so-called practical men in their pursuit of professional ends.

Current architectural education in 'accredited schools' is not on the whole either liberally or broadly informed. It has accepted almost exclusively in its curricula the framework of existing conditions and seeks in the context of 'real' situations of structure, site, etc., to provide 'designer' personnel without performing the

175 necessary research into the changing conditions of the

environment. This method is not practical because it makes the obsolete an ingredient of the future. Formal invention remains without a foundation in new realities.

Professor Muller, a zoologist and Nobel Prize winner, speaking of the slow emergence of scientific thought, comments that: 'At one time instead of a rational system of knowledge, man erected pretentious edifices of misinformation. Within these walls they imprisoned themselves, tied up by bonds of emotion and hopeful compulsion. Inside the puppet show went on, in which the leading roles were played by spirits and the main mode of operating was magic. Even the areas of knowledge in which real progress had been achieved – astronomy, mathematics, medicine – were perverted to the pseudo-sciences such as astrology, numerology and exorcism.' Something very similar is still going on in the design of the environment. In the rush to give new shapes to old errors, new errors continue to be added to the old.

Pseudo-Consensus

A typical technocratic simplism is evident everywhere in a free economy employing increasingly sophisticated technologies. The employment of pseudo-consensus as an instrument of decision is particularly insidious. Opinion polls, now a substitute for meticulous observation which takes longer, create new myths of consensus daily about something which can then be manipulated as an instrument to deceive the public later.

In the foreseeable future, it appears quite unlikely that a meaningful consensus on any aspect of techno-logical complexity can be arrived at on the popular level until statement of the social goals involved (true or false) has been carefully prepared beforehand and launched through information media. Consensus in respect of highly abstract goals such as freedom from fear or want, about which there can be little argument, is politically unequivocal. But at the *means* level of consumer-serving technologies it is questionable whether consensus can be so universally acceptable. Despite this it currently operates on a pre-established and carefully maintained mass-production supply level. At best this is a temporary consensus, for varying periods, until a better or simply a more profitable technology becomes available to government or to great corporations who then decide to produce a new commodity to be as 'hard-sold' as a political goal (good or bad).

Perhaps the practitioners themselves are gradually realizing that they have become obsolete, organized on the one hand as they are in splinter groups of specialty, while on the other their brashest representatives, irrespective of their training, do not hesitate to become generalists and cross the boundaries of their own making in order to operate at any scale in the environment-shaping process. Such excursions into the unknown more often than not wind up in exercises distinguished only by an individual's aestheticism, historicism or scientism, or in collective endeavors in simplicism or in unprofessional compliance to immediate demands.

In the architectural profession, 'urban design' is perhaps the most widely spread and most debilitating fashion of them all – pseudo-artists and pseudo-humanists are bad enough under any circumstances, but today picturesque expediency has been extended in a period of critical transition through the activities of innocent, or perhaps more accurately, desperate, professionals entrusted with gigantic projects and responsibilities. Not even the most affluent society can afford to leave critical urban situations at the mercy of simpletons, any more than we can afford to applaud the shenanigans of the playboys (and girls) of the western world, however artistically talented.

Abstract slogans such as 'beautification' cannot be readily translated into meaningful action while still operating at the level of superficial trivia. We read occasionally that beauty-parlor techniques are being applied as cures to cases of cancer. A similar folly characterizes the design of the environment. 'Beautification' and 'Urban Renewal' as both are now being practiced have the same relationship to urban design as chiropractice to medicine; when rarely they do good, it is only by accident and not for the given reasons. This pseudo-activity has cumulative effects: pseudo-professionals of all kinds (their number is growing as more and more people jump on to the 'urbanology' bandwagon) produce pseudo-realities to deceive innocent men further. Pseudo-plans produce pseudo-reconstruction, urban renewal and, worse, pseudo-cities. The projects newly designed are only slightly less random than
the old bits of blight. We can take pop-art in our

stride, but can we do the same with pop-architecture and pop-cities?

Urbanization thus faces a double threat: from inept professionals as well as from inherited chaos. With the assistance of vast federal funds the first have invaded the ranks of hastily mobilized bureaucracies at all scales and by trying to resolve the disorder through technology have in fact added new computerized problems to the old ones of *laissez-faire.*

Technophiles and Technophobes

This suggests that until there is an adequate supply of rationally trained humble and moral personnel with the opportunity and ability to cope with new realities, technological society will remain to one degree or another at the mercy of either the technophobes or the technophiles, a rough approximation today of the two-party system within the professions. The danger from the latter is no less than from the former; thoughtless arty games are being joined by the half-baked numbers games of technocrats.

Conversely to examine technology mechanistically is to underestimate the scope of its impact by merely measuring its scale. Put differently, it implies concentrating on techniques which offer relatively few problems in their purely quantitative nature and ignoring the social, qualitative transformations which have occurred in the past and will continue to occur and present tremendous problems in the future. The technocratic over-simplifications of breaking down all problems into separate and easily analyzable parts (an ancient and obsolete game) ignore our need to tackle complexity as a whole.

Specialists and Generalists

The process of the design of environments must involve new goals and means in both the sociological and technological context. The triggering of this design process is a process in itself. It may be described as a search for new parameters. A legitimate question to try to answer at this point is: is a designer to be a professional, an artist, a technician, a tradesman or a businessman?

It is not irrelevant to imagine a broader spectrum for design activity which could include all of the above as special complementary functions or a combination of some or all in a new generalist function. The immediate

178

proposal is quite simply that the preparation for any activity, new or old, should be systematically and rationally conducted.

Methodology for Understanding

The bulk of essential knowledge for the environmental designer of the future, under whatever name, lies today outside the design professions and design schools, and what is required as a first step, therefore, is a means of access to this information. The second step may then naturally follow: schools of environmental design with a superstructure of advanced study similar to the current set-up of the sciences. Advanced post-graduate work, post-professional practice in research as a career in itself, could quickly lead to significant activities. Only work at a high level of sophistication can produce the intellectual ferment which must be fed into the professional schools. The designers' tasks can be formulated by pressure both from the top, the advanced special studies, and from the bottom, the great liberal spread of college education. As our higher education improves, the depth and spread of knowledge and interest will increase. Most scientific and professional schools have traditionally been nurtured from these two sources. The design professions, however, seem to have escaped this time-honored process and have for some time been at the mercy of the market place, which, through the fashion mongers now welcome in academic life, has made deep inroads into the universities themselves.

Comprehensive Plan-Design

Liberal preparation at college level is as important as post-graduate environmental studies. A comprehensive, responsible and far-reaching program of research and education in environments should now be developed in great universities, which are communities where the necessary diversity of skills and knowledge can be made available in a climate of inquiry, removed from political and market pressures.

The necessary steps in a systematic design process do not of course exclude aesthetics or inhibit the creative mind. On the contrary, they release the mind from drudgery. Rationality as a system of procedure in problem solving does not inhibit inspiration. Inspiration is a special moment in a rational process which acts as an accelerator on the path towards the desired goal. The two are inseparable and complementary.

179

Equally, discipline is not necessarily restrictive but can build a matrix for the greatest freedoms within it.

The re-definition of the field to include the comprehensive design of environments eliminates the questionable separation of Architecture and Landscape Architecture, Industrial Design, Urban Design, Regional Design, etc. These divisions, only recently established, are already obsolete. They can no longer serve any useful purpose for they only deal with the physical scale. What is now needed is a commitment to the study and design of the human habitat in all its complexity that can produce qualitative variations and help build intellectual bridges between many disciplines.

It is clearly the responsibility of universities to produce a new variety of professional excellence in a broader spectrum of environmental studies and a greater understanding generally of human ecology in a man-made environment. A comprehensive environmental design program should attract the diverse intellectual resources of the college and bring to any segment of design a greater diversity of talents. At this time design is almost uniquely identified with 'Art', which all too often merely attracts the facile or ambitious. Environmental designers can no longer be content with conventional means concerned with form-making through the intuitive process of an individual artist. The systematic structuring of new realities has become a priority for designers. The formulation of ends requires many collaborators, combining incisive intuition with disciplined intelligence and high skills.

Visual order is only one of many analogous orders. It appears necessary therefore to remove all vestiges of the 'Art' mystique from courses at the college level. Perhaps the best way to accomplish this is to revive and develop courses that cut across departmental boundaries. A greater variety of students might then participate in problems of order making, employing media as varied as writing, music, logic, mathematics and visual constructions, stimulated by intellectual and emotional conditions which do not exist in their later professional involvement.

Just as the future strength of design lies in its interdepartmental studies at the graduate and post-graduate level, so may it also derive comprehension of team work from the workshop of the performing

180

arts, which today should not be limited to stage performances, and which may prove to be the most effective catalyst at the college level, inviting collaboration between diverse gifts and talents. In any case, it has become obvious that the spectrum of physical environments is no longer confined to traditional engineering or 'Fine Arts'. It may even be asserted that the best works of innovation in modern societies are performed by quite unexpected protagonists, whom we cannot label, within new frameworks of their own evolution and invention.

A more constructive framework could be provided in more flexible curricula to allow the introduction of interdisciplinary courses at any level as needed. It seems that, as in all pursuits of knowledge, no single university department can any longer be 'all things to all men'. This applies equally to Urban Theory or Design Process. The problems require complementary activities in many universities and institutions. Universities have lately made any number of bridgings between their departments of natural and social sciences. Applied sciences must follow suit.

Intelligence and Intuition

The creative aspect of a gifted individual has to be revealed through the educational process as a system of work. Teaching methods have been developed, based upon self discovery and practice; the feed-back process in learning should not be limited to intellectual means but should include the 'intuitive' processes. Indeed, is man not discovering that the line between the so-called intelligent and intuitive ways of achieving ends is not so easily drawn? If urban culture can bring together individuals of special and different gifts to work together, this may reveal that some tasks are actually simpler, but not more mysterious, for those endowed with talent than they are for the intelligent. This integrated creative activity might help us to decode the apparently unfathomable ways of art. Man may even see issues of great stature from unexpected new liaisons, (born out of wedlock according to convention).

Another priority educational device which might follow the earlier suggestions is a catalytic college course bridging several departments concerned directly or indirectly with physical environments. Such a course in Human Ecology would recognize the man-made urban

181

habitat as a growing inescapable reality and give the study of design of human habitats equal status with the natural and social sciences and the humanities.

This meeting of the minds would have the healthy effect of at least modifying, if not eliminating, the myth of artistic detachment and might lead to the abandonment of the star system which tries to manufacture excellence and heroes, like any other commodity, and is overloading these artificially created paragons with arbitrary demands so great that these might corrupt even the genuinely superior person. The problems facing both the schools and the professions do not originate to any great extent from within the schools. The remedies suggested here will be as hard to initiate in the universities as in the ranks of the practitioners; neither are any longer immune from the growing pressures from outside. The quest for truth and excellence has been deeply affected by fashion and opportunism even in the groves of academe.

Perhaps a moratorium to inquiry into the nature of the creative process is now in order, until a more propitious time when urban society is less self-conscious about art and more confident in its value judgements – when social purpose may have become clearer. The artist is the 'truth-teller' as Robert Graves describes him, who can push solutions to problems further than the less gifted. Lethaby's aphorism makes the complementarity of art and science clear: 'Science is knowing, art is doing.'

There is growing evidence that in the universities a new generation of valuable generalists or bridge-builders is already emerging. New application of talent and the acquisition of new skills for the process of design, it seems, are being made possible. This in turn suggests that the architectonically gifted, synthesis-oriented student can and must be allowed to play an important role in the bridge-building process of interdisciplinary studies proposed.

Such studies now suffer from, among other things, conflicting methods of presenting material for joint discussion, a combination of verbal and graphic images at many levels of abstraction – ideas, descriptions, data and diagrams, schematic plans, architectural plans – all of which can present many semantic hurdles, which

To put it briefly: Art is solving problems that cannot be formulated before they have been solved. The shaping of the question is part of the answer.
    That is how the creative process works even in the most exact fields, just as it does in the recognized art forms.

Piet Hein, 'Of Order and Disorder, Science and Art and the Solving of Problems', *Architectural Forum*, December 1967

Semantic Hurdles

seem difficult to overcome.

A recent series of seminars of the kind proposed (Yale Seminars, 1966) showed that these difficulties fall into two categories. The first, verbal communication, becomes an issue when familiar words are placed in an unfamiliar context and a 'new jargon' is developed that is suspect to several participants. However, in spite of differences in background, an understanding among most seminarists developed after relatively short periods of 'thinking together' about Urban Design. This suggests that for the purposes of interdisciplinary, advanced studies of environments, mutual understanding will grow as fast as the extension of such studies. There is evidently no need to invent either a new lexicon or vocabulary for educated, literate people, focused on new problems. The work-method itself will clarify meaning and some of the jargon of today may become, through usage, a useful language tomorrow.

The second problem of 'General Visual Semantics' may be relatively more difficult to overcome. Literacy, in conventional graphic techniques now employed, will have to be extended through the mastery of new media in order to establish a new information technology. This will be more comprehensive and effective than techniques currently employed by any profession and will approximate more closely the combined images and techniques used in the fields of information and communication, such as film, radio, TV; visual and audio-visual media.

Urban System, Eco-System

Within the framework of the problems and methodology under discussion here, every means must be tried to wean away environmental designers of every kind from false images of their involvement. Two of the most deceptive semantic stereotypes are the words 'City' and 'Urbanism', which immediately conjure up the images and symbols of historic cities – autonomous man-made closed systems, secure places in a generally hostile environment of nature. Now the roles appear to be in danger of being reversed, and the man-made urban habitat threatens other natures as well as humanity's. In any case the 'City' in the historic sense is being replaced by open-ended systems of social, cultural and technological interaction and interdependence appropriate to accelerated growth and change. It is now really

183

a Global Urban System depending increasingly on communication and information sub-systems which must 'find their own appropriate form', to paraphrase Louis Kahn. This Urban System is no longer composed of separate, autonomous 'cities' with country in between but is a complete eco-system. A new urban structure with its own ecology is in the making, and this scope must be the focus of studies of the environment.

The urban matrix has become a complete new environment, man-made and potentially man-destructive. An Urban Ecology and new functionaries are needed to define and shape it. No single profession is fit for the complex task of developing an urban system, leading to an urban model. Before we can approach this ultimate goal, demonstration components of a new potential order at many scales are urgently needed to test its validity. 'Demonstration Cities' as end products of some predetermined magnitude are not suggested here. The framework which we have in mind when speaking of demonstration requires entirely different resources and ranges than those empirical, remedial, piecemeal steps so far promised or implied have suggested. There is no reason to doubt that what we have in mind, large-scale simulations, is within our grasp. New realities are not old realities. Visible, tangible prototype urban components in an urban matrix on an existing metropolitan scale of sufficient scope is an essential first step forward. Later, new realities demonstrated in action will be the strongest argument in favor of a sympathetic look at the unfamiliar. That this will require means beyond any single university's, corporation's, city's or any state's capacity does not need to be argued here.

Model for Education

In summary: designers now require a two-part program of study: first, Theory of Urban Design which is based on predictable changes in science, technology, social structure, and mores; second, appropriate techniques to aid them in the performance of tasks of increasing complexity. A Theory of Design may reasonably lead to new forms of commitment instead of commitment to new forms. Theory, in any case, must always be tested against real situations (when commitment must be translated into action). Designers must learn from other disciplines techniques of prototype programming which, like technology itself, is not exclusive or particular or

It is conceivable, then, that we might hit upon another idea which could serve as the organizing principle for many fields of scholarly inquiry. ... It is simply the idea of survival ... for the first time in history, the future of the human race is in ... question ... it is the message which a growing number of scientists are trying ... to get across to us.

Professor Richard A. Falk, quoted in John Fisher, 'The Easy Chair', *Harper's*, September 1963

The real accomplishment of modern science and technology consists in taking ordinary men, informing them narrowly and deeply and then, through appropriate organization ... more even than machinery ... the tangible manifestation of advanced technology ... arranging to have their knowledge combined with that of specialized but equally ordinary men. This dispenses with the need for genius ... [on the other hand creates the need for this new] complex ... job of organizing specialists ... (for) ... specialists on organization.

J. K. Galbraith, *The New Industrial State*, Boston, 1967

Design is wholly abstract, and is ruled by abstractions: architects do not build buildings, they think about them. But the subject of design is form in the world, and especially the inter-action between environmental form and human behavior.

Frank Eugene Kupper, 'A Theoretical Framework for Environmental Design and Form', Center for Advanced Studies, University of Illinois, 1967

local, but quite universal, generalized and anonymous, at levels of need which may be described as constant. No country need sacrifice culturally and geographically established variants while attending to this priority. A declared broader purpose backed by appointments of widely recognized excellence to guide the post-graduate studies program should go a long way to correct our situation. Social, economic and technical issues, it is true, have to be finally resolved in physical terms: visible, comprehensible order – 'a broadened architecture'. But we cannot begin from the wrong end.

Revolutionary times are times of priorities. One such high priority must be rational and inspiring goals for organizers of environments for urbanizing man. Only from these can come viable principles and methodology to be translated into the production of unprecedented prototypes to leaven the current infatuation with bigger and better stereotypes. A commitment to the study and design of the human habitat can help build intellectual bridges between many disciplines.

It remains, however, the designers' responsibility to make visible what others may only know about conceptually. 'Comprehensive' design will need 'comprehensive designers', in the words of Buckminster Fuller, to employ complementary processes: amassing new knowledge and data, identifying new urban components, developing new theories, learning new skills, and above all making commitments to the achievement of many unfamiliar ends. The only temporary embarrassment may be that the majority of mankind will find the new too baffling to deal with, or worse still, be deemed too simple in the beginning to warrant systematic study. Planning and action are complementary components in the design process; planning shapes ideas; design gives shape to environmental events. In the physical world inhabited by man, the process is never complete: nothing is finished; everything is only begun. Each human life is a system of feed-back from reality to imagination.

The designer's role in the feed-back process may become catalytic through the universities' intellectual bridge-building. He stands at the intersection of force vectors in culture which may be labeled as Science, Technology, Humanities and Art. Designer Training is by definition a university function. The Urban Designer's task is to transform new complexities into visible order. Humanity now has the tools for the resolution of complexity; planning, prediction and preventative action has at last become a reality. Environmentalists can and must join the company of Decision Makers.

A summary and description of some guaranteed
norms for all in an urban environment. Urbanism as
evolution toward community.

It is not my intention to be original, and what I am saying is common knowledge. But I should like to mention vigilance once again. I want especially to remind all the young, the healthy and active, for whom this book is meant, of their responsibility for the fate of man. Comrades and friends! Brothers and sisters! Ladies and gentlemen! Please pause at your pursuits and recreations for a moment! Not all is well with the world! . . . Comrades and friends, brothers and sisters, ladies and gentlemen! Civilization is in danger!

Anatoli Kuznetsov, *Babi Yar*, New York, 1966

[Reporting the murder of a woman who screamed for help]
. . . Forty people heard the screams. Eighteen of those interrogated replied that they did not want to be involved.

CBS Radio News, 31 January 1968

Man is that animal who himself draws the lines that he himself stumbles over.

Piet Hein, 'Of Order and Disorder, Science and Art, and the Solving of Problems', *Architectural Forum*, December 1967

Talk is cheap, the price of action is colossal.

Peter Weiss, *The Persecution and Assassination of Jean-Paul Marat as Performed by the Inmates of the Asylum of Charenton Under the Direction of the Marquis de Sade*, New York, 1965

There lies before us, if we choose, continual progress in happiness, knowledge, and wisdom. Shall we, instead, choose death, because we cannot forget our quarrels? I appeal, as a human being to human beings: remember your humanity, and forget the rest. If you can do so, the way lies open to a new Paradise; if you cannot, nothing lies before you but universal death.

Bertrand Russell, 'Man's Peril', BBC lecture, December 1953

The study has come full circle. The authors' commitment, a theory about the role of the man-made environment, brought out the issues discussed in the book in general terms, and it suggested several vitally important priorities to help restructure the urban habitat that mankind is making its own. Following the injunction of our own commitment, this short summary can now bring into focus some of the organizing principles which can reasonably become operational once such a theoretical base has been established. We have outlined a strategy and its related tactics. The priorities among operational components have now become visible. In accordance with our commitment the strategy puts human ends above all else, and from them we can devise tactics for environmental organization, relegating the mere means of technology to their proper place in the scheme of things.

Throughout the book we have emphasized this because any attempt to deal with a diseased urban tissue must be preceded by a new concept of order and must be tackled with perhaps entirely new techniques. In the process of redeploying man through his environment, the natural and the man-made have become joined. The surface of the earth and its atmospheric envelope have become our habitat. Many millions of people move about and interact with strangeness as only a few nomads did in the past.

Man's fate as a social being is still open. Of course, a new breed of nomads may in the immediate future follow the preferred seasons or shuttle between town and wilderness, everywhere enjoying standard comforts and instant communications, moving like checkers without rules over an endless board in an unstructured environment. If this were to happen, the technology of communications would be doubly destructive, not only undermining historic city concentrations through overcrowding but also eroding the countryside through dispersion with its endless transportation lines. If this happened, something more than the fate of the environment, as we know it, would be at stake; the humanness of human beings could also be threatened.

We're fast moving to a national society if we have not already obtained that station. This is no longer a city based society, no longer a city state. We can call it a nation state and maybe later an international state. The city is now like a house. It's a commodity for accommodating interaction . . .

Paul Weiss, Yale Seminars, 1966

Ours is a vision and an activity together . . . we think the past preserves itself in the future . . . we are the culture of living change . . . what we are changing is the division of life. We are making a unity – a complete culture.

J. Bronowski, *Science and Human Values, the Abacus and the Rose, A New Dialogue on Two World Systems*, New York, 1965

Immense economic growth in technologically advanced countries after the Second World War was not generally anticipated, and only recently has this phenomenon been accepted as something which should and could be maintained. The even more formidable increase in population has, in spite of this economic growth, become menacing. Having failed to control population growth, the discrepancy between technology and social need has itself grown immeasurably. Consequently the widening gap between the haves and have nots has become a new and unexpected component which has not been mastered even in the most affluent societies. This phenomenon is as damaging between nations as it is within them. Technological society has not as yet devised appropriate measures to deal with the unpleasant fact that the rich are getting richer and the poor relatively poorer.

Even more disturbing and more difficult to adjust to is the growing discrepancy between the informed and wise minority (those who have correct responses to new realities) and the less-informed majority who, although not necessarily illiterate or irresponsible, have the wrong responses but remain inside the vital decision-making process. This discrepancy, being a product of technological growth, may prove the most difficult to overcome in social evolution because it involves institutional adjustment to technologies which respond neither to politics nor ideology. Even institutions of higher learning theoretically dedicated to the search for truth are at this time in danger of being downgraded by accepting too quickly new technology at its face value without examining its possible after-effects. The gap between the desirable and the possible may become greater and the human condition as a consequence may become worse.

Perhaps in the process of adjustment to the inevitable, however difficult, some of the less painful problems will be solved. Mankind may learn quickly enough, for instance, that the availability of information through technological media alone is not enough to create human purpose and that direct, constant interaction between people, individually and in community, as well as concern for the well-being of all things in the environment, is required. This is central to our theme and why we emphasize the provision of the full gamut of human experience in the form of direct interaction between work, leisure and learning, between the private and the public realms and between the participating and the temporarily alienated. Identity is the complementary opposite to anonymity in the spectrum of community. Both these characteristic options in complementarity must be maximized to obtain their full potential, thus inducing participation and involvement.

Community in Concourse

Public concourse, the collective interaction, for the structuring of man-made environments of variety, is emphasized as a goal because we believe that too little attention is given to it at present. Concourse involving simultaneously expected events and surprising adventures and discoveries cannot, of course, be prescribed any more than urban life itself. But opportunities for concourse may be slowly expanded through the provision of inviting and readily available facilities. Functional and physical components, man-made places and unspoiled pockets of nature, must be within easy reach of all, rich or poor, at every age and stage of development.

Today the mobility of the adult is greatly increased, but one never sees any mention of the corollary fact that the child's mobility has simultaneously been greatly reduced largely as a result of the hazards introduced by the new means of adult locomotion. The child's daily orbit has been even more sharply curtailed than its mobility.

A. E. Parr, 'Urbanity and the Urban Scene', *Landscape*, Spring 1967

Guaranteed Urban Norms

These essential urban components were described as hierarchies of places and hierarchies of movements, 'containers' and 'flows'. To create the hierarchy of untrammeled, independent, safe and varied movement (flows), everyone must be within easy walking reach of an 'exchange' where the pedestrian may become a passenger, free to move further afield in the urban environment. In our model the ability to move easily on foot and to travel in comfort and safety thereafter, if desired, is a basic urban right. Without cheap, if not free, mass-transit, proliferation of ghettoes can only be accelerated. This and pedestrian precincts containing basic public services of housing, health, education, welfare and information are all integral physical urban

192

components of social security and may be considered as *guaranteed minimal environmental norms* which technological society could reasonably provide along with guaranteed minimal income. Based on these norms every station in a public transportation system then becomes a point of transfer between many modes of movement, public and private, mechanical and pedestrian – a modern agora and gateway at the same time, an 'exchange' and a place of public concourse.

Public-transit and public-service components may naturally work together within integrated flow and container systems. Both require public investment and control. Exchanges thus born of public service will, at certain magnitudes, generate many other urban functions. Public funds and facilities then become the pump-primers for civic places inviting many other activities and investments. A health center, a hospital, a school, a college, courts of justice or housing may be typical prime-use nuclei of place. Collectively, all these meeting places containing basic public services can revitalize and humanize whole sectors of social decay. Public initiative and private enterprise jointly can make, without usurping each other's function, such places the expression of community, inviting involvement, increasingly meaningful choices and deserving pride.

The priority of flow systems and free travel between social, cultural and service facilities, between residence and employment, recreation and learning, is the natural extension of the notion of public welfare. The distribution of Social Security checks, as Daniel Moynihan has observed, 'does not of itself become an instrument for providing services for the urban lower classes.'[54] A comprehensive, free, channeled movement system between community facilities is essential. It can transform passive private consumers into citizens.

Public transportation and the publicly subsidized ordered urban systems of flow may be one of the major operations through which the growth of the public sector of the economy in non-Communist countries, from the present level of roughly 30 per cent in advanced countries to anywhere between 40 and 50 per cent, may be realized. The result may be that the government will distribute half of the national income.

Karl Deutsch, 'Baselines for the Future', *Daedalus: Journal of the American Academy of Arts and Sciences*, Summer 1967

Urban Warp and Woof

All these public-service components are prime urban-structuring systems. The warp of intensity/density/frequency and mix of use of place complement the woof of places of retreat and rest. It is out of this complementarity that our urban cloth is woven to clothe the rich and poor alike. The ingredient of mix in place is a commitment to interaction, complementarity and maximization of opposites, versatile agents in developing both a sense of community and tolerance of strangeness – an all-inclusive urban process in which man becomes more human.

The maximized experience of the man-made can complement the rediscovery of the wonders of the natural. One kind of tolerant encounter may lead to another. The self-reliance first learned close to home may help to build the greater community of mankind. The immediate priority, in our view, is to provide these for the urban poor who are currently deprived of both rewarding exploration and formal education and are corrupted in degrading environments. This double deprivation cannot be corrected by schooling alone, however good or integrated, or by the remodeling of slums.

. . . If we have a much larger opportunity in our society, and I think we will in the next ten years, the choices we have as a society will be in making investment in the kinds of commerce which we now try to economize on.

John Eberhard, Yale Seminars, 1966

55. Gunnar Myrdal, 'Too Late to Plan?', Bulletin of the Atomic Scientists, January 1968

. . . Development is much more than a matter of encouraging economic growth within a given social structure. It is rather the *modernization* of that structure, a process of ideational, social, economic and political change that requires the remaking of society in its most intimate as well as its most public attributes. . . . The conditions of backwardness must be attacked with the passion, the ruthlessness and the messianic fury of a jehad, a Holy War.

Robert L. Heilbroner, 'Counterrevolutionary America', *Commentary*, April 1967

Contradiction into Complementarity

We already have much information on some specific urban social problems and the means for collecting more have been devised. What remains is to consider the urban environment as a whole, as an instrument of social purpose and sociological evolution through which humanity may obtain the missing humane components. Without appropriate physical organizing principles and new means of measuring socio-technical interactions, many of the social remedies now proposed will vanish like needles in the urban haystack. We will have bought expensive cures without having solved problems which will require even more expensive prevention later.

In the United States today, surprisingly at this time of crisis in human affairs, there is an inappropriate tendency to advocate little plans and tiny economies for the gravest social matters while gigantic technological expenditure on hardware for 'little' wars and other unconscionable enterprises are dipping ever more deeply into the public purse. A generally responsible and idealistic public servant spoke of 'fun-city' at a time when proliferating riots and rising crime, daily traffic jams and rising road deaths, all evidence of conspicuous technological failure, were becoming unmanageable hazards for the majority of Americans. Comic relief can, we suppose, be occasionally therapeutic, but humane priority under critical conditions demands, as Gunnar Myrdal wrote, 'not the courage of illusory optimism but the courage almost of desperation . . .'[55]

The approach to urban problem solving proposed in this book tries to bring into focus the ingredients of crisis prevention and to outline some simple means of transition from dangerous urban obsolescence to conditions which are tolerable. The urban model suggested was an attempt to structure the 'third ecology' of the man-made environment before mankind will have reached a point of no return in its evolution, far short of human potential. The most promising method for preventing ecological mayhem, if not the extinction of all living things on earth, undoubtedly must start with the containment of stereotypical scatteration and emphasize the implementation of planning for an excellent and comprehensive urban compactness.

Such a system, prototypical in essence, would be more likely to put optimum human resources, including technology, into equilibrium with natural resources.

Stepping Stones

Perhaps public meeting places, points of arrival, departure and exchange within the urban complex everywhere in the world, with their potential concourse activity, may become stepping stones for all men and merit the most massive investment. Airports, now operating in a global network, are neither exchanges nor stepping stones but launching pads for those who need and can occasionally afford the fastest available transportation. It seems reasonable today to extend the whole hierarchy of movement down to the slowest, to think of structuring the urban land and water transportation systems immediately in order to serve the poorer many with stepping stones for their daily rounds and postpone speeding up the richer few.

Which Johnny Does What?

The constant search for new values, the comprehension of new realities, is proceeding apace among enlightened scientists and artists. Their activities are similar in effect and directed toward complementary goals. The creative act can come out of inquiry or doing. The main body of professionals engaged in diverse day-to-day tasks remain, by training or temperament, unsuited for systematic research or creative prototyping. The survival of many professions is in jeopardy because to a large extent the purposes for which they were originally established and the means which they have learnt to employ have become suddenly and simultaneously obsolete. The next stages of comprehensive design, requiring many and probably most unexpected kinds of protagonists, will no doubt be slow and painful for all well-established professions. These are, alas, not exempt from the dismal law of social evolution: institutions always lag behind realities.

Shape of Excellence

Excellence has always been the goal of creative men, but its structure and shape have periodically changed. Excellence today has many faces, new and old. Mobility, the dramatic masquerade of modern man, is still only the complementary opposite of ancient tranquility. Man still needs peace of mind, leisure and security. Mobility, in the modern world, is obtained

196

through highly complex technology, at great cost, and with an immense collective effort in which the passenger traveler plays no personal, active or creative part. He remains a passive consumer. Tranquility is the opposite in every respect. It can only be enjoyed by individual actions which initiate and control what happens.

A different but analogous complementarity of maximized opposites in cultural and technological terms is exemplified in a great symphony orchestra, which demands sophisticated, costly organization and environment for many listeners, in contrast to a guitar player under a tree, who is satisfied with simpler conditions. Both kinds of events remain incomplete without the proximity of a variety of facilities for leisurely enjoyment of meeting, refreshment, promenade and rest which makes a pleasant prelude or epilogue to all such events. They belong in pedestrian realms in the urban system, vital places for public meeting, the transfer points between many means of movement, including walking. Pedestrian realms are special places where men become persons instead of statistics. These environments demand that the manifestations of technology within them be visibly and audibly subservient to social purpose. It is only in such places that community may rediscover its substance and reality: humanity at its highest potential.

This book has described different ways of journeying back to community in the urban setting. Perhaps least damage will be done to both humanity itself and other living things if man finds a new urban symbiosis. It was written in a time of troubled transition from one epoch to another, in the midst of crises born of disillusionment and expressed in cynicism and opportunism, in protest and violence against existing order. We share much of the prevailing disillusionment with the present, but have a vision of environments in the future which will provide greater freedom of choice instead of the mendacious rationalizations and unfulfilled promises of the mass-cultures of great powers. The young generation of today is the caretaker of the future. It will without doubt build in good time institutions corresponding to new realities, able to adjust to the new ecology and to the new aspirations of humanity everywhere and so lead the march out of chaos toward community.

Crystal: Solid having a definite internal structure which is the result of the arrangement of the atoms of its constituents . . . a definite external form . . . which is the manifestation of the internal structure. . . . In their internal structure, crystals are not considered to be 'solid', i.e., one continuous mass, but to be formed by the arrangement of the atoms in a latticework, each having a relatively fixed position in space . . .

Columbia Encyclopedia (Second Edition 1956)

A regular solid, a pentagon-dodecahedron which has twenty corners, thirty edges and twelve sides and which may grow (repeat itself in any direction), is analogous to the structure of the authors' argument. The forty corners of two dodecahedra approximate our commitment, from which radiate sixty edges (issues) which in turn frame twenty-four planes (actions). These were described as structure of concepts in the Prologue. The listing of the component pairs under three categories is given here together with graphic images of the crystal structure and growth.

Fig. 15
Structure of Commitment

2 dodecahedra
20 corners each
40 commitments

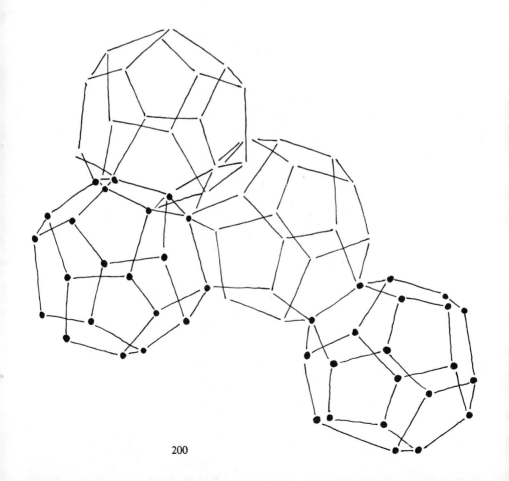

Structure of Commitment into Lattice Grid

Strategies
Social Goals
Sociological Ends

Community – Privacy
Community – Individual
Anonymity – Identity
Controls – Freedom
Continuity – Change
Variety – Uniformity
Maximization – Consensus
Contact – Communication
Exploration – Guidance
Option – Focus

Tactics
Organizing Principles
Organizing Characteristics
Operational Principles

Public – Private
Prevention – Cure
Rules – Randomness
Interdependent – Autonomous
Compatibility – Discord
Mixture – Uniqueness
Cohesive – Divisive
Locus – Orbit
Fields – Territories
Place Proximity – Space Availability
Localization – Deployment
Density – Dispersal
Intensity – Diffusion
Open – Closed
Flexible – Rigid
Mobility – Tranquility
Conservation – Construction
Prototype – Stereotype
Invention – Implementation
Frequent – Intermittent
Hierarchies – Clusters
Local User – Outside User
Pedestrian Access – Vehicle Access
Pedestrian Distance – Vehicle Distance

Means
Functional Hierarchies
Physical Hierarchies
Technological Components

Flows – Containers
Exchanges – Targets
Prime Purpose – Crevice Fillers
Urban – Ex-urban
Public Services – Private Enterprise
Meeting Places – Communication Systems

201

Fig. 16
Structure of Issues

2 dodecahedra
30 edges each
60 issues

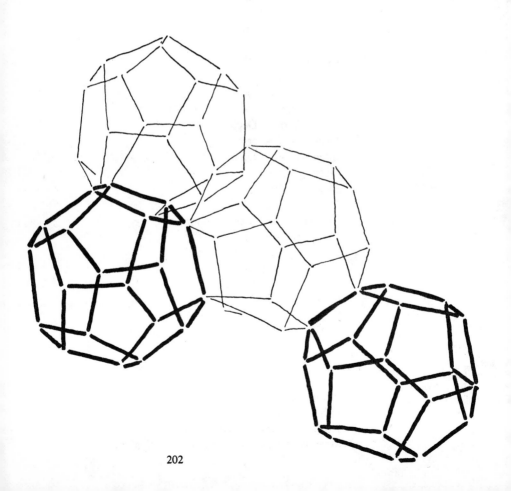

Evolutionary Clocks
Third Ecology
Complementarity – Contradiction
Commitment to Concourse
Dynamic Order
Maximization – Consensus
Prevention – Cure
Confrontation – Communication
Public – Private
Prototype – Stereotype
Cohesive – Divisive
Tranquility – Mobility
Community – Privacy
Mixture – Uniqueness
Hierarchies – Clusters
Public Transit – Private Car
Open System
Priorities – Commitment
Ends – Means
Social Purpose – Urban Components
Building Bridges
Design as Catalyst
Change and Growth
Synchronizing Clocks
Constants and Variables
Programme – Process
Options – Optima
Man-full – Car-free
Bi-Polar System
Socio-structure – Techno-effects
Ecologies and Ideologies
Community and Individual
Controls and Freedom
Community in Concourse
Conservation and Construction
Interdependence – Autonomy
Cohesion – Diffusion
Compactness – Dispersal
Maximization – Consensus
Variety – Uniformity
Localization – Deployment
Proximity – Access
203   Planless Planning

Fig. 17
Structure of
Priorities

2 dodecahedra
12 planes each
24 priorities

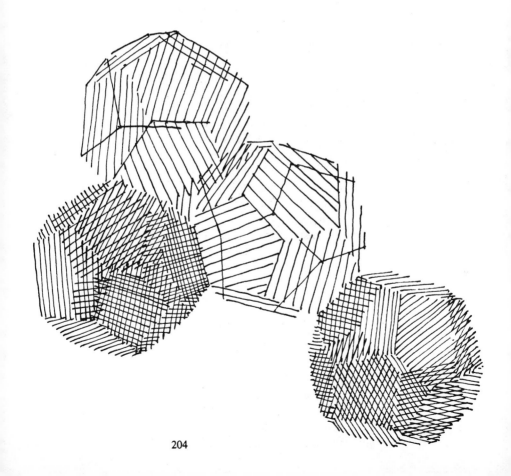

204

Territories – Fields
Techno-fallout
Specialties – Staples
Methodology and Understanding
Locus and Orbits
Syndrome – Diagnosis – Therapy – Prophylaxis
Search for System
Sorting Complexity
Model in Action
Theory and Practice
Urban Weights and Measures
Metabolism and Pollution
Technophiles – Technophobes
Flows – Containers
Exchanges – Targets
Prime Purpose – Crevice Fillers
Urban – Ex-urban

Structure of Priorities

Sociological Ends

Construction – Conservation
Community – Individual
Controls – Freedom
Maximization of Opposites
Confrontation – Communication

Organizing Principles

Change – Growth
Prevention – Cure
Public – Private
Cohesion – Concourse
Mixture – Uniqueness
Hierarchies – Clusters
Territories – Precincts

Organizing Characteristics

Complexity – Simplicity
Identity – Anonymity
Tranquility – Intensity
Exploration – Education
Leisure – Work
Proximity – Access
Prototype and Open Systems
Flows – Containers
Public Transit – Exchanges
Meeting Places – Learning Places
Prime Use and Crevice Fillers
205   Public Places – Social Services

So far as I know, there is very little literature on the art of 'combination' forecasting as against the extrapolation kind.

Daniel Bell, *Daedalus: Journal of the American Academy of Arts and Sciences*, Summer 1967

The true-structure is here a fictitious or heuristic tool . . . for our operational purposes . . . the notion of an operational principle to link these two entities . . .

E. F. Haden, M. S. Han, and Y. W. Han, *Resonance-Theory for Linguistics*, Monton, 1962

All the levels of classification in fact have a common characteristic: whichever, in the society under consideration, is put first it must authorize — or even imply — possible recourse to other levels, formally analogous to the favored one and differing from it only in their relative position within a whole system of reference which operates by means of a pair of contrasts: between general and particular on the one hand, and nature and culture on the other.

Claude Lévi-Strauss, *The Savage Mind*, Chicago, 1966

It might possibly be more effective to start with new kinds of physical technological structures, where government would fit in because of the nature of the structure . . . not as a 'final' solution but merely as a way of playing through the idea of using techno-logical possibilities in order to achieve social and political ends.

Harvey Perloff, *Daedalus: Journal of the American Academy of Arts and Sciences*, Summer 1967

I think one of the problems is that you're not simply dealing with two contrasting categories. Closed and open in what respect. For instance, physically closed or visually closed or audibly closed. . . . Actually closure or opener has probably six or eight dimensions.

A. E. Parr, Yale Seminars, 1966

There is also usually implied in the term, systems analysis, the notion of optimizing some aspect of the outputs. . . . There are a number of mathematical devices for simplifying a search of this kind.
    A similar phrase, systems approach, refers to a much less defini-tive procedure. It is simply the idea of viewing a problem or situation in its entirety with all its ramifications, with all its interior inter-actions, with all its exterior connections and with full cognizance of its place in its context. The two ideas are related because a systems analysis attempts to deal with a problem comprehensively; in setting up the mathematical model one uses the systems approach. However, one uses it primarily as a guide and as insurance against overlooking an important factor.

Alexander M. Mood, 'On Some Basic Steps in the Application of Systems Analysis to Instruction', *Socio-Economic Planning Science*, Vol. 1, 1967

This new tinge to modern minds is a vehement and passionate interest in the relation of general principles to irreducible and stubborn facts. All the world over and at all times there have been practical men, absorbed in 'irreducible and stubborn facts'; all the world over and at all times there have been men of philosophic temperament who have been absorbed in the weaving of general principles. It is this union of passionate interest in the detailed facts with equal devotion to abstract generalization which forms the novelty in our present society. Previously it had appeared sporadically and as if by chance. This balance of mind has now become part of the tradition which infects cultivated thought. It is the salt which keeps life sweet.

A. N. Whitehead, *Science and the Modern World*, 1926

For the end rules the method.

Francis Bacon, *Novum Organum*, 1620

It seems that very broad generalities can be translated into something approximating an urban system in which the abstractions are broken down into various levels of reality. The spectrum of our 'urban' abstraction is analogous to the spectrum of verbal abstraction in the 'General Semantics' of A. Korzybski and Wendell Johnson. This was devised to get discussion of any subject in a meaningful context by clarifying the semantic level of any issue raised.

The parameters and components of an urban system can take the form, in a structure, of a schematic frame. This can then be used to depict a continuous process of growth and change. Theoretically this design system must have no limits but be open-ended in all directions toward new goals, technologies and organization models. It may have added to it or have subtracted from it any components, whether constants or variables, in accordance with the governing commitment. The latter may vary from particular problems to general concern. The structure of the system therefore must be flexible enough to accommodate at any stage of the planning-design process a spectrum of components: those to be preserved, others which may be modified or improved, others of an obsolete nature which must be removed, and those which have to be discovered or invented. It could be a portrait of the system for which we are searching: a complex of purposes, processes and products which might assist the evolution of man-made environments. It should be an instrument for defining programs and describing the plan-design process, for establishing priorities and finally for correlating all three simultaneously. At the moment we are content to represent this multi-dimensional complexity diagramatically in a two-dimensional lattice-grid for the purposes of a book.

The two-dimensional grid is a composite of two major components. The vertical ends–means spectrum is calibrated from human goals and strategies at one end, organizational principles, operational components and tactics in the middle, and functional, technical and physical components at the other end. This may be called the programming spectrum. It is horizontally a plan-design-action sequence which includes operational priorities and specifications of physical facilities to be

Fig. 18
**Structure of
Design Process**
Commitment into Lattice-
Grid

Urban parameters can be
organized in categories.
Every component in each
category can be organized
in accordance with the
principle of comple-
mentarity of maximized
opposites. The diagram
here follows a develop-
ment from the authors'
commitment, to a typical
set of the complementary
parameters (see ch. 5,
fig. 4) in a lattice-grid and
finally a number of
priority components
governed by the
commitment. (The number
of categories and
components will vary with
each different problem
and commitment.)

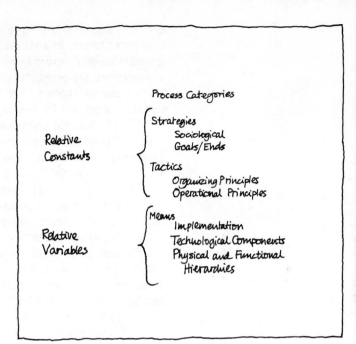

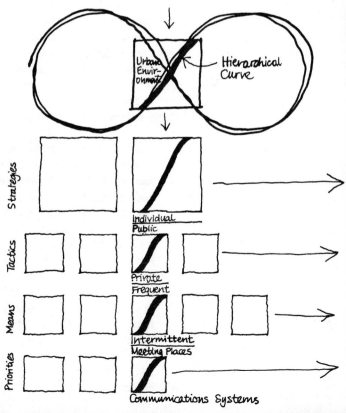

209

provided and technologies to be employed. The lattice-grid puts together in a simple way components of a complex dynamic order in which the governing commitment, the programming process, the plan-design process and functions and techniques are shown to be interdependent and interacting at all times.

The lattice-grid will contain as many variable 'boxes' therefore, for each problem, under the major groupings indicated above, as the commitment demands to satisfy the desired number of ends and means.

The various verbal abstractions have been given their appropriate semantic levels (in the 'general semantics' sense), and grouped in appropriate categories: bio-social, physical, technological, etc., which the declared purposes dictated. Some examples of realities behind the various abstractions of the commitment mentioned earlier follow. Every grid is a 'yardstick' and an 'outline of specifications' for the model, made explicit in the first place by the declared purposes.

This yardstick may be extended in the vertical or horizontal dimensions in either direction in the two dominant spectra of program and process and in the sub-spectra of functional, technical and physical components. These sub-spectra we describe as hierarchies, families of components of varying quantities in dimension, number, size and scale or qualities of character lying on the curve between maximized complementary opposites which we will now briefly discuss.

Complementarity and Maximization

Our commitment embraces not only interaction between isolated components in the urban system, but also interaction between complementary opposites within each component. These are maximized at each end of the particular spectrum of complementarity as viable options. It is precisely this maximization of option in a system of interaction and complementarity which is now recognized as an essential condition in the evolution of human culture as well as of the man-made environment. The lattice-grid could describe a macro-system in evolution on an ecological scale of a global community or describe a micro-system of urban environments for an individual growing, changing child.

In summary, complementarity and maximization of option are translated in the grid more precisely as:

complementarity of goals, complementarity of organizing

principles and complementarity of operational components irrespective of scale. Every physical component, which is the end product of the design process, becomes related in the grid to a 'higher' level of abstraction of human goals and every goal to the 'lower' level of the physical reality of physical means.

The 'loops' in the figures 5 and 6 in chapter 6 are schematic, intended to represent complementarity interaction: a continuous process. In reality, these could not intersect symmetrically in the square representing an environment. Most likely the hierarchy curve would modulate the 'environmental condition' (schematized by the square) toward the desired maximization of its opposite. A perfect symmetry of loops with their intersection at the centre would indicate complete equality of the components plotted. The hierarchical curve can be plotted as a sequence of magnitudes of a given functional hierarchy to show increments of physical components at each stage of its development.

It must be repeated that the physical 'quantities' which are in reality the 'environment' (and therefore the square representing it in the grid) may never reach the extreme levels of maximization. The operational spectrum is a hierarchy within limits of compatibility between intolerable extremes. These levels of tolerance, in most cases, could be identified and be given their proper values in relation to the problem. In this way the 'quality' of an environment is defined in terms of selected 'quantities'.

The conceptual models of urban order come therefore out of the 'vertical' programming spectrum in our grid and the 'horizontal' action process, it seems, must follow. However, the design process may begin at any level of the programming spectrum after the declaration of human purpose has been made. The search for a system and a model may find its beginnings in grand strategy, in methodology or in practical engineering. Any level may be a departure point for research, structuring of a method, or improvement of techniques of decision making and action. But the vital primary directive device for any design process must remain the declared goals.

The grid may therefore assist us in grasping a purposeful urban system from which could be developed a viable

Fig. 19
Commitment into
Lattice-Grid
Parameters and Priorities
Complementarity and
Maximized Choices

The Structure of the Design
Process (preceding diagram)
can now make a sketch
portrait of a Commitment.
This represents the authors'
commitment described in
Appendix 1.

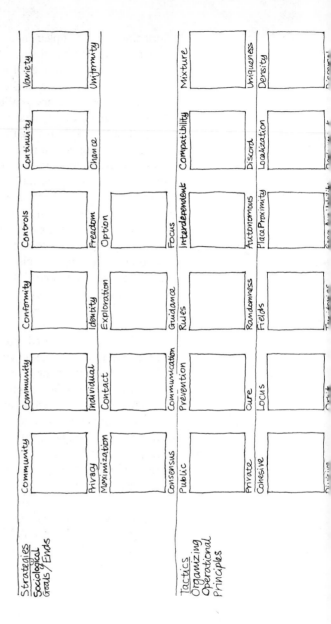

212

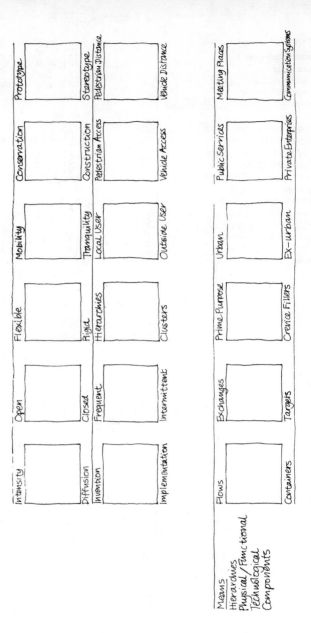

213

Fig. 20
Meeting Places in Lattice-Grid
Hierarchy of Exchanges between Movement Systems

A priority component in the lattice-grid. The hierarchy of meeting places operates throughout the urban system. The numbers representing typical location-dimension of each meeting place are plotted in relation to typical urban territories which they serve and functions which they contain.

1. Dwelling
2. Cluster (of dwellings)
3. Sector (cluster of communities)
4. Sub-core (cluster of sectors)
5. Core or Spine (city or metropolitan central functions)

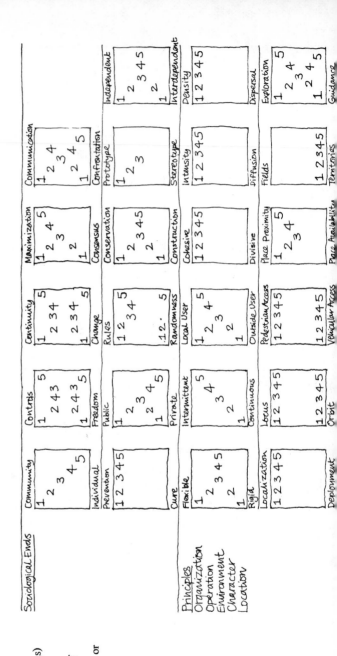

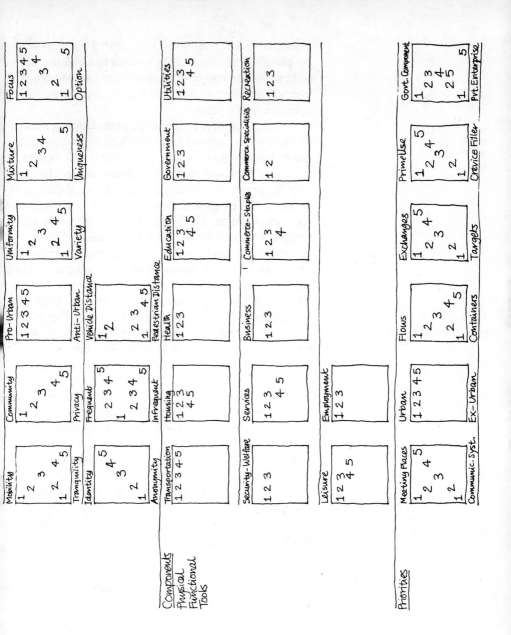

organized model and finally a structured physical order. By plugging into the grid the various bits and pieces collected in the course of research, one can transform a mosaic of random distribution in a general frame of reference into a pattern.

Projection of a future urban plan-design is not too different to the method long employed by archaeologists and paleontologists who try to transform the random mosaic of remnants of all kinds discovered in 'the dig', with the assistance of scientific and historical data, into an integrated pattern: the reconstruction of a vanished scene in evolution. The system proposed is a tool which integrates various pieces of human problems into a pattern which can then be developed into an urban environment. The archaeologist must reconstruct what has been lost; the environmental designer must learn to structure something which does not yet exist. Prediction is a process which is similar in method to reconstruction. The study of the reality of the past and future complement each other and help to define the present.

Now we can narrow the analysis by examining some applications.

The means–ends parameters, which emerged in the study's commitment-system-grid-model sequence, show up finally in the grid in six boxes of complementary interaction. The operational tool consists of six pairs of operational physical complementary components that structure the hypothetical urban model. These are all physical components and are described here in pairs of complementary function:

Flows – Containers
Exchanges – Targets
Meeting Places – Communication Systems
Urban – Ex-urban
Government Components – Private-enterprise Componer
Prime Use – Crevice Filler

All these may be modulated, refined and made specific in hierarchies of maximized opposites according to principles of organization dictated by the commitment which governs them. In this manner the hierarchy of Meeting Places and where one could expect to find them, which is basic to the authors' commitment, can be plotted in the lattice-grid. Equally physical and functional components in hierarchies for each could be determined through the application of the design system.

It is possible to test the yardstick of commitment-system-grid-model developed as a tool of criticism. At one recent stage in this study a series of seminars was held as a trial run in this direction. The participants in this exercise represented many fields directly and indirectly concerned with urban affairs. Among them were professional city planners with diverse biases carried over from their basic disciplines: law, economics or sociology; natural scientists with special interest in ecology, behavioral sciences and biometeorology; applied scientists in public health, physical and mental; a philosopher and a political scientist and some maverick architects. The seminar discussions were triggered off by the presentation of a variety of projects from all over the world at many scales, ranging from metropolitan regions to special components, from schematic plans to actual projects. The seminars were carefully documented and digested. The results broadened the framework of problems and suggested many new parameters for inclusion in our commitment and model.

The critique which follows each example reaffirms, as far as we are able to do so briefly, our commitment and the complementary urban parameters discussed earlier.

The seven models, Reston, Hook, Cumbernauld, Milton Keynes, Dublin University, Berlin Free University and Tokyo, are discussed in a sequence unrelated to their size or location. They have been graded for our purposes between a very low and very high incidence of viable parameters in each model.

Reston, Virginia

Designers: Whittlesey, Conklin and Rossant
Location: Fairfax, Virginia, 4 miles east of Dulles
Airport, 18 miles west of Washington, D.C.

Program

General Principles
There is a provision for housing for all income groups.
The town is created on the basis of private enterprise.
It will be served by privately owned and operated
vehicles. The pedestrian paths are separated from the
traffic road.
    After Reston reaches the population limit, it will
stop growing and another town will be generated to
continue overall growth.
    The town is subdivided into seven villages. There
is a village-center which is designed to serve, besides
Reston, Fairfax County which contains 500,000 people.

Facts and Figures
Area: 6,800 acres
   (4,100 acres residential
   1,100 acres public and parks
     900 acres industrial
     400 acres golf courses
     200 acres conserved nature
     100 acres lakes)
Population: 75,000 people (by 1980)
Density: 11 per acre average
      60 per acre to 2·8 per acre range

Fig. 21
Reston
Diagramatic Plan

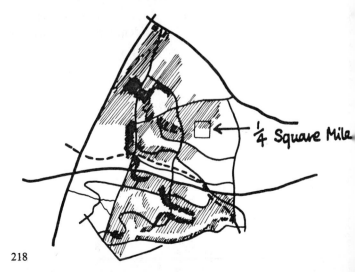

¼ Square Mile

Fig. 22
Reston
Diagram of Organization

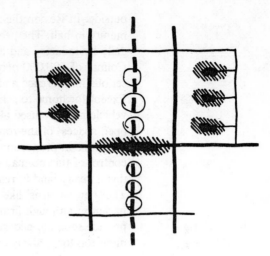

Reston is the first of three U.S. 'new towns' which
received much publicity and which was sufficiently
complete in 1967. The other two, Columbia in Virginia
and Valencia in California, share certain features with
Reston. None of these three towns proposes any
fundamental innovations or solution to urban living;
they appear to be suburban developments, well-designed
stereotypes to meet market demand. These towns are
not 'urban', because they lack the necessary population,
and the density of population distribution in the project
area is far too low to support the variety of services and
events of urban character. Their close proximity to
Washington, D.C., or Los Angeles means that there are
many competitive choices.

In spite of some lip-service to social integration
and variety, Reston appears to be designed for single-
class and economic-level occupancy, providing in all
cases a representative type of housing and school
stereotypes of established profitability and acceptability.
Reston is entirely auto-centered, inviting a great deal of
automobility. The placing of industry close to housing is
questionable. Residents of these developments will find
employment in the larger region and the local Reston
industries will probably find most of their working force

outside. In Reston the industrial zone cuts the community in half. The peak-hour traffic problems created daily by industry and a 'village center' to serve Fairfax County of 500,000 people may prove formidable – a serious interference and hidden cost to the residents. Except for home-to-school walking distance, a motor vehicle must be used all the time. An excess of 'green open spaces' of the romantic tradition is unlikely to invite use in proportion to the cost of upkeep and control of this no-man's-land. One can only assume that this is really land in reserve for future development. The 'new suburbs' like Reston contain a curious paradox; although firmly based on auto traffic, they provide separate pedestrian routes as well. Paths are often too long, always uneventful, leading to a very limited number of staple targets, and are passive and scenic in character. All facilities and events, designed apparently for pedestrian enjoyment, become more and more scattered and difficult or tedious for purposes of access. Soon after this critique was first made in 1967, the original Reston 'management', which must be given architectural credit for design standards, ran into financial difficulties and was taken over by a corporation creditor. A comparison between the area and population statistics of the three 'new towns' shows the progressive quantitative decrease in population density:

Reston	6,800 acres	75,000 pop. (12 per acre)
Columbia	15,200 acres	110,000 pop. (7 per acre)
Valencia	44,000 acres	250,000 pop. (5·6 per acre)

This suggests in general two anti-urban trends: a progressive decrease in density and increase of traffic in and out, but more importantly the increase of private interests in control of public-scale territories – bigger and better company towns, a concept which was dismissed as socially undesirable long ago.

(Proposed British 'New Town' – not built)

'The intention was to design a new town, ultimate ten-year population 100,000, in the south-east of England within a 100 mile radius of London. A location farther north or west would fall under the influence of Birmingham and tend to pull midland population south rather than provide a population release for the London area. It is to be an autonomous town, providing amenities to industrial and commercial interests. It is not to be a residential commuting satellite to London.'

General Statements – Four Main Aims of the Town
'1. Urbanity: the town should have a coherent and compact structure without sacrificing standards of open space. A linear central area projecting along main pedestrian routes into the inner residential areas was substituted for the earlier new town-planning concept of a nuclear central area with radially dispersed neighbourhoods.
2. The Motor Vehicle: the vehicular traffic is separated from pedestrian with precedence given to the latter. This separation is horizontal in all but the central area where the car parks are covered.
3. Town and Countryside: the compact town will stand out and complement the surrounding countryside. Its linear form produces its own green belt.
4. Population Balance: every effort should be made to achieve a balance of population in relation to age groups, family structure, and employment . . .'
'. . . The planning has been based on a system of main pedestrian ways, independent of the roads and without crossings at road level. Along these pedestrian ways are grouped the main non-residential activities and buildings, the children's play areas, the local shops and services and the primary schools. Pedestrians could move inwards along these ways, which lead directly into the central area; vehicles could move in the opposite direction from culs-de-sac and development roads, outwards along the residential distributor roads, and thence on to main collector urban motorways which would take them across the town and beyond it. London Airport is within an hour's motoring distance. Primary schools and all their play areas are sited inside the residential areas. Secondary schools have their building

221

and hard play areas inside, but would have been disposed to place their playing fields mostly in the belt of town open space outside the residential areas. Small local industrial estates and service areas are sited within the residential areas, adjoining the collector urban motorways.'

Major Industrial Areas: 'There are three major industrial areas, and these are sited at the corners of the town.'

Fig. 23
Hook
Diagramatic Plan

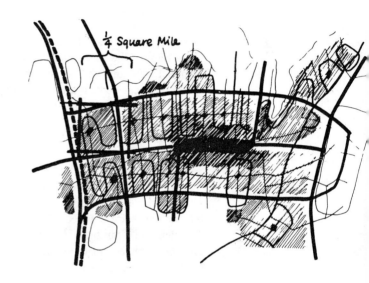

Fig. 24
Hook
Diagram of Organization

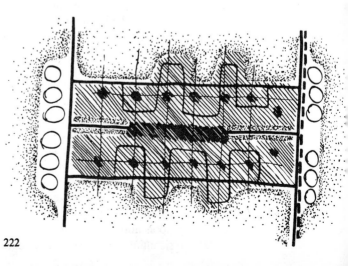

Architect: Hugh Wilson
A 'new town' in Scotland, twelve miles from Glasgow
with a target population of 70,000

The general planning principles are very similar to those
of Hook. The center of Cumbernauld, however, has
some new and specific characteristics: 'On the ridge and
upper southern slope of the Cumbernauld hill 200 feet
above the reconstructed Glasgow–Stirling trunk road,
will rise a structure nearly half a mile long, 200 yards
wide and up to eight stories high. Elevated over a
unidirectional vehicular system, the multi-level development, with provision for most of the commercial, civic,
religious, cultural and recreational uses for a population
of 70,000, will be the largest single employment source,
traffic generator and land-space user in the town.' The
town is structured by three major instruments of
physical planning:
1. the exploitation of the topography and the recognition
of climatic and geologic determinants;
2. the layout and hierarchic ordering of the paths of
motion;
3. the decision to create a 'super-core' as a community
focus, having, in addition to its cohesive effect on the
town, an effective regional potential. This distinguishes
Cumbernauld from the previously built 'new towns' in
Britain.
The site characteristics and access patterns combine to
establish the nature of housing at Cumbernauld. The
density range is 60 to 100 persons per acre, with every
attempt being made to achieve privacy and proximity to
the ground. 'The Central Area: Perhaps the most
radical departure which Cumbernauld makes is the
structure and intent of the Central Area of commerce
and concourse. . . . This is not only the basis for the
tightly-knit "compact town", but the manifestation of
the Cumbernauld developers' ambition for this center to
draw substantial regional patronage.'

223

Cumbernauld
Diagramatic Plan

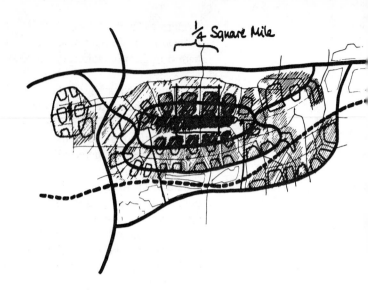

¼ Square Mile

Cumbernauld
Diagram of
Organization

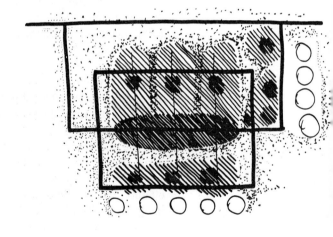

Critique

Hook, although not built, and Cumbernauld are both
what the English planners have described as prototype
towns and are of historic interest in the sequence of
development of New Towns Systems in Great Britain.
They illustrate the time lag between theories developed
in the twenties and thirties and actual execution almost
a generation later. The idea of 'autonomy' was super-

224

seded. Cumbernauld was carefully planned to fit into the natural environment and at the same time fit into existing main lines of transportation to and from the adjacent metro-center. The main organizing elements are clearly the circulatory systems, kept separate throughout, of pedestrians between all sectors. The linear 'center' is accessible to rubber-wheeled vehicles, mainly private cars, and has parking facilities for approximately one third of the residents' automobiles in the center and in dead-end streets from peripheral roads. It appears that the car-road and parking system may in the near future become typically overstrained because of the reliance on the free-running car transportation. The access to highways and railroads makes easy industry location within 'walking distance' and 'very short drive distance' questionable.

It seems that the centers may become stereotype staples in content and character without a genuine urban mix, variety and vitality. The very costly 'Castle Hill' center structure of Cumbernauld is not being extended fast enough and is, several years after completion, surrounded by a no-man's-land waiting for events. The scattering of schools within the residential areas and around the town's periphery, a short walking distance from dwellings, limits the experiences for the children, who are not induced by the plan to explore the 'adult world in action' in the center.

In the case of Cumbernauld, tight clustering of essential facilities 'plugged into' the complex core would have a declared advantage over inclement climate. It should be noted that the structure of Cumbernauld Center, containing all essential 'meeting place' activities, is by far the most complete and thoughtful of any project to date. On the other hand, as a system around a combination of ancient citadel and Milan's *galleria*, it does not operate as an 'exchange' so much as a better, weatherproof version of 'downtown'.

New Towns in general appear to run the danger of attracting a highly homogenized population of the very young professional white-collar families who may, as in the case of many suburban developments in the U.S.A., prove to be transients. The declared intention of attracting the elderly and generally a more socially and economically varied population may not be realized.

(under construction)
Buckingham County Department of Architecture and
Planning. Ministry of Housing and Local Government
Architect: Frederick Pooley

Program

General Statement
'A tremendous growth in the south-east region and the
evergrowing dominance of central London as a centre
has created tremendous transportation and housing
problems. A lack of suitable available land for development in and around London has resulted in heavy
pressure for development in the metropolitan green belt.'

General Proposal
The proposal is intended to make a maximum contribution to the problem of the south-east and to act as
a 'counter magnet' to the metropolitan area of Greater
London, providing sufficient facilities to avoid commuting out and to maintain the metropolitan green belt.
'The plan recognizes that the desire for maximum choice
in housing, work, and leisure is expressed in a need for
mobility. The plan explores the implications of an efficient
public-transit system and permits its economic use.
      'The plan seeks many diverse patterns of com-
munity to develop and change by neighbourhood contact (the street or cluster), by district identity (centred
on public transport stops, shops, and community
services), and civic identity achieved by a common
point of contact for all citizens in the city centre.'

Specific Proposal
'The site is approximately 22,950 acres of agricultural
land of not high value, approximately 45 miles north-
west of London. The site is close to a main highway and
railway line, ensuring easy access to London and the
Midlands for goods and passenger traffic. Close
proximity to three airports – Birmingham (54 miles),
Luton (23 miles), and London (48 miles).
      'Designed as an urban complex to house a popu-
lation, after 29 years, of 250,000 people. A "linear"
system of planning capable of independent growth is
adopted. The city consists of three principal parts:
1. a central area complex;
2. 4 circuit linear housing sectors;
3. 4 main industrial areas.

Each sector is further divided into townships. Each township contains 5,000 people with an average density of 50 people per acre. The regional centre provides facilities for housing, education, health and industry. Each township provides adequate shops, clinics, libraries, churches, nursery and primary schools. The open spaces between the townships have parks and playing fields at 8 acres per 1,000 persons (minimum) as well as stadia with parking, hospitals, high schools, and agricultural land.'

'Industry occupies 3 separate areas:
1. 4 main industrial areas at the extremities of the city;
2. 1/8 of the industrial provision is in housing areas;
3. some service industry is located in the central area.
Transportation consists of a free, public mass transit system, elevated above ground level, consisting of 4 circuit routes connecting the townships with the city centre, main industrial areas, and railway lines. Stops are located at a central point in the townships – no dwelling being more than 7 minutes' walking distance away. A peripheral road serves the townships, city centre, and main industrial areas and joins to the main spine route. A complete traffic segregation at all levels permits easier integration of local communities. Services are to be carried by ducts and to have easy access, without interfering with the roads. The form of the plan suggests that a whole-city heating system would be economically feasible. Existing villages lying within the main residential areas will be incorporated into the appropriate townships. Villages within open spaces will be maintained and improved – but no expansion will be allowed. The village falling within the city centre will be in a conservation area. Surrounding countryside will form a "white area" around the city, to be retained in agricultural use.'

Fig. 27
Milton Keynes
Diagramatic Plan

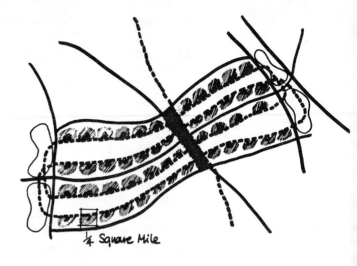

¼ Square Mile

Fig. 28
Milton Keynes
Diagram of
Organization

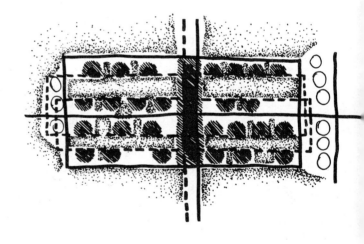

Critique

Compared to Hook and Cumbernauld two major
planning principles become apparent: Milton Keynes is
much larger and is organized around an efficient, free
public-transit system in addition to private automobiles.

Modular organization centered on transit stops or
stations could be repeated along the major existing lines
of road and railway transportation between London and
Birmingham, each some 50 miles distant. The 'townships' linked by a suspended slow monorail system
could support a fully developed spine segment. The
228 main, central exchange point joins short and long

haul systems. Easy, fast access to both historic magnets is provided which could induce a metro-spine growth.

However, the implied autonomy of Milton Keynes seems forced, as are the 5,000 population township modules. The dimensions are arbitrary and could inhibit growth and change of the larger community They are too small to sustain adequate staple services and supplies within walking distance and too large for purposes of neighborhood identity and meaningful community interaction. The monorail for staple travel is complemented by a ring road for rubber wheels going to random targets outside the New Town. There may be some conflict developing between industrial traffic to the designated peripheral industry locations and the surrounding horticultural land. Perhaps employment proximity is incorrectly linked to the local system and would be more effective as part of the metro-corridor between Birmingham and London, which could be the next step in a hierarchical structure in a system of interaction and interdependence. The preservation and integration within the protective transportation residential outer ring of historic villages and farms provides conservation of the natural and man-made in a complementary manner.

Dublin University

'Proposal for a System' based on a competition organized by University College, Dublin, 1963 Architect: G. DeCarlo. Collaborators: Barp, Greig

Program

Problem: 'The original study was made for an international competition organized by University College, Dublin, in 1963. It was for a plan of the new buildings of the University on a large, flat, well-treed site. Housing for students was included. The aim of the proposal was to resolve the fundamental requirements of a University:
1. Flexibility.
2. Social contact at all levels.
3. A distinctive educational environment in relation to the city and to its immediate setting. The university should be sufficiently strong in character to start an intellectual interaction with the city.'

229

System of Organization: 'A system was proposed, organic, relevant and continuous in time, to give clarity to an architectural principle.'

Functional System: 'In order to stimulate social contact, a common basis of disposition of elements had to be found to create one organism with a clear structure. Each faculty and communal building is broken down and classified by individual rooms according to their need, ranging from community to privacy in four degrees: 1. Communal; 2. General; 3. Particular; 4. Specialized.'

Flow System: 'The structure of the circulation system is a basic part of the space and social organization of the University. It is based on a time-distance factor between all elements, of ten minutes on foot. . . . The basis of the circulation system is a central spine which all elements cross or join in equal relationship. . . Related to the hierarchy of space is a hierarchy of routes running parallel to the main spine giving the pedestrian a wide selection of paths . . .'

Pedestrian Circulations: 'The principal circulation everywhere is on foot. The circulation is centered in the double central spine in which are placed the lecture halls and the classrooms, the communal facilities, and other public rooms. Along this route everyone passes through a series of varying spaces which at every point has a clear identity within the system, defined by the character of the element that touches or passes over the route. Once in any particular element, one can pass from one side of the main route to the other, and enter the lecture halls without touching the main route, yet remaining in visual contact with it.'

Parking: 'Cars park at each end of the spine.'

Growth: 'The plan is capable of complete rearrangement while still maintaining the order of the systems.'

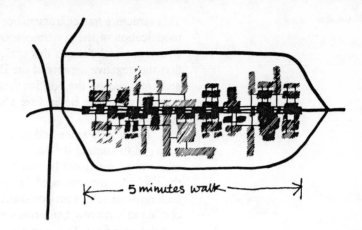

Fig. 29
Dublin University
Diagramatic Plan

K— 5 minutes walk —→

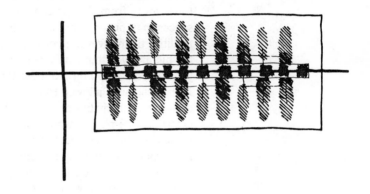

Fig. 30
Dublin University
Diagram of
Organization

Fig. 31
Dublin University
Diagramatic Revision

Max Technology

Max Concourse

Max Technology

Max Concourse

Max Technology

Max Concourse

Max Technology

¼ Mile

231

This structure has characteristics which, with minor modification of the system proposed, could become the structure which follows this critique. We will describe first the negative aspects of the Dublin project separately and second the positive aspects which this university and the Berlin Free University hold in common.

The central spine and its many components are too rigid to contain the various servicing flow systems which may eventually be required. The same is true of the vehicular movement of different kinds. In the single underground tunnel proposed there appears to be a conflict in a narrow band containing both people and technical services. The growing specialized technical requirements may be more demanding in the laboratories away from the spine, while maximum concourse spaces may prove to be technically the simplest. The facilities themselves are correctly located in relation to the hierarchy of human function (community to privacy), yet are located too far from the service spine as planned. If the scheme is allowed to have the desired flexibility allowing the activities of individuals and groups to determine the plan, it would most probably develop as troughs of concourse and human interaction along main routes where greatest community is most likely: the constants. The technological variables, growing and changing functions, would probably develop as was proposed, only they would bring with them their own service spines. The reduction in the size of the bulky traffic/service mono-duct in its central position would have the additional advantage of inducing easy bridging of the spine concourse by university teaching and research facilities. The scheme could ultimately develop into a net or grid of main service lines and high-level community-interaction spines, and thus be a 'multidirectional' system of spines and sub-spines. This project accepts the criteria of an urban situation like Berlin Free University, an urban micro-system in social organization: a concourse spine of high intensity, density and variety with twenty-four hour occupancy. It provides the complementary components of privacy, leisure and tranquility. It is organized in a hierarchy of exchanges.

Competition project, September 1963
Architects: Caudilis, S. Woods and Josic
Collaborators: M. Scheidhelm, J. Greig

'The competition program called first for facilities
(departments of natural sciences and arts) for 3,600
students on a 30 acre site in the centre of Berlin as an
extension to the existing buildings and later expansion
to accommodate approximately 72,000 students.'

Governing Principles
'We consider the university as a place and a tool. Many
of its functions are known, others are not. We suppose
that its principal function is to encourage exchange
between people in different disciplines with a view to
enlarging the field of human knowledge. Our intention
then, in this scheme, is to provide, within one organization, maximum possibilities for contact and interchange
in the community university, while ensuring privacy for
each specific function. . . . The system adopted is one in
which a series of parallel ways is established following
the principal direction of the university, existing and
projected. These main stems run N.E.–S.W. and are
about 200 feet apart (about one minute walking distance). They contain and serve all those functions and
places which would benefit from easy contact with the
rest of the university, including auditoria, exhibition
spaces, lounges, libraries, lecture halls, cafés, etc. The
main stems are interconnected at convenient intervals
by secondary ways. Those places and functions which
require privacy and tranquility are located away from
the main ways. . . . In the beginning the system exists
only as an approximate right-of-way for circulation and
services. It is a structuring device, which exists only
where and when it is required.'

Structure
'The form of the University building is a three-storied
matrix of enclosures and open courts. A fourth level
can be added for some housing. All roofs are accessible
as public or private terraces.'

Circulation
Mass Transit: A subway line is tangent to site with two
convenient stations. Vehicular: Internal vehicular circu-

lation is restricted entirely to service (underground). The privately owned vehicle is excluded entirely with provision for convenient perimeter parking. Pedestrian: The internal circulation based on the system of parallel primary arteries and secondary crosspaths is entirely pedestrian oriented, with mechanical aid for pedestrians connecting the main levels of circulation.

Fig. 32
Berlin Free University
Diagramatic Plan

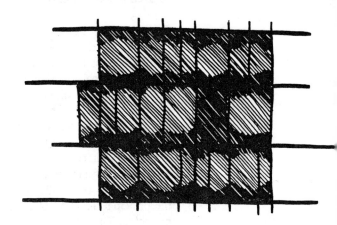

Critique

This is an open-ended grid system accommodating omni-directional growth in three dimensions. It provides linkage systems for two basic hierarchical components: containers and flows which can grow either in a linear or in a nodal fashion, leaving great freedom for future unforeseen developments. The general principles become readily visible. Two overlapping grids create a complementary system of flows and hierarchies: first, social intercourse channels, and second, technological service ducts. Both designed to induce and enable high-density/intensity use. Mixed-use 'containers of functions' would in turn induce a twenty-four-hour (urban) life. The Berlin grid divided into departmental territories and community channels could grow in sectors and convey a sense of completion to the pedestrian at any stage before the ultimate high density is reached. The pedestrian 'preferred' levels are designed to assist maximum variety of pedestrian motion and to provide options of either leisurely promenade and concourse or quick short cuts towards desired targets.

234

The proposal for this university is close to other diagramatic projects by the same authors, which employ similar organizational constants throughout. The Berlin University, with its overlays of complementary spines and sub-spines, is the nearest to a rational urban system made for a 'real' situation we have encountered. Increase in dimension or complexity in any variable parameters would not violate the system and could be dealt with.

Architects: Kenzo Tange Team

In the intröduction to this comparative critique we suggested that urban parameters which we regard as constants may be applied to systems and models irrespective of their size. Even then, the jump from 100,000 or less to ten million may be hard to take. Unlike the modest proposals of 'new towns' or new universities within old towns, which could be absorbed and modified if they failed, the Tokyo bridge extension of the already largest, densest metropolis in the world can be likened in its impact on a whole country's economy and cultural evolution to a full-scale war. We believe, however, that in spite of these dimensional discrepancies, the organizational similarities between the last project discussed and Tokyo will become apparent.

General Statements
'The concentration of people into pivotal cities of ten million or more is a necessary result of the advance of civilization and economic growth of the Twentieth Century. It is clear that the principal function of Tokyo is carried out in the center of town. The three downtown wards contain the economic pivot of the nation. The telephone, the radio, television, the portable telephone, the video-telephone – all these indirect means of communication give rise to a greater demand and need for direct communication . . . since transportation is necessary for direct communication, the transportation system is the basic physical foundation for the functional operation of the city . . . *individual transportation is not only the ideal*, but the necessary pattern

235

for the variable flow in an open urban organization. The problem raised by automobile traffic requires that we discover a means for bringing the city structure, the traffic system, and architecture together into an organic whole.'

General Proposal
'1. To shift from a radial centripetal system to a system of linear development.
2. To find a means of bringing the city structure, the transportation system, and urban architecture into organic unity.
3. To find new urban spatial order which will reflect the open organization and the spontaneous mobility of contemporary society.'

Specific Proposal
'We reject the concept of the metropolitan civic center in favor of a new concept which we call the civic axis. In effect we are proposing that the radial structure of Tokyo be replaced by an axis which develops linearly. It is only natural that the axis should begin at the present center. The cost of construction over the bay will doubtless be greater than on land, but there would be a minimal risk of land speculation. Cyclical system will permit the flow of 200,000 cars per hour. Parking 40,000 cars per square kilometer link, 23 links provide parking for 920,000 cars, 100,000 workers in each link, 1 car per 5 workers. The architectural prototype would be a system consisting of cores laid out in a grid of squares approximately 200 meters on the side and of 10 or 20 storey office buildings resting on the cores. We like to think of our plan for Tokyo as a plan for creating land values.'

Critique

The vast bridge structure is designed as an omni-duct joining two high-density metropolitan concentrations. It would provide new high-density real-estate values at the outset in an orderly and controlled manner, inviting the continuation of a highly urban mixture of use throughout the spine. The indicated residential island ribs may be considered as one of many possible variants and is not an integral part of the project. The dimensions and complexity of the bridge-spine match the existing city's density and growth potential. These

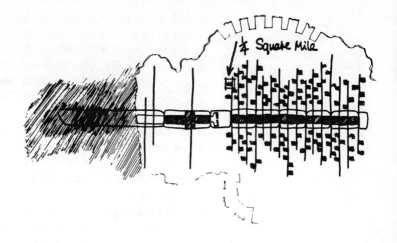

Fig. 33
Tokyo: Metropolitan
Bridge Extension
Diagramatic Plan

¼ Square Mile

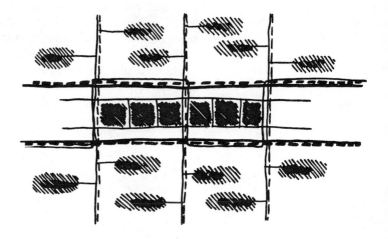

Fig. 34
Tokyo: Metropolitan
Bridge Extension
Diagram of Organization

appear economically viable as a direct result of the
proximity and accessibility of new to old. The high
intensity-density-frequency of use of the metro-spine
has its complementary components out in the water on
a smaller neighborhood or sector scale.

The enormous dimensions and scope of the project
preclude any specificity in the system at this stage. The
hierarchical organization of pedestrian concourse,
circulation and technical systems become immediately
237 visible in the modest university structures, but are not

explicit in the gigantic metro-bridge. It appears at first glance to be an omni-duct containing but not ordering the highest imaginable intensity-density-frequency and mix of use. However, its multi-layered structure can accommodate rights-of-way for pedestrian, passenger and service flows in all directions. The Berlin one-minute walking distance square is analogous to Tokyo's 200-meter module. At some preferred pedestrian level the whole could be served by many transportation systems including, one may guess, one level entirely devoted to private automobile circulation.

Unlike Berlin, in which the grid structure will contain relatively predictable events to accord with a university's growth, the Tokyo grid provides a departure point for all sorts of unexpected events, some of which could hurt, but in the end could be absorbed in the giant matrix without destroying it. The pedestrian and passenger exchange systems are implicit but not spelt out in Tokyo. The authors' commitment to uniquely automobile 'individual' transportation involving a million cars seems quite arbitrary and unnecessary and would no doubt prove impossible. The governing principles in both Berlin and Tokyo, in spite of their dimensional difference, are unequivocally urban.

A postscript must be added to the above critiques. The selected examples and the sequence of their presentation here can now be further related, through their analysis, to certain operational parameters stressed throughout the book: pedestrian realms generating human contact and concourse which are related to transportation exchanges of the urban system, as opposed to targets which invite concentrated intermittent use. In the light of these criteria, Reston may be seen as an automobile realm with scattered unrelated targets. Hook is a centripetal organization with a town-center target and scattered school targets. Cumbernauld's center begins to look like an exchange because of its variety of use and compactness of form. Dublin University is a pedestrian realm inserted into a road-vehicle city system with emphasis on its concourse-spine. Berlin Free University is a pedestrian realm with a concourse-grid and is clearly an exchange between road-vehicle and subway metro-passengers and local pedestrians. Tokyo, actually a bridge spanning Tokyo Bay between two metro-concentrations, becomes in essence an exchange system as a whole as well as the sum of exchange sub-systems in its modular structure.

The governing principles and data for each model given here are either selected quotations or paraphrased or edited extracts from the original programs. Interested readers are referred to the source material (p. 240) for more detailed information.

The information on each of the seven projects is taken from the sources listed below:

RESTON

'Lake Anne Village Center: A Planned Community Nucleus', *Progressive Architecture*, May 1966.

'Progress in Planning', *Architectural Forum*, July 1964.

HOOK

The Planning of a New Town, London County Council, 1963.

CUMBERNAULD

'Cumbernauld: A Citadel of Many Levels for Both Men and Machines', *Architectural Forum*, August–September 1964.

Geoffrey Copcutt, 'Planning and Designing in the Central Areas of Cumbernauld New Town', *The Pedestrian in the City*, ed. D. Lewis, Princeton, 1966.

MILTON KEYNES

Northampton, Bedford and North Bucks Study, London, 1965.

Buckinghamshire County Council: The Case for the Monorail, Aylesbury, 1965.

North Bucks New City, Aylesbury, 1966.

R.I.B.A. Journal, July 1970.

DUBLIN UNIVERSITY

Giancarlo de Carlo, *Proposal for a University Structure*, Venice, 1965.

BERLIN FREE UNIVERSITY

'Berlin Free University', *Le Carré Bleu*, I, 1964.

'Concours pour l'université libre de Berlin', *Architecture d'Aujourd'hui*, February 1964.

'University for Berlin', *Architectural Review*, April 1964.

TOKYO–METROPOLITAN BRIDGE EXTENSION

'A Plan for Tokyo', *The Japan Architect*, April 1961.

Gunter Nitschke, 'Cities Stasis or Process', *The Pedestrian in the City*, ed. D. Lewis, Princeton, 1966.

'Una Proposa por Tokyo', *Architektura*, October 1961.

The following are definitions of 'jargon' words which apply in the context of this book.

ACCESS: An urban measure based on the time-distance of approach and amount of effort needed to establish contact with the assistance of a technological medium.

ANAMNESIS: A careful record of physical and medical history of a patient, first introduced by Hippocrates, who paid attention to instances that might or might not be associated with the disease.

BRIDGE BUILDING: A process through which previously isolated institutions or fields of inquiry are made to interact, generating new principles, new solutions and new fields of knowledge.

CLUSTER: A group of dwellings of any kind sharing communal facilities and having a territorial identity.

COHESIVENESS: An organizing principle of distribution according to which functions are interrelated in territorial proximity to generate human contact or 'concourse'.

COMMITMENT: A set of declared goals necessary as a theoretical basis for action. (The commitment of this study is described in the 'Grid'.)

COMPLEMENTARITY: A methodology whereby unrelated but interacting principles resolve conflict, translating it into two maximized opposites in a non-contradictory relationship.

COMPONENT: Functional and operational physical elements or constituents of environments which are constituent parts or elements of a system.

CONCOURSE: The 'milling around' in public meeting places which generates a variety of social experience, without direct contact (see MIX).

CONFRONTATION: First-hand experience; meeting of people face to face, encountering 'events'.

CONTACT: Direct, 'private' contact between individuals.

CONTAINERS: Urban components operating as territories or places of human contact at any hierarchical level.

CREVICE FILLERS: Urban components of a 'servicing' nature, depending on the existence of neighboring places of special purpose, which can extend time-occupancy and generate variety and density of use.

DENSITY: The measure of the numbers (not necessarily residents), at any time, of a territory or place.

DIVISIVENESS: An organizing principle of distribution according to which places may be distant in space but are in contact through technological systems.

DYNAMIC ORDER: A state in which processes of complex function and interdependence operate in time and space.

ECOLOGY (THIRD): The ecology of the man-made environment created by culture and technology.

EXCHANGE: An urban component functioning as a transfer place between any number of vehicular and pedestrian movements.

FIELD: The sphere of action which operates or exerts influence in an area independent of territory.

241

FLOWS: Urban components which operate in all forms of movement at several scales.

FREQUENCY OF USE: The measure of intensity relating number and convenience of access.

GRID: A two-dimensional description of a multi-dimensional lattice which correlates parameters, processes and components of the urban system.

HIERARCHY: An organizing system which ranks or grades things or events in a sequence of successive importance or scale (see SYSTEMS ORDERING).

INTENSITY: The relation between the number of activities and convenience of access in a given place: the measure of intensity and frequency of use.

LAISSEZ-FAIRE: The doctrine, in economics and politics, that an economic system functions best when there is no interference from government. Later a philosophy of individualism and utilitarian ethic; then a tenet of the conservative opponents of socialism. Here it includes opposition to planning by government in any form.

LATTICE: A multi-dimensional, abstract structure of interlaced elements which correlates parameters, processes and components. Here this is translated into a two-dimensional grid for the graphic purposes of a book (see GRID).

LEARNING: Accumulation of knowledge from the environment by formal or informal means; structured and directed by others or unstructured and spontaneously self-discovered.

LEISURE: Creative activity of any kind with no profit motivation.

MAXIMIZATION (OF CHOICE): A condition which is increased or magnified to the highest possible degree within a spectrum of organized choice between opposites, thereby producing option instead of consensus or conflict in chaos.

MINI–MIDI–MAXI: A description of magnitudes, borrowed from the popular jargon of fashion, to describe short, intermediary and long haul urban transit systems and the relative dimensions of vehicles involved.

MIX: An organizing principle in which functions of maximum variety are brought together in territorial proximity to generate maximum interaction between them and to offer maximum choice.

MODEL: A structured order, explanatory, descriptive and predictive, applied here to human ecology.

MOSAIC: 'Pieces' randomly presented within a frame but related to each other by chance.

NEIGHBORHOOD: An urban territory composed of several 'clusters', with social identity, with separated pedestrian and vehicular paths and its own transit 'exchange'.

ORBIT: Path of communication (movement) relating targets of interest independent of location, proximity or territories.

PARAMETER: A quantity which is constant (as distinct from ordinary variables) in a particular case considered, but which varies in different cases (*Columbia Dictionary*, Columbia University Press, New York, 1950).

PATTERN: A step in the process of ordering 'places'. A relative order of purposeful relationships which follows the random stage of 'mosaic'.

PLACES: Physical settings in the natural or man-made environment which may be occupied continuously or intermittently by people, having function, character and form with which individuals or communities may identify or be identified.

PROXIMITY: An urban measure based on the time-distance and effort needed to establish contact without the assistance of any technological medium.

SECTOR: An urban territory composed of several 'neighborhoods', with its own 'exchange' of character or functional identity linked to neighborhood exchanges and other sectors' exchanges by public transit systems.

SPECIALTIES: Facilities and supplies dependent on a great variety of consumers and choices, unusual and luxury items.

SPECTRUM: A band of compatibility in an abstract range between two maximized opposites, which represents real qualities or events, and permits these to interact in a complementary (non-interfering or destructive) manner (see HIERARCHY).

STAPLES: Mass-produced necessities, consumer goods or entertainments dependent on mass-consumption.

SYMBIOSIS: The habitual living together of organisms of different species. The term is usually restricted to a relationship beneficial to at least one of the participants and harmful to none (*Columbia Dictionary*).

SYSTEM: An aggregation or assemblage of parts joined in regular interaction or interdependence; . . . an organic or organized whole (*Webster's Third New International Dictionary*, 1961).

SYSTEMS COMPONENT: A related part in a system. If this part is a system in itself, it is considered as a sub-system to the whole.

SYSTEMS ORDERING: A process through which components are related progressively through an increasing application of rules. From a stage of random presentation or 'mosaic' to an emerging interrelationship of 'pattern' and finally to an 'ordered structure'. If this order is a model of processes it is a 'dynamic order'; if it is a sequence of successive scales it is a 'hierarchical order'.

TARGET: An urban component functioning as a terminal destination place of special purpose.

TECHNOLOGY: '. . . A composite of technical, psychological and economic concepts . . . a social-economic power structure . . .' (Professor Suranyi-Unger). 'Technostructure' (Professor J. K. Galbraith).

TERRITORY: A part of the physical environment which corresponds to a set of functions related in spatial contiguity.

TRANQUILITY: an environmental state of maximized relief from interference in a place of ease which provides repose and opportunity for leisure.

UNIQUENESS: A condition in which special areas are assigned a sole function with minimum interference from, and maximum independence of, other functions.

243

URBAN: Functional components which require little land but are dependent on close proximity and convenient access all the time to large numbers which generate variety and concourse.

EX-URBAN: Functional components which require economic space availability and easy access for many for intermittent, peak-load use.

URBANISM: The human community characterized by intensity and frequency of contact by means of direct intercourse and indirect communication systems. These require the use of the most sophisticated technology available at any time. The measure of this conditon is greater choice for the greater number.

Some other books published by Penguins are described on the following pages.

**Man and Environment
Crisis and the Strategy
of Choice**

Robert Arvill

What will the world look and be like tomorrow? Must the
landscape be an extension of today's spreading deterioration?
More air fouled by noise and poisoned fumes; more water
polluted by chemicals and oil slicks; more land crushed under
the sprawl of towns, super-highways, airports, factories,
pylons, and strip-mines? Is man bound to build a stifling
steel-and-concrete hell for himself? Or can effective steps be
taken now to preserve our open spaces, seashores, and life-
sustaining elements from the assaults of technology?

This is a book about man – about the devastating impact of
his numbers on the environment and the decisions and actions
he can take to attack the problem. The author is an expert on
conservation and planning. Land, air, water, and wildlife are
treated by him both as valuable resources in very short supply
and as precious living entities. He contrasts present management of these resources with man's future needs. British
experience and examples from all over the world illustrate
the critical and practical aspects of the problem. Past
conservation programmes are reviewed and evaluated and the
book offers a complete set of proposals for regional, national,
and international action on environmental protection. The
approach is farsighted, informed, urgent.

Urban Choices:
The City and Its Critics

Roger Starr

A probing review of America's urban problems and their possible solutions by an articulate professional who has dealt firsthand with the intricacies of city planning in the nation's largest metropolis. Roger Starr denounces what he considers the simplified and utopian solutions to city problems put forth by such critics as Lewis Mumford, Jane Jacobs, Herbert Gans, Marya Mannes, and Peter Blake. Drawing on his experience as Executive Director of New York's Citizens' Housing and Planning Council, Mr. Starr proposes his own direct and highly reasonable—if somewhat controversial— line of attack on the ills that plague America's cities in this period of unprecedented social and economic change. Among the areas that come under his scrutiny are housing, transportation, unemployment, racial tensions, poverty, architectural planning, air and water pollution, and urban politics. Originally published in hardcover as *The Living End,* the book has been fully revised for this Pelican edition.

LOS ANGELES

Reyner Banham

A look at the architectural ideas and facts that have shaped Los Angeles. Reyner Banham recognizes that while Los Angeles is often dismissed as an aesthetic disaster it has a more creative architectural record than any other American city except, perhaps, Chicago. Considering it as an environment for architecture, he sets the works of designers as diverse as Frank Lloyd Wright, Charles Eames, Richard Neutra, and Simon Rodia in their proper landscape of mountains, plains, beaches, and freeways, and shows the complex interplay of powers and concepts—from Spanish-style ranches to the Environmental Goals Program—that have created the city as it stands today. This volume is an addition to the widely acclaimed Architect and Society series. Reyner Banham is Professor of the History of Architecture at University College, London.